THE MONKEY AS MIRROR

Emiko Ohnuki-Tierney, *Emiko.*

THE MONKEY
AS MIRROR

Symbolic Transformations
in Japanese History
and Ritual

PRINCETON

UNIVERSITY PRESS

Copyright © 1987 by Princeton University Press
Published by Princeton University Press, 41 William Street,
Princeton, New Jersey 08540
In the United Kingdom: Princeton University Press, Guildford, Surrey

All Rights Reserved

Library of Congress Cataloging in Publication Data will be
found on the last printed page of this book

ISBN 0-691-09434-9

Publication of this book has been aided by a grant from
the Paul Mellon Fund of Princeton University Press
and the Japan Foundation

This book has been composed in Linotron Palatino
Clothbound editions of Princeton University Press books
are printed on acid-free paper, and binding materials are
chosen for strength and durability. Paperbacks, although satisfactory
for personal collections, are not usually suitable for library rebinding

Printed in the United States of America by Princeton University Press
Princeton, New Jersey

DESIGNED BY LAURY A. EGAN

Contents

v

PART THREE: BASIC STRUCTURE, PROCESSUAL-
CONTEXTUAL STRUCTURE, AND MULTIPLE
STRUCTURES OF MEANING

PART FOUR: FROM THE MEDIATING MONKEY TO THE REFLEXIVE MONKEY: HISTORICAL TRANSFORMATIONS AND RITUAL STRUCTURE

List of Illustrations

Preface

NO OTHER WORK have I enjoyed more than that done for this book. In part this was because the monkey symbolism and monkey performances were, to use an American colloquialism, "a lot of fun." Also, it was because the book began and ended as the fruit of collegiality: many of my colleagues patiently listened to my talks, read parts or all of the manuscript at various stages of its development, and generously offered their insights.

My thanks are first to Mr. Murasaki Yoshimasa, Mr. Murasaki Shūji, Mr. Murasaki Tarō, and other contemporary monkey trainers, their friends, and their families, all of whom generously opened the door for me. As detailed in Chapters 5 and 8, not only did they let me observe their training sessions and actual performances, they were most generous in sharing their experiences, information, and photographs with me. I cherish the many hours during which we discussed their interpretation and my interpretation of the meaning of the monkey performance. I am particularly grateful to Ms. Kumi Kobayashi of Suō Sarumawashinokai, who has kept me in touch with their activities by mail. She also obtained archival materials not available in the United States.

The final stage of manuscript writing was undertaken during the 1985–1986 academic year with a fellowship from the John Simon Guggenheim Foundation, and during the fall of 1986 at the Institute for Advanced Study, Princeton, under a grant from the National Endowment for the Humanities. My research in its early stages was supported by the Institute for Research in the Humanities at the University of Wisconsin and by the Graduate School, University of Wisconsin, Madison. My fieldwork was supported by the Wenner Gren Foundation for Anthropological Research. I gratefully acknowledge these institutions for their generous support. While the major part of my archival research was done at many archives in Japan, library grants from the Asian Library of the University of Michigan and from the Far Eastern Library of the University of Chicago supported me in the final stage of my archival work. I am indebted to them for their assistance.

This project began as a fortunate accident. In 1981, while I was conducting fieldwork on illness perception and health care in Japan, I had the opportunity to observe the then recently revived monkey performances in Hikari City, Yamaguchi Prefecture. Although I was fascinated by them, I had never seriously considered such performances as a topic of research. In 1982, Professor E. Bruner invited me to present a paper in his plenary session of the American Ethnological Society, which was to meet in Baton Rouge, Louisiana, in 1983. The session was intriguingly entitled "Text, Play, and Story: The Construction and Reconstruction of Self and Society." The invitation was too attractive to refuse, and I started the monkey performance project—the only "play" I had some data on. So began my struggle and my fun. I thank Professor Thomas Sebeok, who was instrumental in bringing about my initial encounter with the monkey performance, and Professor Bruner for his invitation.

It is embarrassing to list all the talks I gave on different aspects and stages of this research. The first was at the 1983 American Ethnological Society meeting. Other talks were given at the Third Decennial Conference of the Association of Social Anthropologists, Robinson College, Cambridge University; the Wenner Gren Conference on "Symbolism Through Time"; the departments of Anthropology and

East Asian Programs at the University of Chicago; the University of Illinois, Chicago Circle; the University of Tokyo; the University of Michigan; the Institute of Social Anthropology, Oxford University; University College, London; the Nissan Institute of Japanese Studies, Oxford University; the University of Iowa; and the University of Rochester. I thank my colleagues who arranged these talks and those who patiently suffered through them, asking probing questions and offering suggestions.

Professor J. Vansina, who has quietly insisted on the diachronic dimension of culture, has been most influential in the writing of this book. He read the entire manuscript more than once and offered his usual profound insights and criticism. Several others served as readers for publishers, including Professors A. Appadurai, J. Fernandez, J. Peacock, and H. Ooms, and their constructive criticisms were most helpful to me as I revised the manuscript. Professor T. Najita shared with me his knowledge of social mobility in Tokugawa, Japan. Professor D. Greenwood encouraged me to see the relevance of this work to minority groups in general, and Professor Y. Tuan read some chapters and offered useful comments. Professor H. Kawakatsu prompted me to think more carefully about the relationship between the special status people and the "professionals" (Chapter 4). Dr. A. Waswo offered useful comments on the section on Japanese history. Professor E. Swanger shared with me information on the medical use of the monkey. Professor T. Umesao offered insightful remarks on Japanese ethologists' attitude toward macaques. Professors N. Miyata, M. Itoh, and T. Moriya all helped me in locating historical sources, while Professor M. Yamaguchi provided me with provocative suggestions during the initial stage of this project. Professor S. Kita offered his brilliant insights and also helped me to locate Japanese paintings with monkeys. The staff members at the Monkey Center in Inuyama, Nagoya, kindly shared their knowledge; Mr. T. Ōtake, in particular, not only shared with me his own long-term study of the monkey in Japanese culture but also sent me a number of photographs of monkeys found in various artifacts housed in the museum of the Monkey Center. Mr. D. Krupa exercised his editorial skill on the manuscript, Ms. T. Kishima helped me in numerous ways in the early stages of research, and Mr. K. Yano assisted me in the final checking of the references.

If I have been fortunate in receiving feedback from my colleagues, I have also been most lucky in receiving professional advice and criticism from various editors. I thank Mr. Peter Agree for his interest in my work as a historian. Ms. Sue Allen-Mills read not only the final version of this book but also a preliminary version almost a year ago, and she offered me invaluable suggestions. Above all, I am most grateful to Mr. Walter Lippincott, Jr., for his warm encouragement and sustained interest in my work over the years, and to Ms. Margaret Case, for her expertise as a historian and editor. Ms. Janet Stern did an admirable job of editing the manuscript, and I thank her for it.

My gratitude is due also to two professional photographers who generously offered their photos, some of which are used as illustrations in this book. They are Mr. Y. Azuma of the Mainichi Newspaper, Inc., and Mr. H. Sawada of Shiran Tsūshin Kōgyō. Finally, I thank Professor Robert J. Smith, who sent me Photo 11 as it appeared on the cover of the magazine from which it was taken.

With such generous input from the contemporary monkey trainers and from the most exceptional scholars and professionals in anthropology, Japanese Studies, and publishing, I have no excuse for the shortcomings of this book, all of which are simply my own.   E. O.-T.

Princeton

A Note to the Reader

FOLLOWING the Japanese practice, I have rendered Japanese personal names with the surname first. A Japanese word is italicized only the first time it appears in the text, except in those instances when it reappears in quotations or in book titles, or when the meaning of the word itself is under discussion. Japanese words commonly used in English, such as shogun, kabuki, and Tokyo, generally are spelled as they are in English, and so are not italicized the first time they occur.

Part One

Introduction

1

Theoretical Setting

IN THESE YEARS of post-colonialism and post-scientism, we have seen major turns of direction in anthropology. We have finally emerged from an ahistorical period during whose long reign we largely ignored historical dimensions of culture and concentrated only on the notoriously artificial "ethnograpahic present." We have begun to examine seriously how culture changes or does not change over time—sometimes over periods as long as centuries or millennia.

As we have begun to confront historical processes, somewhat ironically we have also become aware that history "in the raw" was an erroneously held ideal in the past; we do not simply "reconstruct" history from "objective facts" recorded in archives. We are fully aware that both ethnographic and historical representations are incomplete, partial, and over-determined by forces such as the inequalities of power—the forces that are beyond the control or consciousness of the individuals who are involved in the complex process of representing and interpreting the "other," be it historical or ethnographic.[1]

---

[1] In the past—and I suspect that it will continue to occur—we have had cases of academic construction or misconstruction of other people's history by academics. A most drastic example is the fabrication of the "Aryan invasion" as a historical fact, as Leach (n.d.) delineates. Even when "stories" of the past are told by the "natives" (Geertz 1980) or when an anthro-

3

These epistemological questions about knowledge and the process of its production are at least in part responsible for forcing us to confront the multiple voices in every culture. We no longer assume that there is a single thought or behavioral structure common to all the members of a given society at all times. We are faced with profound differences between men and women, young and old, and dominant and minority groups—let alone individual variations—within the same society. The multiple voices in almost all societies are constrained by inequalities in power. Such is the case in Japan, as discussed in this book. There has never been a homogeneous culture, and there are a number of ways to represent a culture.

These developments in the way we view societies have forced anthropologists also to realize that there has never been a simple or primitive culture. This realization coincides with another—that anthropologists will become extinct if they continue to specialize only in relatively isolated or small societies that are virtually gone from the twentieth-century world. As a corollary, anthropologists have started to pay more serious attention to the erroneously labeled "complex" societies—industrialized sectors of the world, often with long traditions of written record.[2] Our task, then, is to study these societies that have long had writing systems, but to be aware of the complexities and constraints involved in ethnographic and historical representations.

---

pologist analyzes native perceptions of historical events (Sahlins 1981, 1982, 1985), the distinction between "myth" and "history" becomes a fine one (cf. Leach 1965, 1967). White (1983) uses the term "metahistory." A similar denial of the "objectivity" in "history" is expressed by McNeill's (1986) term "mythistory." But I am not sure that a new label is necessary here. These epistemological questions are most succinctly expressed in Clifford (1983). See also Kuhn (1962).

[2] Appadurai (1986) provides us with a penetrating explanation, in which academic politics plays no small part, as to why the study of complex non-Western societies has been a second-class citizen in anthropology. See also Hannerz (1986).

At this critical moment in the conceptual development of anthropology, I join the optimists who nevertheless try their best to understand the ethnographic and historical other. Thus, while the research embodied here represents my own struggle with these epistemological and theoretical problems, I attempt in this book to make sense of ethnographic and historical information, rather than to make epistemological questions the focus of my research. It is an anthropology of Japan, a post-industrial society with a high degree of intra-cultural variation, contrary to the stereotypical image of "homogeneity." Futhermore, its oldest documents date to the beginning of the eighth century, making Japan a fertile ground for historical anthropology.

Using Japanese culture as an example, I examine multiple structures of meaning—that is, culture—and how they are transformed through history, on the one hand, and expressed in myth and ritual, on the other. In this book, I use the term *history* to refer to interpretations of the past based on its records as best one can represent it on its own terms.[3] Specifically, I am interested in the relationship between history and culture, and in the relationship between the structures of meaning involved in historical processes and those expressed in myth and ritual. In examining the structures of meaning as expressed in ritual, I am particularly concerned with the construction of multiple structures of meaning as engendered by different readings of ritual performance by different social groups.

To examine these relationships, I have chosen a study that consists of three interrelated parts: the monkey metaphor, the special status people, and the monkey performance. The special status people, as I refer to them in this book, are a heterogeneous group of people who are often

---

[3] Since historians and anthropologists belong to the contemporary culture, some argue that the past is interpreted only from the perspective of the contemporary culture. Although the past and the present are mutually determined, many of us try our best to understand the past on its own terms.

referred to as the outcastes in Japan. The monkey performance has been one of the traditional occupations of this social group. Both the monkey and the special status people have long been intrinsically involved in Japanese deliberations of the self and other; they have been reflexive symbols.

My task in combing through historical data on the monkey metaphor, the special status people, and the monkey performance was to determine the "dominant" meaning of each in a given historical period. While all three have been and remain multivocal symbols, certain of their meanings received greater emphasis in different historical contexts, as indicated by the relative frequency of appearance in an assortment of media—folktales, icons, folk religions, paintings, and the like.[4]

Throughout history, the monkey has been an important and complex metaphor in Japanese culture (Chapter 3). It is the animal considered to be most similar and therefore closest to humans. Its very proximity as perceived by the Japanese has made it in turn a revered mediator during early periods in history and a threat to the human-animal boundary in later periods, fostering ambivalence that is expressed by mocking the animal. As a mediator, it harnessed the positive power of deities to rejuvenate and purify the self of humans. However, seeing a disconcerting likeness between themselves and the monkey, the Japanese also attempt to create distance by projecting their negative side onto the monkey and turning it into a scapegoat, a laughable animal who in vain imitates humans. The monkey as scapegoat is best expressed in the contemporary Japanese "definition" of the monkey as "a human minus three pieces of hair." By shouldering their negative side, the monkey cleanses the self of the Japanese. As a scapegoat, it marks the boundary

[4] As I will discuss below, my focus in this book is on folk culture; therefore, I do not closely examine Buddhistic doctrines and other sources pertaining to the intellectual elite alone.

6

between humans and animals. Both as a mediator and a scapegoat, the monkey therefore has played a crucial role in the reflexive structure of the Japanese.

The monkey as a reflexive symbol is not simply a histo-rial relic. On the contrary, it continues to be a dominant symbol of reflexivity in contemporary Japan. As if to reaf-firm the centrality of the monkey in the Japanese structure of reflexivity, we observe that while its characterization in contemporary Japan as "a human minus three pieces of hair" continues to remain strong in people's minds, a new meaning is emerging—the monkey as a clown who turns it-self into an object of laughter while challenging the basic as-sumptions of Japanese culture and society (Chapter 8). A clown is a truly reflexive figure who can distance himself from the self, rather than simply act as an agent for the re-flexive structure, as mediator and scapegoat do.

In sum, because the monkey's depiction in art, literature, and other historical sources has sensitively reflected Japa-nese delibration about the self and other throughout his-tory, we can tap a significant part of the Japanese structure of meaning by examining the transformations of the mean-ing of the monkey—as a metaphor for humans in relation to animals and as a metaphor for the Japanese in relation to foreigners.

One major form of the monkey's participation in Japa-nese culture is the monkey performance, during which a trained monkey performs tricks and dances at the trainer's command. The history of the monkey performance is simi-lar to the history of monkey symbolism itself. It started as a religious ritual at horse stables, during which a monkey danced to heal ill horses. Gradually, it was replaced by a monkey performance in the street, becoming a form of sec-ular entertainment with abivalent values and meanings.

Historical study of the monkey performance (Chapter 5) necessarily involves historical study of the special status people (Chapter 4). Contrary to the stereotypical image held by people both in and out of Japan, historical sources testify that traditional Japanese arts, especially the performing arts, owe a great deal to individuals from this group, and that their lowly status with its intensely negative meaning has a relatively short history. Above all, their ancestors are so heterogeneous, including artistic and religious specialists as well as craftsmen, that it is impossible to lump them into a single category. These artistic and religious specialists were, in early history, mediators between humans and deities, but in later history, they too, like the monkey, were turned into scapegoats, marked by impurity. The history of the special status people and that of the monkey performance together reveal a process whereby play, music, dance, other entertainments, and various forms of art and performance gradually lost their religious significance.

When I first began this study, I had no idea whether there were different meanings earlier in history or when changes in meaning took place. As my research progressed, it became clear that the meanings of the monkey, the special status people, and the monkey performance all went through a similar transformation twice in history, and that these two transformations in meaning coincided with two periods of great change in Japanese culture and society at large: the latter part of the Medieval period and contemporary Japan. (Both periods will be discussed in more detail in the next section.)

It should be noted that a shift in dominant meaning takes place gradually during a long period. In fact, during the latter part of the Medieval period and the beginning of the Early Modern period, two meanings of the monkey and the special status people—mediator and scapegoat—existed side by side, and only after the beginning of the Early Modern period did the scapegoat become the dominant meaning. Similarly, in contemporary Japan, the meaning of the monkey as clown has just emerged and is now competing with the meaning as scapegoat.

While the historical transformations of the multivocal symbols constitute one half of this book, the other half is devoted to the analyses of monkey performances. As noted above, the monkey performance began as a religious ritual conducted at stables, during which a trained monkey danced to music in order to cure horses. It was a healing ritual with a monkey as a shaman who harnessed the power of the Mountain Deity for healing purposes. The monkey was assigned this role since it was believed to be a messenger from the powerful Mountain Deity. While the stable ritual continued to be practiced well into the twentieth century, since the Medieval period the monkey performance has also been a street entertainment. Its repertoire has included not only dances but other acts, often sensitively reflecting society and the events of the time. For example, a monkey performance during wartime Japan included a scene in which a monkey carries a toy cannon and dashes into presumed enemy territory, only to drop the cannon on the way—a most extreme and sacrilegious act incurring hearty laughter from spectators. In contemporary Japan, one group of trainers is attempting to revive the traditional form of monkey performance, emphasizing only dances. The other group of trainers has adapted the performance to the contemporary culture of Japan, jabbing at the hierarchy in Japanese society and the line between humans and animals. Thus, the highlight of this group's performance is the staging of "ordered disobedience," during which the monkey voluntarily refuses to take orders from the trainer.

The monkey performance is full of important polysemes. The monkey may be interpreted as a beast, as a messenger from the Mountain Deity, or as an animal who outsmarts humans. And the monkey performance itself may be either a superb artistic performance or an act falling short of human behavior. There are many other symbols yielding many readings.

My concern is how these polysemes of symbolic objects

9

and behaviors are read by the different individuals and social groups that constitute the spectators. To this end, I will
examine monkey performances in different contexts, that
is, in different historical periods and in different performative contexts, both as sacred ritual and as street entertainment. I will also examine how polysemic symbols are read
by ritual participants—at times uniformly and at other
times with different meanings—and what factors determine the structure of meaning during a performance. In
particular, I will argue that during certain performances,
the trainers from the special status group and the spectators
from the dominant Japanese group read the symbols in the
performance differently, so that a structure of meaning and
its inversion are simultaneously present.

A broader implication of the multiple structures of meaning during a performance is encompassed by this question:
Do we assume the "text" to be out there "objectively," that
is, do different individuals and social groups read the same
text differently, or is the text constructed as it is being read?
A related question is: What is shared or public? In the case
of the monkey performance, this study indicates that it is
not the particular meaning or structure of meaning during
a performance that is shared by ritual participants, but
rather the pool of meaning, that is, polysemes, from which
the participants draw at times the same meaning and at
other times different meanings.

This tripartite research project turned out to be fertile
ground for critically examining existing theories about symbols, ritual, and history. In this regard, I will attempt to examine how culture—its symbolic structure, form, and
meaning—changes over a long period. More precisely, I
will be concerned with what in culture changes and what
does not change, and with why particular changes take
place and how they relate to historical contexts. My strategy
in approaching Japanese culture and history from this angle

is to focus on the reflexive structure—perhaps the most important structure of meaning in any culture. I will attempt to examine how Japanese culture—as expressed through its concepts of the self and other—interacts with historical forces, and how the dialectic between culture and history has unfolded over the past millennium.[5]

Most important, I will examine the cultural transformations over the past millennium to see how they represent structural transformations, and thus stability of the structure, on the one hand, and how they represent historical transformations, and thus changes over time, on the other. The key to probing into this question is a qualitatively long enough time to study the culture. Only by studying a culture over a long enough period can we determine if a historical event ordered by culture indeed alters it. A dramatic historical event, such as the arrival of Captain Cook in Hawaii, may indeed be ordered by culture (Sahlins 1985). Thus, a display of fireworks or reordering, as it were, at the time of a significant historical event, is often to a great degree shaped and ordered by the structure of the received categories. But how the firework retains its form or dissipates in the air can be determined only after a considerable time has elapsed since the event. For the purpose of determining structural changes, then, a culture with a long recorded history, such as Japanese culture, provides us with strategic ground.

The findings of this research indicate that changes in the meaning of the monkey and of the special status people represent not only structural transformations but also historical changes. As noted previously, such changes in meaning have taken place twice during the past millen-

[5] In his work on Japanese culture and society, R. Smith (1983), in a most trenchant way, elucidates how history ("tradition" is his term) is created through interactions between historical events and the concepts of self and other.

nium, thus enabling me to compare and contrast the two types of transformation to see in what way they represent structural stability and in what way they represent historical changes.

In addition to the relationship between culture and history, I am also interested in the relationship between the structure of meaning as expressed in historical processes and that expressed in the myth and ritual/performance of different historical periods. In short, the relationship between culture and history on the one hand and that between history and ritual/performance on the other constitute the two major concerns of this book.

The Two Transitional Periods in Japanese History: A Sketch

The theoretical discussion just presented constitutes the backdrop against which my tripartite research was conceived. Now I will briefly characterize the two transitional periods in Japanese history when the major transformations in culture and society took place—the late Medieval period and contemporary Japan.[6] Specialists in Japanese history will undoubtedly find the following description too general and perhaps detractive. However, I am including it here because I am addressing theoretical concerns in anthropology and related fields, and thus I anticipate that readership will not be confined to Japanese specialists.

[6] Throughout the book, I use the conventional periods in Japanese history. It is beyond the scope of this book to discuss historicity (the people's conception of history) in reference to the conventional schema in Japanese history of punctuating the flow of time. As this study indicates, a major transformation of Japanese culture and society took place during the latter half of the Medieval period. Therefore, one can argue that this era, for example, should be demarcated as a separate period. Along the same lines, it is worth noting here that throughout history each emperor, as he or she was installed, began a new era—a convention expressive of the cyclical notion of history.

The Late Medieval Period and the Beginning
of the Early Modern Period

Japanese society has been highly stratified since the Ancient period (300 B.C. to the twelfth century), and much of the basic structure of culture and society was formulated during that period. However, historians who compare the Ancient, Medieval, and Early Modern periods (see Figure 1 for the chronology of these periods and sub-periods)[7] often point out the extraordinary character of the Medieval period, especially its latter half (Yokoi, in H. Inoue et al. 1978:167–70; Yokoi 1982).

Great waves of change began about the mid-thirteenth century, culminating in political chaos during the Nanbokuchō period in the later half of the fourteenth century, at which time two emperors reigned simultaneously. This era was followed by a long period of cyclical conquests, and finally by the political hegemony established by Ieyasu. Shortly after Ieyasu seized control of the entire nation, Japanese society started on a path toward rigidity, which terminated the dynamics of the latter half of the Medieval period.

In contrast to the Ancient period and the Early Modern period (1603–1868), both of which were characterized by societal rigidity, the Medieval period was marked by greater mobility and flexibility, as manifested, for example, in the existence of multiple structures of stratification and in the availability of several institutionalized means of achieving a social status beyond one's ascribed status at birth. As we will see in detail in Chapter 4, this flexibility provided con-

[7] There is a great deal of variation in assigning dates to each period, often depending upon which event is considerd by each scholar to be significant enough to signal a new period. I generally followed Samson (1943), except for the beginning date for the Early Modern period; I adopted the date of 1603, instead of his 1615, since 1603 is used more often in Japan.

Yayoi Period (Agriculture) (300 B.C.–A.D. 250)

Ancient Period
(Gen-Kodai)

Tomb Period (State Formation) (250–646)

Nara Period (646–794)

Heian Period (794–1185)

Medieval Period
(Chūsei)

Kamakura Period (1185–1392)
(Nanbokuchō Period 1336–1392)

Muromachi Period (1392–1603)

Early Modern Period (1603–1868)
(Kinsei)

Modern Period (1868–Present)
(Kin-Gendai)

Figure 1. Chronology in Japanese history.

siderable opportunities for the special status people; indeed, some of them transcended their status at birth through their talents and not only became famous but also changed the course of history in the arts, performing arts, architecture, and a number of other fields.

14

This trend reached its peak during the Muromachi period (1392–1603) and was most clearly manifested in the concept of *gekokujō*, literally "the below conquering the above." Gekokujō, derived from the dualistic cosmology of yin-yang and the five elements, does not recognize the absolute supremacy of any particular element in the universe (see Chapter 6). This metaphysical-ontological perspective gave rise to a literary genre called the literature of the gekokujō, which enjoyed much popularity among the common people (Satake 1970; Sugiura 1965). Moreover, the theme enticed some Japanese to translate and transform it into a pragmatic philosophy of life, thereby making it possible for persons of low social status to surpass those above them. At any rate, some scholars (e.g. Kuroda 1972) argue that Japanese society went through a profound change during this period—a change that gave rise to a society, in the subsequent Early Modern period, that was governed by the military elite, who had conquered "the above."

Inner dynamics during the Medieval period were expressed outwardly as well. The Japanese during this period were most open to outsiders; they were curious about foreign lands and cultures. Under the direction of Zen monks, they reestablished trade and cultural contacts with China in about 1342 (Putzar 1963:287). In their ships, they visited foreign countries, and they even founded Japanese colonies. They also engaged in extensive trade with other peoples, bringing in foreign goods that had high symbolic value to them. Such fluidity in both culture and society was unprecedented; it was also unique until the contemporary period. This dynamic tendency was soon overtaken by the opposite tendency, however, as manifested in the consolidation of Japan into a highly stratified society during the Early Modern period. Inner dynamics were eliminated and the country was closed to outsiders.

It is important to recognize, however, that opposing

forces were also at work during the Medieval period, with its emphasis on ascribed status, hierarchy, and a system of meaning that included purity and impurity *as moral values.* These principles, already present during the Ancient period, were highly developed in the Early Modern period.

During the long Medieval period, then opposing forces and principles in both society and culture were struggling against each other. The nature of society and culture was closely related to the status and symbolic meaning of the people who were relegated to a marginal position in society—the special status people. It was during this long period of transition that gradual but fundamental changes took place in the meanings of the monkey, the special status people, and the monkey performance.

Contemporary Japan

World War II ended with the first and only defeat the nation of Japan ever experienced. Drastic changes were brought about by the occupational forces. While these changes were basic in nature, they were imposed from without. It is perhaps for this reason that we see "indigenous" changes emerging only in contemporary Japan, that is, Japan since the early 1970s. The change is most conspicuous in the image of the *self* of the Japanese in relations to the *other*, that is, other peoples. The technological and economic successes of Japan carry immense symbolic meaning for the Japanese, who for the first time in history seem to feel that they have "conquered" the West—the dominant other whose technological advancement had been a source of awe since the opening of Japan in 1868. Nevertheless, any assessment of contemporary Japan must be tentative. Waves and ripples have not yet settled enough for us to evaluate if they are to have an impact upon the fundamental structure of the culture. There is no doubt, however, that it is a period of transition.

LIMITATIONS AND ORGANIZATION OF THE BOOK

The scope of this book is hopelessly immense. In focusing on the monkey metaphor, the special status people, and the monkey performance, I am attempting, in fact, to interpret Japanese culture through its entire history—an impossible task indeed. A macro-study such as this one often involves sweeping generalizations, both in terms of history, in its setting aside of fluctuations within a particular historical period, and in terms of culture, in its de-emphasizing intra-cultural variations of all sorts. I have not paid enough attention to the nature of the production of cultural and historical texts, nor have I explicated in detail my method of interpretation. I do not pretend that I have written a definitive work on the subject, topically or theoretically. I hope only that some of my arguments have broader implications for those readers interested in symbols, rituals, and the study of culture through time.

To talk about "the Japanese" or "Japanese culture" is to commit the anthropological sin of lumping the whole population under one umbrella. A major focus of this book is indeed intra-cultural variation and its effect upon the perception of ritual. The two specific groups of Japanese dealt with in this book are the dominant Japanese and the special status people. By "dominant Japanese," I mean the agrarian population who initially occupied southwestern Japan but later became the majority population throughout Japan. Most historical sources focus on this group. Of the people who constitute the dominant agrarian population, my emphasis is on the folk, not the intellectual elite. Also not included in this book are other subgroups of the Japanese, such as fishing and hunting populations, both of which constitute small segments of the total population. In terms of the specific concerns of this book, differences between men and women do not seem significant and therefore are excluded from discussion.

17

I have deliberately written a short book. In order to treat comprehensively in this book the findings of my research that have broader theoretical implications, I have decided to relegate to separate treatments the detailed findings and analyses of my 1981 and 1984 field observations of the monkey performance.[8]

Since the monkey metaphor and the special status people are not confined to Japan, readers may wonder about the relationship of the structure of meaning assigned to the monkey and the special status people in Japanese culture to that in other cultures. Again, comparative perspectives and theoretical points not directly relevant to the central concerns of this book are not included here.

For the same reason, the organization of the book is unconventional. Chapter 2 compares and contrasts different meanings of the monkey, in an attempt to establish a hierarchy of meaning, that is, different levels of abstraction. Recognizing that there is no strict line between description and analysis, I have chosen to focus in Part Two on the historical and ethnographic setting, so that my arguments elsewhere are not interrupted by a detailed substantiation of my points. I knowingly subject the reader, then, to detailed information relating to the meanings of the monkey in different historical periods (Chapter 3), to the history of the special status people (Chapter 4), and to the history of the monkey performance (Chapter 5) without justifying these details as they occur. The arguments in Chapter 2 are then carried to Chapter 6; here, using the information presented in the previous three chapters, I place the monkey, the special status people, and the monkey performance within the broader context of Japanese cosmology, with

---

[8] For example, I plan to examine the transformations in Japanese culture of the monkey from the well-known Chinese novel of the Ming period, *The Journey to the West* (Yu 1977–1983), from the time it was introduced to Japan to the present. The *songokū* (the monkey in the novel) is a popular television series in contemporary Japan.

particular emphasis on the reflexive structure. Chapter 6 therefore constitutes the analytical conclusion to Part Two whose organizational framework is historical.

In contrast to the diachronic scheme of Part Two, Part Three presents a sychronic analysis of the monkey performance. Chatper 7 focuses on the interpretation of the monkey performance in the late Medieval period, while Chapter 8 concentrates on the monkey performance in contemporary Japan. These two chapters primarily examine how the polysemes of monkey and special status people, which we saw in historical contexts in Part Two, are expressed ritually.

Part Four, which consists only of Chapter 9, brings together the arguments presented in the preceding chapters, with an emphasis on history and symbolism. It summarizes my understanding of multiple structures of meaning in ritual and history. In regard to the latter, I argue that in our interpretation of historical changes in symbolism we should go beyond the transformational model, and that we must recognize the critical importance of studying culture over a long period.

2

The Monkey as Metaphor
for the Japanese

THE JAPANESE MACAQUES (*Macacus fuscatus* = *Macaca fuscata*) is characterized by a red face, red buttocks, and a short tail. It is found on all of the islands of the Japanese archipelago except Hokkaido, which belongs to a different ecological zone. To the Japanese, macaques used to be familiar animals that came to the fields and even to settlements. With urbanization, they have retreated to the mountains. Contemporary Japanese only see them in zoos. Consequently, the Japanese conceptualization of the animal today is based almost exclusively upon its culturally defined characterizations transmitted through various media. Yet, the monkey has remained an important animal in Japanese culture. Above all, it continues to serve as a powerful metaphor for the Japanese and, in general, for humans as defined in Japanese culture (see Chapter 3). In this chapter, I examine the Japanese characterization of the monkey, focusing on why the monkey has served as a dominant reflexive symbol throughout history.

WHY THE MONKEY?[1]

In most cultures of the world, the question of who humans are occupies a central place in the thought structure of the

[1] A question raised by Professor Sahlins during a talk I gave at the De-

people, irrespective of whether such intellectual specializations as philosophy, theology, and so on have developed. The reflexive question "Who are the humans?" is
often framed in terms of the relationship between humans
and animals (cf. Willis 1974). The distinction between humans and animals, or between culture and nature, is assigned a complex structure of meaning in every culture
(Lévi-Strauss 1966, 1967). In the Judeo-Christian tradition,
the Supreme Deity, God, is the creator of an order whose
basic dyad is the sacred and the profane, with the latter
comprising humans and nonhuman animals. Transgress-
ing the demarcation line between humans and animals
is against the order created by God; it is a blasphemy.
Thus, transformations or metamorphoses between animals and humans are transgressions against the sacred
order.

But in most other religions of the world, including those
of the Japanese, many of the beings of nature, such as animals, are deified. In native Shintoism, deities are natural
phenomena and animals. Buddhism recognizes no sharp
line between or hierarchy of humans and animals (cf. La-
Fleur 1983:29). In this type of cosmology, metamorphoses
between humans and animals are more frequent, and the
line of demarcation is generally more lax (see Ohnuki-
Tierney 1981a for a detailed discussion of this topic).
Yet in every culture the line is drawn, often in a complex
way.

The monkey is unique as a nonhuman being in Japanese
culture precisely because there is no other animal so intimately involved in the Japanese deliberation upon the crucial distinction between humans and nonhuman animals.
Unlike the Sun Goddess, who is so clearly sacred that she
has little to do with the problem of distinguishing between
humans and nonhuman beings of the universe, the mon-

partment of Anthropology at the University of Chicago prompted me to
think further about the question "Why the monkey?"

key presses hard at the border line, constantly threatening human identity and forcing contemplation of such questions as "Who are we?" and "How do we differ from animals?"

The unique role played by the monkey in Japanese culture comes from its dual meaning—the monkey as simultaneously similar to, yet distinct from, humans. Similarities that the Japanese see between the monkey and humans force them to create distance and differences between the two.

THE MONKEY AS METAPHOR FOR HUMANS

The Monkey as a "Human among Humans"

The Japanese notion of humans is most succinctly expressed in the two characters for humans, which are combined to form the term *ningen*: the character for *nin* means "humans" and that for *gen* means "among." In the Japanese conception, an individual human cannot be conceived of without reference to others, since humans exist only in the company of other humans. This notion of humans, common to both the folk and the intellectuals throughout Japanese history, is articulated by Watsuji Tetsurō (1959:esp. 1–67). Watsuji explains that ningen is dialectically defined by both humans (*hito*) and society (*shakai*). Thus, the term ningen means at once both humans and society (see also Plath 1982:120).

If the two characters for humans express the concept of humans as dialectically defined vis-à-vis society, the avoidance of pronouns and the use of a particular speech level in daily discourse and in writing clearly express the dialogically defined self of the speaker/writer vis-à-vis the addressee. Thus, the Japanese usually avoid the use of "I" or "you," although there are several equivalents for each. Instead, when they talk or write about themselves, they use humble forms, as expressed in prefixes and suffices, but when they talk or write about the addressee, they use elevated forms. The reason for this is that, in the context of polite discourse, the other, or the addressee, is by definition higher in status than the speaker, even when the two are of equal social standing. If a son is talking to his parents, he uses polite or deferential forms to them because of the parents' higher status within the family. However, when referring to his parents in conversation with someone outside the family, he must use humble forms, since a member of his own family must be placed in a lower position than that of an outsider.

While this description expresses only the basic principle of the speech level in a system that is quite complicated, the basic notion is that the relative status of the speaker/writer and the addressee determines the choice of the level of speech, which in turns makes it unnecessary and undesirable to use pronouns (for details, see Miller 1967).

In this system of discourse, a context-free utterance rarely exists. The self cannot be defined in the abstract. It cannot be without reference to the specific other. As a corollary, the self is never constant; it changes depending upon the specific other.[2]

The dialectical and dialogical conception of the self underlies other types of day-to-day transactions as well. It is expressed in the incorporation of the wishes of others into decision making. For example, a person who is asked where he would like to dine would suggest a restaurant that serves the type of food known or guessed to be preferred by the person who asked the question. A better example of Japanese decision making is the process of group decision making. For the Japanese it is not a process in

[2] The relational perception and definition of self is well-expressed in the term *kanjin* (between people) proposed by Hamaguchi (1982), who translates the term as "contextual" (Hamaguchi 1985).

which isolated individuals state their own opinions. Instead, every opinion of a Japanese is expected to incorporate his or her perception of the opinions of others. Thus, the underlying principle of Japanese decision making contrasts with the basic assumption prevalent in American society that the collective good is somehow achieved through maximization of the individual goals. In Japanese group decision making, on the other hand, the resultant collective good is often less than individual members' goals but something that every member can psychologically live with. By the same token, if a group decides against a proposal, it may mean that at least one is strongly opposed. Majority rule by a slim margin seldom takes place.

The most crucial aspect of Japanese decision making is the *nemawashi*, which literally means "to dig around the root of a tree." It is a process in which a proponent of an idea engages in extensive but informal negotiations to persuade others involved in the decision making. Only later are the important decisions presented for formal decision making, during which there seldom is a vote. Nemawashi is a normative process, constituting a vital part of decision making.[3]

Given this Japanese conception of humans, the monkey, a group animal par excellence, is indeed an apt metaphor for humans. Seen in this light, the seemingly insignificant hunter's taboo against hunting and killing a lone monkey (Hirose 1979:47–48) takes on significance. I think that a lone

[3] The consideration of others' wishes or feelings in decision making and informal negotiations before formal decision making both occur in the United States, for example. However, the difference between Japan and the United States is that the nemawashi is an institutionalized process, and the Japanese expect it as a normal part of decision making, while a similar process in the United States seems to be a covert pattern, not explicitly recognized and sometimes even denied. It is important to recognize that the difference in decision making processes derives from the conception of the individual in the respective societies.

monkey is like a lone human, antithetical to the very basic notion of humans. It is unusual, hence a taboo.

In this connection, it is noteworthy to recall Asquith's study in which contemporary Japanese ethologists are compared with Euro-American ethologists. Asquith points out that Japanese ethologists study "the society of monkeys" by focusing upon their cooperation for survival and their joint ownership of resources, rather than upon the survival of the fittest—the characteristic that receives greatest attention among Euro-American ethologists (Asquith 1984:39). She further points out that Japanese ethologists assume that monkeys have souls and personalities. Japanese ethologists perform memorial services for dead monkeys, and a temple in Osaka, where such services are held annually, houses some 20,000 monkey tombs (Asquith 1984:41). The beliefs and attitudes of Japanese ethologists, according to Asquith, contrast markedly with those of Euro-American ethologists, in whose society the question of the ownership of a soul has been a focus of intensive discussion since Descartes. I might add that Japanese ethologists may not personally believe that monkeys have souls, but collective behavior such as that represented by memorial services for dead monkeys is not out of place in contemporary Japan.

The monkey is the animal that comes closest to humans as defined in Japanese culture; therefore, the monkey is the only animal that is addressed and referred to in adult language by the use of *san*—the address form used for humans.[4] The proximity that the Japanese see between them-

---

[4] I was reminded by an anonymous reader who reviewed the manuscript of this book for a publisher of the use of *san* in referring to monkeys. I am grateful to the reviewer. Indeed, in the language of children, other animals are also addressed and referred to by *san*, but the monkey alone qualifies for the human status in adult language.

selves and the monkey is also evident in the following historical development of Japanese art.

Gibbons and Macaques in Visual Art

The contrast in the way gibbons and macaques (both linguistically classified as monkey, or *saru*) are presented in early Japanese art is an unexpected source of information about the monkey (macaque) as a metaphor for humans in opposition to nature/deities, and the monkey as a metaphor for the Japanese in opposition to foreigners.

Gibbons, not part of the fauna of Japan, were never actually seen by people during the early periods of Japanese history but became an important motif in art through somewhat unusual circumstances. Mu-Ch'i, a Chinese Zen priest-artist who lived during the thirteenth century (exact dates of his birth and death are not known), emigrated from the Szechwan province of China to Kyoto in Japan. Although unrecognized in his own country, he became very influential in Japan. In particular, three of his paintings, labeled *The Goddess of Mercy* (Kannon), *Monkeys*, and *A Crane*, respectively, were considered masterpieces. The painting of the mother and infant monkeys, which were gibbons, was dated about 1291, and it gave rise to an artistic tradition known as "Mu-Ch'i's monkey," or *Bokkei-zaru* (Bokkei means Mu-Ch'i in Japanese). Tōhaku and other well-known Japanese painters, who, I assume, never saw a live gibbon, drew gibbons in nature using Mu-Ch'i's gibbons as their model, thus perpetuating the tradition of "Mu-Ch'i's monkey."[5]

It is significant that Mu-Ch'i's gibbons were almost always drawn against the background of nature, while macaques were depicted in human settings, as we shall see

[5] For details of Mu-Ch'i's life, see Toda (1978); for more information on Tōhaku, see Doi (1973) and Nakajima (1979).

shortly.[6] In other words, gibbons represented nature, which in folk Shintoism signified deities. Furthermore, I even venture to suggest that to the Japanese of the time, Mu-Ch'i's gibbons represented the Chinese art tradition (*kanga*), which in turn represented the Chinese, who were then the most significant foreigners. Ultimately, then, Mu-Ch'i's gibbons symbolized the other to the collective self of the Japanese in the reflexive structure briefly outlined in Chapter 1.

The history of macaques in Japanese art is quite different from that of gibbons. There are some paintings in which macaques are portrayed in natural settings. For example, two macaques are walking on a mountain in the *Yūzū Nenbutsu Engi*, a Buddhistic picture scroll from the fourteenth century (Komatsu 1983:4–5). More frequently, however, macaques are pictured either as anthorpomorphic caricatures or in human settings, that is, among humans or among human-made objects. For example, the *Hōnen Shōnin E-den* (Illustrated Deeds of St. Hōnen) (Kadokawa Shoten 1961) provides examples of monkeys in Buddhist paintings. The paintings illustrate the life of Hōnen (1133–1212), founder of the Jōdo (Pure Land) sect of Buddhism, during the twelfth and thirteenth centuries, as envisioned in the early fourteenth century.[7] Naturalistically drawn

---

[6] One exception to this general rule is a painting by Tosa Mitsunobu (?–1521?) entitled *Kōshin-zu* (Picture of kōshin) (reproduced in Iida 1983:31). It depicts the three monkeys see no evil, hear no evil, and speak no evil, but the three "monkeys" are gibbons, not the macaques of the three-monkey icons of later periods. I suggest that Mitsunobu's painting emphasized the Chinese origin of both the kōshin and the three-monkey theme.

[7] The forty-eight volumes in which this series of paintings appears were reportedly edited by Shunshō between 1307 and 1317. Therefore, we may assume that the paintings reflect the early fourteenth-century perception of the lives of Hōnen and his contemporaries during the mid–twelfth to the early thirteenth centuries.

monkeys appear in these volumes, but they are always in human settings; they play, for example, on the roof of a temple or around a temple gate (reproduced in Kadokawa Shoten 1961: Plate 14). Similarly, in another illustrated biography of a Buddhist monk, *Ippen Shōnin Eden*, dated about 1299, there is a scene of a naturalistically drawn monkey tied to a stable (reproduced in Miyamoto 1981:81). A number of other illustrations of monkeys in human settings appear in the picture scrolls of these periods, supporting my argument that the monkey is unique in its closeness to humans.[8]

Symbolic oppositions represented by gibbons and macaques generally can be arranged in a hierarchy of meaning:

LEVEL	MACAQUES	GIBBONS
4	self	other
3	culture	nature
2	humans	deities
1	Japanese	foreigners

I need not explain Levels 1 and 2. At Level 3, I introduce the opposition nature:culture, which currently is not in favor in anthropology. But it remains a useful analytical framework as long as the concepts are contextualized in terms of a given culture, and as long as it is used with the recognition that there is no "nature" "out there in the external world";

[8] For paintings in which monkeys are depicted in human settings, see Shibuzawa (1965:238–39; 1966a:244–45; 1966b:82–83, 228–29; 1968:50–51, 92–93).

In the twelfth-century *Chōjū Giga* (Scrolls of Animal Caricatures) (Kaneko 1969), monkeys, together with hares and other animals, are drawn in animal forms but wear pieces of human clothing and engage in human activities. Although monkeys are depicted in these scrolls, the scheme of the scrolls is to present all animals in human clothing and demonstrating human behavior. Therefore, they present neither positive nor negative evidence for my argument that the monkey is unique in its closeness to humans.

rather, "nature" is always culturally defined. Relegating a more extensive discussion of the nature:culture opposition in Japanese society to a later section of the book, I simply wish to point out here that in Japanese cosmology, the sacred consists of the beings of nature, including animals. It is culturally defined to be "out there," beyond human society. It is this nature that is represented by gibbons.[9] Also belonging to "out there" or "the outside" are foreigners, represented by the Chinese in earlier times and Westerners in later periods. These foreigners and deities of nature were opposed collectively to the Japanese and to humans, whose realm is "the inside," that is, within human society.

It is well to note here that the problem of sacred and secular enters only at Level 2. In other words, the distinction between sacred and secular does not govern the meanings at higher levels of abstraction, indicating that religion is subsumed under a broader cosmological framework of self and other. I explore implications of this finding in later sections of this book.

The structure of meaning represented in the hierarchy above, however, underwent fundamental changes as Japanese culture and society experienced significant transformations, as noted in Chapter 1. The political power of the Imperial Court in Kyoto ended when the shogunate in Edo (Tokyo) established political control over Japan at the beginning of the seventeenth century. Soon the shogunal government legally codified a four-caste[10] system, consisting of

---

[9] Generalizations based on the evidence from art may seem at first to contradict the evidence from poems. Poems by aristocrats and intellectuals during the Heian period (examples are given in Iida 1973:215–19) depict the "monkey's calls" as an aesthetic representation of nature. However, during this period, the auditory image of the "monkey's calls" was directly copied from Chinese poems and should not, therefore, be taken to reflect the Japanese image of the macaques.

[10] For further discussion of castes, see note 7 in Chapter 9.

warriors, farmers, manufacturers, and merchants; there were, in addition, two other castes below merchants. Also significant was the closure of the country to outsiders at the very beginning of the Early Modern period. The government forced Japan's isolation, known as *sakoku*, by restricting trade and closing ports, and by the effective proscription of Christianity—the religion of Westerners, who by then were the most important foreigners in Japan.

These changes were paralleled by significant changes in culture in general, and in art in particular. In art, the naturalistic style of painting began to flourish both as an indigenous movement, known as *shijōha*, and as a result of the influence of Western paintings. Most important, with the transfer of political power from the Imperial Court in Kyoto to the shogunate in Edo, the center of culture also shifted to Edo, and this meant the end of the *Yamato-e* tradition in art in the seventeenth century. Yamato-e, the so-called "Japanese style" that embraced various art styles, including the kanga tradition of Chinese origin, was identified with the Imperial Court. Many distinguished artists of the Yamato-e school were *machishū*; these were wealthy townsmen in the Kyoto, Osaka, and Sakai regions of western Japan who gained civil control over those cities.[11] The shift of the center of culture to Edo also meant the birth of the *ukiyo-e* tradition, developed by Edo's newly established merchant class, known as *chōnin*. During the Early Modern period under the Shogun, however, the merchant class in Edo was rigidly defined in the feudal caste system as the class at the bottom of society; only the outcasts, regarded as being outside society, were below the merchants. The flexibility available to the machishū during the previous period no

[11] For a detailed study of the machishū, see Hayashiya (1978); for a good summary of social history and its impact on the art of the time, see Mizuo (1965:55–75).

longer existed (see Kita n.d. for a detailed treatment of this topic).

These dramatic changes in Japanese society and art during the seventeenth century are reflected vividly in the paintings of gibbons and macaques. The end of Yamato-e meant the disappearance of Mu-Chi's gibbons from Japanese art, except for a few sporadic exceptions.[12] With the rise of naturalistic painting, Japanese macaque for the first time began to be drawn against natural backgrounds, just as the gibbons had been. Thus, macaques became a major motif of paintings by such famous artists of the Early Modern period as Maruyama Ōkyo, Nagasawa Rosetsu, Kawai Gyokudō, Watanabe Nangaku, and Mori Sosen (cf. Hirose 1979:169–82). In addition, macques continued to appear in human settings in various other visual art forms. Thus, we see monkeys and their trainers for the monkey performance depicted in the ukiyo-e woodblock prints of eighteenth- and ninteenth-century masters such as Suzuki Harunobu and Katsushika Hokusai (see Chapter 5).

As foreigners were closed out of the day-to-day universe of the Japanese, then, so too were gibbons, who had represented foreigners. The Japanese and macaques were isolated from the rest of the world during the Early Modern period. The "nature" in which macaques were placed in the paintings of this time was not the "nature" of the previous period. The fundamental change in the cosmology of this period was the absence of the other against which the Japanese had once viewed their collective self.

With this brief discussion of the proximity that the Japanese see between themselves and the monkey, I now move

---

[12] One such exception is a painting by Masunobu, dated about 1770, which is housed at the Elvehjem Museum of Art at the University of Wisconsin. In this painting, a gibbon is depicted as naughtily interrupting a flower-viewing party.

to a discussion of the distance that they create between the two.

The Line between Humans and Monkeys

Perceiving such a close relationship between themselves and the monkey, the Japanese attempt to establish a dividing line by creating a distance between the two. I think this is reflected in the fact that, in oral tradition, monkeys seldom possess humans—a role assigned to other animals such as foxes, badgers, and snakes. And, unlike foxes and snakes—animals that also are believed to be messengers from deities—monkeys seldom metamorphose into humans, as documented in a recent study by T. Nakamura (1984).

With the aim of elucidating the Japanese concept of animals, Nakamura examined hundreds of Japanese tales that involve animal metamorphoses (different versions of the same motif are subsumed under one tale in Nakamura's study). Nakamura compared Japanese conceptions of animals, as represented in these tales, with those of the West, as represented in Grimm's fairy tales.

The most striking contrast between the Japanese tales and Grimm's tales is that in the former animals frequently become humans, while in Grimm's tales they seldom do. This contrast implies that in the West, the demarcation line between humans and animals must be kept sharp, so that lowly animals may not be transformed into humans. Some animals in Grimm's tales may don human clothes, but that does not constitute metamorphosis. In Japanese tales, on the other hand, animals are frequently allowed to become humans.

Of the 134 pre-Early Modern tales Nakamura examined, 42 show humans becoming animals, while in 92 cases animals become humans. Even more revealing of the cosmology is the nature of each metamorphosis: human metamorphosis into animals in Japanese tales occurs less frequently than animal metamorphosis into humans, but when it does occur, it is portrayed as a form of transcendence; profane humans become sacred birds, for example.

On the other hand, Nakamura's findings also indicate that the Japanese are not confortable with metamophoses between monkeys and humans. Of the 42 cases in which humans metamorphose into animals, only 3 involve a monkey, and all 3 cases, humans are transformed into monkeys as a form of punishment. Of the 92 cases in which animals become humans, again the monkey is involved in only 3 (T. Nakamura 1984:11–12).

These 134 tales are from early historical periods, but the frequency of human-monkey metamorphoses in tales from the Early Modern period is also revealing. Of the 60 cases of human metamorphosis into animals, the monkey is involved in only 1 (T. Nakamura 1984:221). Of the 156 cases of animal metamorphosis into humans, the monkey is involved in only 2 (T. Nakamura 1984:190).

A comparison of the frequency of metamorphosis between humans and monkeys before and during the Early Modern period indicates, then, that the incidence of metamorphosis was slightly higher during the earlier periods. The shift in frequency of metamorphosis parallels the shift in the meaning of the monkey. During early historical periods, the Japanese attitude toward the monkey was positive enough to view it as a mediator between deities and humans; this view was manifested in the belief that the monkey was a messenger sent to humans by the Mountain Deity. Later in history, the monkey's meaning turns increasingly negative, and the monkey becomes a scapegoat figure; this view is expressed succinctly in the Japanese proverb in which the monkey is caricatured as "a human minus three pieces of hair." The phrase suggests that the

33

monkey is a clever animal, similar to but not wise enough to qualify as a full-fledged human. Thus, when proximity is emphasized, the monkey is seen as being close to humans in its role as mediator, but when distinction is important, the Japanese drive the monkey away by turning it into a scapegoat that they can laugh at.

The Monkey as an Anomalous Symbol and the Hierarchy of Meaning

Before I present in Part Two historical and ethnographic data on the different meanings assigned to the monkey, let me first try to sort these meanings out, since it is imperative to recognize that these meanings belong to different levels of abstraction (cf. T. Turner 1977). The hierarchy of meaning, as I call it, is shown in the diagram below.

Levels	Meaning	
5	clown/trickster	
4	mediator	scapegoat/trickster
3	a marginal member	
2	a member of the sacred	
1	a member of the nonhuman	

Let me first explain the conceptual relationships between these meanings at different levels of abstraction. At the least abstract level, the monkey is classified as one of the non-human beings of the universe. At the next level, it is one of the sacred beings, that is, one of the millions of deities in the Japanese pantheon. However, the proximity which the Japanese see between the monkey and humans makes the monkey a peripheral deity close to humans, as shown at Level 3. As with the symbolic oppositions represented by

34

gibbons and macaques, at the higher levels of abstraction, the sacred/secular distinction is no longer a governing principle.

Levels 4 and 5 are corollaries of the structurally peripheral or marginal position (Level 3) assigned to the monkey in Japanese culture. The following schema is presented as a general discussion of the objects and beings that are assigned a peripheral position in the symbolic structure of a people (for several types of anomaly, of which marginality is one, see Ohnuki-Tierney 1981a:119–29).

LEVEL 4

A. Negative power

    Impurity ⟶ Taboo/Scapegoat (−)

B. Positive power

    1. Symbol of reconstruction/rejuvenation

        ⟶ Prophet/savior/creator (+　+)

    2. Mediation ⟶ Mediator (+)

LEVEL 5

C. Ambivalent/dual power

    1. "Practical" power of destruction/creation

        ⟶ Trickster (+　−)

    2. Metaphysical power of reflexivity

        ⟶ Clown (+　− ⟶ +)

Because an anomalous symbol, such as the monkey in Japanese culture, is not a normal or full-fledged member of a category, it is most often assigned negative power or meaning, such as impurity. From a semiotic perspective, it is *labeled* taboo; when it is people who are symbolically anomalous, such as outcastes (Level 4 A), they are labeled scapegoats.

On the other hand, an anomalous status frees the object

or being from structural constraints. It is often capable of traversing categorical boundaries—a freedom not accorded to the central members of the category. In some cases, freedom from structural constraints empowers anomalies to construct a new system. They represent prophets, saviors, and creators of a new, often utopian world (Level 4 B.1). While reconstruction of the entire system occurs infrequently even in ritual contexts, anomalous symbols regularly are assigned the less powerful but nevertheless positive role of mediation; freedom to traverse culturally codified categorical boundaries enables anomalous beings to mediate between members of different categories (Level 4 B.2).

Although the terms are broadly used in anthropology and related disciplines, I use *trickster* and *clown* to represent "symbolic," "mythical," or "real" figures or types who possess ambivalent or dual power (Level 5). While the two concepts are too closely interrelated to distinguish between them easily, trickster is used here to stress the "practical," rather than the metaphysical, power of figures that are assigned dual power. The distinction between "practical" and "mythical" should be strictly "from the native's point of view." A trickster is a figure who plays practical jokes on people, tricks them into doing things, is mischievous, or in general is characterized by both positive and negative qualities and powers. The primary characterization of a clown, as I use the term, is its role as metasocial commentator, to borrow Geertz's phraseology. Clowns are figures who philosophically comment upon the basic assumptions of the people. But, importantly, they do so by carrying a negative semiotic sign, that is, by being, for example, silly, impotent, or insignificant. We might say that if a scapegoat becomes capable of laughing at itself, rather than simply being laughed at, then conceptually it elevates itself to a higher level of meaning—that of a clown, a figure that is capable of being reflexive about its own follies.[13]

In this book, we will see that most of these meanings are assigned to the monkey because the Japanese are aware of the simultaneous proximity and distance between themselves and the monkey. When they allow proximity, they view the monkey as a deity that is close enough to humans to be a mediator. When they are threatened and wish to keep the monkey at a distance, they regard the animal negatively, as a scapegoat. Somewhat unwittingly, the Japanese also assign the clown and trickster figures to the monkey. As I will demonstrate in Chapter 7, in the Medieval monkey performance, the monkey is a scapegoat who innocently fools the audience and thereby plays the role of a clown. As a result, the world is toppled upside down for the audience. In the contemporary monkey performance, the monkey is unquestionably a clown who is funny and silly, while at the same time jabbing at the basic assump-

[13] Various terms, such as trickster, clown, fool, jester, and culture hero, have been used to refer to such figures. However, each term has a slightly different emphasis from the others, as Hastrup and Ovesen (1976) illustrate through an incisive structural analysis of these terms. Furthermore, a figure of ambivalent meaning or power in a particular culture is not always an exact replica of similar figures in other cultures, both in ethnographic details and in the significant conceptual features that define the figures.

It should be pointed out that my use of these terms is somewhat different from that of others. For example, Handelman (1981:330) writes that "the sacred clown type" is "composed of sets of contradictory attributes: sacred/profane, wisdom/folly, solemnity/humour, serious/comic, gravity/lightness, and so forth." Lévi-Strauss (1967:223) defines the trickster as "an ambiguous and equivocal character" who is both mediator and scapegoat at the same time. While he cautions against allowing the term trickster to serve as a label for a universal category, Beidelman (1980:28) characterizes tricksters as those who "exemplify certain forms of supposed disorder and mischief, sometimes even malevolence, though ultimately commenting on morality and order by their play with boundaries and ambiguities of these key concepts." In the Japanese examples, tricksters do not always have the reflexive element (see Chapter 3).

tions of the contemporary Japanese. When scapegoats and clowns become reflexive agents, their commentaries may aim at the immediate social hierarchy, but they may also aim at basic cosmological assumptions, such as the assumption of human superiority over animals. At a yet higher level, these reflexive agents may remind us, as the Japanese monkey does, of the basic duality of our universe—a universe in which evil and impurity are integral parts but which also embraces good and purity.

Part Two

Meanings through History

3

The Monkey in Japanese Culture:
Historical Transformations
of Its Meaning

ALTHOUGH ALL the meanings discussed above have been present, I believe, from the earliest times in Japanese history, at different times in history, a particular meaning becomes dominant. Briefly put, in earlier periods the dominant meaning of the monkey was that of mediator between deities and humans. Later in history, its meaning as a scapegoat became increasingly dominant, until by the seventeenth century the monkey became fully a scapegoat, onto whom the Japanese projected the negative side of human nature that they saw in themselves. The process of transformation was quite complex and developed gradually throughout several centuries, roughly between the middle of the thirteenth century and the end of the sixteenth century. During much of the interim period, the two dominant meanings—mediator and scapegoat—apparently coexisted with equal force. Since the monkey's role as a sacred mediator remained strong well into the transitional period during which the monkey's role as a scapegoat started to become dominant, I will discuss the early and transitional periods in one section and the later period in another.

THE MONKEY AS MEDIATOR IN EARLY AND TRANSITIONAL PERIODS

Saruta Biko (Monkey Deity)

Perhaps one of the oldest sources of evidence linking the monkey with the role of mediation is the Saruta Biko, the Monkey Deity, who features prominently in both the *Kojiki*, compiled in A.D. 712, and the *Nihongi*, compiled in A.D. 720—the first publications to contain accounts of mythical-historical events of early periods. Saruta Biko appears in an episode in which the Sun Goddess (Amaterasu Ōmikami), considered to be the ancestress of the Japanese, decides to send her grandson to earth to govern there. As the grandson, accompanied by several other deities, is ready to descend, a scout, who has been sent earlier to clear their way, returns to report his encounter with Saruta Biko at "the eight cross-road of Heaven." The scout describes Saruta Biko as a deity whose nose is seven hands long and whose back is more than seven fathoms long, whose eyeballs glow like an eight-handed mirror, and from whose mouth and anus a light shines (Sakamoto, Ienaga, Inoue, and Ōno 1967:147–48; for descriptions of Saruta Biko, see also Kurano and Takeda 1958:127; Philippi 1969:138, 140, 142; and Shimonaka 1941:118). Saruta Biko explains to the scout that he has come to greet the heavenly grandson.

This episode indicates that in Japanese myth-history, Saruta Biko serves as the mediator between deities and humans and between heaven and earth. Indeed, the location of Saruta Biko at "the eight cross-road" is a spatial symbol of his mediation role.

There are various factors that identify Saruta Biko as the Monkey Deity. First, the term *saru*, which forms a part of his name, means monkey. Second, the deity's physical characteristics include red buttocks, which are a prominent characteristic of Japanese macaques (Shimonaka 1941:118). Third, in the *Kojiki*, Saruta Biko is said to have had his hand caught in a shell while fishing (Kurano and Takeda 1958:131; Philippi 1969:142)—a behavioral characteristic of macaques, who gather shellfish at low tide. It should be added here that a monkey with one hand caught in a shell is a frequent theme of Japanese folktales (Inada and Ōshima 1977:392). The description of Saruta Biko's physical characteristics and his shellfish gathering are cited by Minakata (1972:401) as evidence that Saruta Biko was unquestionably an old male macaque. Others have suggested that, since Saruta Biko welcomes the Sun Goddess just as Japanese macaques "welcome" the rising sun with their loud morning calls, he must be a macaque (Matsumae 1960:44; Minakata 1972:410–11).[1]

The Monkey as Messenger from the Mountain Deity

The monkey also figures in *sannō shinkō* the belief in the Mountain Deity. According to this belief, the function of the monkey, referred to as the "Monkey Deity," or *saru gami*, is to serve as a messenger to humans from various other deities. In particular, the saru gami is the messenger from the powerful *sannō*, or Mountain Deity (Origuchi 1965b:299, 324–25; Yanagita 1951:240; Yanagita 1982d:333–40). The mountains, where deities are believed to reside, constitute the most sacred place in the universe, and the Mountain Deity is consequently one of the most important

---

[1] Some scholars disagree with the identification of Saruta Biko as a monkey. Miyata (personal communication), for example, believes that the deity should be identified as *tengu*, a mythical creature of the mountains with a long nose. Yet another interpretation is that Saruta Biko represents a foreign people (*ijin*).

deities in the pantheon of Japanese folk religions (Blacker 1975; Yanagita 1951:642–44).

Belief in the Mountain Deity was prevalent toward the end of the Medieval period and the beginning of the Early Modern period. Toyotomi Hideyoshi, who in 1590 gained control over the entire nation, was nicknamed Kosaru (small monkey) or Saru (monkey), not only because his face looked like a monkey's, but also because he eagerly sought identification with the monkey in various ways (Ooms 1985:285–87). Tokugawa Ieyasu, the first shogun, officially designated the Monkey Deity as the guardian of peace in the nation, and a festival for the deity was elaborately carried out in Edo during Tokugowa Ieyasu's reign (1603–1616) (Iida 1983:65). Initially, a procession was led by a monkey cart (*saru dashi*), although later a rooster cart came to take the lead.

As we will see in detail in Chapter 5, just around this time, that is, toward the end of the Medieval period and the beginning of the Early Modern period, we see another expression of the monkey as messenger from the Mountain Deity in the emergence of a genre of paintings illustrating rice harvesting and depicting a dancing monkey. The Mountain Deity is believed to descend from the mountain in the spring to become the Deity of the Rice Paddy until the fall, when he again returns to the mountain. Therefore, the dancing by the monkey in the harvesting scene represents the blessing of rice by the Mountain Deity.

There are other visual representations of the monkey as messenger from the Mountain Deity. In several paintings, a monkey holds a *gohei*, a ritual staff with pendant paper strips (Japan Monkey Center 1967:5, 7, 12–13). The *gohei* is used by shamans and Shinto priests in their rituals to summon the spirit of a deity (Yanagita 1951:212–13). In other words, the monkey in these paintings is assigned the role of mediating between deities and humans, just as shamans and priests do.

The Monkey's Association with the Deities of Mediation

The importance of mediation as a meaning assigned to the monkey is also revealed by the fact that the monkey is associated with several deities and a Buddha, all of whom are mediators. Relegating details to footnotes, I will introduce in this section these mediators and their relationship to the monkey.

Kōshin　The term *kōshin* refers to the fifty-seventh day or year of each sixty-day or sixty-year cycle in the Taoist calendar; that is, it stands for a point in time between two temporal cycles. Kōshin became associated with a number of beliefs and practices whose meanings have centered on the concept of mediation, just as the original concept of kōshin stood for the temporal mediation between the calendrical cycles. Since the sixteenth century, the kōshin belief and associated practices have become closely linked to the monkey.

The belief in kōshin may have started in Japan as a result of the diffusion of a Taoist belief (Yanagita 1951:196; for alternative explanations, see Kubo 1961:531–32). The forms of belief in kōshin underwent a series of transformations under the influences of Buddhism, Shinto, and other folk religions. The dominant and most persistent form, however, is the belief encapsulated in the term *kōshin*, the liminal period in the temporal cycle. On the night defined as kōshin, three worms (black, green, and white) that are believed to dwell in a person's body are said to ascend to heaven. There they report to the Emperor of Heaven their host's transgressions during the previous cycle (Blacker

1975:329; Yanagita 1951:196–97). This belief led to the Japanese custom of staying up all night to prevent the worms from leaving the body to report on their host.[2]

This original form of kōshin observance was transformed during the late sixteenth century into an occasion that included a ritual dedicated to the *kōshin-sama*, or kōshin deity. Like many other deities in the Japanese pantheon, the identity of the kōshin deity was only vaguely perceived, but it was assigned the role of overseeing the welfare of the people, especially at times of illness.

As this brief description of kōshin indicates, the meaning and the role of kōshin centered on mediation—between

---

[2] According to Kubo (1961:538), the oldest record of the all-night kōshin wake comes from A.D. 838. Kubo (1961:540), however, suggests that the practice started during the latter part of the eighth century, when Taoism was introduced to Japan. In any event, a number of documents testify that an all-night gathering on the day of kōshin was already popular among aristocrats during the early phase of the Heian period (794–1185), and that it was established as one of the annual events at the Imperial Court (Kubo 1961:540–46). These documents illustrate that the event was full of play (*oasobi*), including poetry reading, music, *go* and *sugoroku* games, and feasts. Although the participants, including the emperors, seem to have understood the cosmological meaning of the occasion, there is little evidence that they made it into a religious ceremony as such (Kubo 1961:542). During these early periods, shortly after the kōshin belief and its associated ritual-play had been introduced to Japan from China, the event had an exotic flavor (Iida 1983:53–54).

While remaining popular among aristocrats, the kōshin belief and the associated all-night observance also diffused during the latter half of the fifteenth century, to warriors and commoners, at least those of high status. The belief and the event have spread even more widely since then (Kubo 1961:549, 606).

A major change in the nature of the kōshin belief took place toward the end of the sixteenth century. At that time, the kōshin belief and practice became religious in essence, and as recorded in a document dated 1595, a religious ritual became a part of the kōshin observance, although which deities or Buddhas were the objects of worship is not clear (Kubo 1961:585). In time, people started to pray to *kōshin-sama*, that is, the kōshin deity (the Japanese use the term *sama*, an address form for humans, in addressing deities), for their protection and welfare. It was an influential deity among the commoners during the Early Modern period (Kubo 1961:342, 607).

temporal cycles, between humans and deities, and between heaven and earth. It is with this mediating deity that the monkey became associated, thereby further reinforcing the meaning of the monkey as mediator.

During the late phase of the Muromachi period (1392–1603), the kōshin belief and associated practices became fused with various forms of belief in the monkey, including the aforementioned Saruta Biko and the Mountain Deity (Yanagita 1951:196). An example of this fusion appears on the amulets used by those believing in the sacredness of Mt. Fuji, which had been closely associated with the kōshin belief. Depicted on these amulets are Saruta Biko and more than sixty monkeys worshipping Mt. Fuji at its foothills (Miyata 1975:148).

But by far the most conspicuous expression of this fusion is seen in the engravings of monkeys on the stone monuments called *kōshin-tō* (kōshin monuments) that were produced as part of the kōshin observance (see Motoyama 1942 for reproductions of these monuments). Although the monuments began to appear during the late Muromachi period (Kubo 1961:586; Yanagita 1951:196), the engravings of monkeys became a standard feature on them only during the Early Modern period.

Saeno Kami and *Jizō*   The mediating role of the monkey is also evinced in its association with *saeno kami*[3] and *jizō*—supernaturals who are mediators. These supernaturals—one a deity and the other a Buddha—are placed at spatial boundaries, especially at the border of a community. As will be explained in detail in Chapter 6, in the Japanese cos-

---

[3] Saeno kami (Roadside Deity) is also called *Dōsoshin*, and is considered to dwell at the boundary of a community, the edge of a bridge, the foot of a hill, and other spatial boundaries. This deity is believed capable of preventing the assault of epidemics thought to come from outside the community (Hirose 1979:244, 265–68; Shimonaka 1941:93, 118; Yanagita 1951:400–401; good photographs of this deity are found in Cazja 1974).

mology, deities endowed with both negative and positive powers were located outside the settlement. Saeno kami and jizō were assigned the roles of guarding against the intrusion of negative elements, such as epidemics, from the outside, and of bringing in the positive supernatural power to rejuvenate life within the community. In short, they were assigned the role of mediating between the community and the outside world.

During the Early Modern period (1603–1868), saeno kami, who had been fused with Saruta Biko, became fused with jizō, a roadside Buddha (cf. Shimonaka 1941:93). The merging of the three deities—Saruta Biko, saeno kami, and jizō—resulted in stone statues of a monkey wearing a bib, which is a trademark of jizō, a guardian Buddha of children (Hirose 1979:268–71).

The Monkey as Guardian of Horses

Perhaps the most important role assigned to the monkey was guardian of horses; the monkey was considered to have the power to maintain the health and cure the illnesses of horses.

This belief gave rise to two related practices. First, warriors began to cover their quivers with monkey hides so as to harness the protective power of the monkey over horses (Yanagita 1982e:99). During the latter part of the Medieval period, when the nation was engulfed in cyclical conquests by regional lords, the monkey was highly valued by warriors as well as by farmers, both of whom were armed and eagerly sought monkey hides for their quivers. Since farmers constituted over 90 percent of the population at the time, it is safe to assume that this was an important role of the monkey.

The second phenomenon this belief gave birth to was *ema* (literally, "picture-horse")—votive plaques on which people drew pictures of horses and offered them at shrines to ensure the health of their own horses. Yanagita refutes a widely held assumption that ema, as offerings to the deities, were substitutes for real horses. Instead, he suggests that ema were considered offerings in their own right (Yanagita 1951:70–71). A large number of ema from various historical periods and regions of Japan depict monkeys pulling horses, providing rich evidence that the monkey functioned as guardian of horses. I might add here that the monkey's healing power was later extended to the oxen used by farmers to plow their fields, as illustrated on some ema that show monkeys pulling oxen (Japan Monkey Center 1967:5).

The historical antecendents of this link between horse and monkey are not altogether clear. Yanagita (quoted in Miyamoto 1981:82) speculates that since horses used by the Japanese in early times were wild, the monkey was employed to tame wild horses. But a more complete understanding of the role of the monkey as guardian of horses requires consideration of the horse's significance in Japanese religions. As Yanagita (1982e:342) explains, Japanese deities were thought to have descended on horseback from the mountains. In other words, horses were not simply utilitarian animals used for work in paddy fields and for warriors to ride; they had religious significance.

If the historical association between the two animals is unknown, we may at least speculate about the symbolic association between them. Like monkeys, horses were mediators who carried deities to humans. For mediator-horses, which nevertheless were wild animals, monkeys acted as ancient shaman-healers. As we will see in detail in Chapter 4, the shamans of ancient Japan performed music and dances during their healing rituals. The monkey likewise performs dances—a cultural act par excellence—and thereby tames another mediator, the horse, which is truly a wild animal. I will continue my symbolic interpretation of the performing monkey in Chapters 7 and 8.

The Monkey's Role in Healing

It should be emphasized here that the supernatural beings associated with the monkey—kōshin, saeno kami, and jizō—are all assigned the role of healing. The monkey's role in healing is most clearly expressed in the belief in the monkey as the guardian of horses. Symbolically, healing is an act of pulling back to life a sick person who is under the threat of death; that is, it is an act of mediation between life and death. Thus, the monkey's role as mediator is evident in its association with supernaturals who possess the power to heal. Moreover, almost every part of the monkey's body has been extensively used as medicine and medicinally, at least since about the sixth century but most likely earlier.

Even today, a charred monkey's head, pounded into powder, is taken as medicine for illnesses of the head and brain, including mental illnesses, mental retardation, and headaches, although this particular use was, no doubt, far more prevalent in the past.[4] The remaining body parts, as well as various representations of the monkey such as small stuffed monkeys (kukurizaru), have been used as amulets thought to be efficacious in treating various other illnesses, as well as childbirth. A monkey made of brick is used still as an amulet by pregnant women at a number of shrines of the Mountain Deity (Japan Monkey Center 1967:2, 6; Minakata 1972:378). Likewise, figurines of the three-monkey theme (see no evil, hear no evil, and speak no evil) are used as charms to ward against illnesses; if one follows these three behavioral taboos, one will live in harmony with other people—a good preventive medicine, at least to some.

---

[4] For a survey of medical uses of the monkey, see Hirose (1979:76–94, 199–202).

The Monkey as Mediator in Folklore

There are a number of folktales in which the monkey is portrayed as a mediator; one example is a tale in Volume 2 of *Zatsudanshū*, a collection of tales published in the thirteenth century. The story is about a hard-working man and a lazy man who once lived side by side at the foot of a mountain.

The hard-working man worked in the field from early morning till evening to grow soybeans and red beans. One day he became tired and fell asleep, whereupon monkeys came and thought he was a Buddha. They gave him yams and other offerings and went back to the mountain. The man took the offerings home. Upon hearing this story, the wife of the lazy man urged her husband to do the same. The monkeys carried him across the river to ensconce him there. While they were carrying him on their arms, the monkeys said, "We should raise our *hakama* [a skirt-like garment for men]," and they stroked their fur to imitate the gesture of raising the hakama. Upon seeing this, the man laughed. The monkeys said that he was a man, instead of a Buddha, and threw him into the river. He was drenched, swallowed a great deal of water, and narrowly escaped his death. Upon hearing of the incident, his wife became enraged. "One should never engage in superficial imitation of others." (Yanagita 1982a:226–27)

In this tale, monkeys act as mediators sent by deities who reward or punish humans depending upon their conduct. It should also be noted, however, that the monkeys are depicted as imitating humans—they imitate the human gesture of raising the hakama garment when crossing a river. The tale, then, has a complex theme. It depicts the monkeys as sacred mediators who on behalf of the Mountain Deity punish a lazy man and his wife for engaging in superficial

51

imitation of their neighbors, while they themselves are imitating humans.

This tale served as a prototype for later versions known as *Saru Jizō* ("The Monkey Jizō Buddha"). In these later versions, the episode of the monkeys imitating humans is absent, and in the version after the Kamakura period (1185–1392), the monkeys mistake each man for a jizō Buddha, the roadside Buddha of mediation, rather than simply a Buddha (Yanagita 1982a:227).

The Monkey in the Names of Human Mediators

Closely related to the positive meaning of the monkey as mediator is the use of the term *saru*, meaning "monkey," in personal names or pen names. The practice started quite early in history. For example, Sarumaru Dayū, which includes the term *saru*, is the name of historical-legendary figures found in various regions of Japan who were religious and literary specialists, including poets and narrators of oral tradition (Yanagita 1979:168–211). The *Sarumaru Dayū-shū*, a collection of poems by Sarumaru Dayū, is dated to the late ninth century. Although some consider Sarumaru Dayū to be a poet of the Genkei period (877–884), both Origuchi and Yanagita argue that Sarumaru Dayū is a name given to a number of itinerant priest-poets who formed a group named Sarumaru (Origuchi 1976b:467–68; 1976c:190; Yanagita 1982e:336–40). As we shall see in Chapter 4, during the early periods in Japanese history, those people involved in the arts and the performing arts were considered mediators between humans and deities, since these activities were primarily of a religious nature. As such, they received high cultural valuation, although their social status was low.

We can infer from the preceding information that human mediators were regarded as analogous to the monkey, who was a sacred mediator. But the use of the term for monkey was not reserved solely for human mediators; other humans also had names with the word *saru* in them, and the practice continued until at least the sixteenth century. For example, the childhood name of the sixteenth-century feudal lord Uesugi Kenshin was Sarumatsu (Minakata 1972:343).

Other Meanings of the Monkey during the Early and Transitional Periods

While the monkey's meaning as mediator predominated during early periods in Japanese history, several other meanings seemed to have been present during these periods, although their sporadic appearance in literature and historical artifacts suggests that they were not dominant meanings.

In a mid–eighth century collection of poems, *Manyōshū*, the monkey appears only once, but it is as a metaphor for people with ugly faces.[5] In *Nihon Ryōiki*, dated to the late Nara and the early Heian periods, there is a story in which a female saint is depicted as having been mocked as a "monkey saint (*saru hijiri*)," because people thought that she was mimicking a sage (quoted in LaFleur 1983:42). Although these examples are limited, the use of the monkey

[5] The appearance of the monkey in poems of this period is very restricted. Only once does it appear in the *Manyōshu*, a twenty-volume collection of some 4,500 poems of the mid–eighth century. In this poem, Ōtomo-no-Tabito, the author, ridicules sober people for having faces as ugly as that of a monkey, while he justifies and praises drunks (Iida 1973:215).

In the *Kokinshū*, a collection of poems by Kino Tsurayuki and others, compiled at the order of Emperor Daigo and published in A.D. 903, the monkey appears in only one poem. There, the voice of *mashira* (the monkey) appears, expressing the sadness associated with the mountains. As Iida (1973:216–17) points out, the poem was written under the direct influence of Chinese poetry, which had just been introduced to Japan, and which was cited by Emperor Uta. Therefore, it is reasonble to assume that the meaning of the monkey in this poem in the *Kokinshū* does not represent the meaning system of the popular culture of Japan at that time.

as a metaphor for undesirable humans is significant in that it foreshadows the monkey as a scapegoat—the meaning that became dominant during the later periods of Japanese history.

The monkey is also portrayed as a trickster, sometimes good but sometimes evil, who uses his wits in an attempt to outsmart others. The monkey as a truly wise trickster appears in a folktale entitled "Boneless Jellyfish" (*Kurage Honenashi*).[6] In this tale, the monkey saves his own life by outsmarting the jellyfish, who tries to take out the monkey's liver.

In another folktale, the monkey appears as a malicious trickster. "The Combat Between a Monkey and a Crab" (*Saru Kani Kassen*), initially formulated around the end of the Muromachi period (1392–1603), was in circulation in a popular edition during the early seventeenth century (Asakura, et al. 1969:216; Shimazu 1933:173) and remains a popular folktale even today. In one widespread version, the monkey takes a rice ball from a crab in exchange for a persimmon seed, explaining to the crab that there is nothing left of a rice ball after its consumption, whereas a persimmon seed will grow and bear fruit. When the crab manages to grow the tree, which bears much fruit, the crab asks the monkey to fetch a persimmon. The monkey climbs up the tree and throws a persimmon at the crab, injuring or killing her, depending on the version. Eventually, the crab (or her children, in the version in which she is killed) and her sympathizers (a chestnut, a needle, a wasp, a mortar, dung, and so forth, depending upon the region) take revenge on the monkey.[7]

---

[6] The prototype of this tale appeared in *Konjaku Monogatari* (early twelfth century) and *Shasekishū* (compiled between 1279 and 1283) (Matsumae 1960:53).

[7] This tale is recorded in Seki (1979:138–40, 141–165, 167–77); Yanagita (1951:240–41); and Yanagita (1982a:391–414). There are a number of other

Even less frequent than the portrayal of the monkey as a malevolent trickster is that of the monkey as an evil deity. A story involving two evil deities, the snake and the monkey, who were enshrined at Minasaka-no-kuni (Okayama), is recorded in both the *Konjaku Monogatari*, a collection of tales dated to the early twelfth century, and the *Uji Shūi Monogatari*, another collection of tales dated between 1212 and 1221.[8]

EARLY AND TRANSITIONAL PERIODS: A SUMMARY

Early Periods

A cursory survey of various aspects of Japanese culture in early times suggests that the dominant meaning of the monkey was as sacred mediator, a meaning that continued to be powerful during the transitional period. Nevertheless, the monkey was also a metaphor for an ugly human, a trickster, and an evil deity during this time.

The monkey in the role of sacred mediator appeared as early as the eighth century, and this remained the dominant meaning throughout the early periods, that is, until

---

tales in which the monkey appears as a similar type of trickster, among them the *Saru no Chūsai* ("Arbitration by a Monkey") (Seki 1979:70–71; Yanagita 1982a:391–414).

[8] For dating of both collections, see Nihon Rekishi Daijiten Henshū Iinkai (1968:678 [vol. 1], 550 [vol. 4]). The part of the story involving the monkey is as follows: "During the annual festival of the shrine, the villagers had been forced to offer a beautiful girl for the deities to consume. One day a hunter from the east passed by and heard the crying of the parents whose daughter was to be sacrificed. Volunteering to kill the evil deities, he hid in a box with his dog. A large monkey flanked by more than two hundred other monkeys opened the box, thinking that it contained the girl, whereupon the hunter and the dog attacked the monkeys. The hunter married the daughter and thereafter they were able to offer an animal, instead of a human, at the time of the annual festival" (the tale reproduced in Iida 1973:198).

the mid–thirteenth century. The stability of this meaning is quite remarkable, since by the eighth century, there had occurred two major historical events that could have had a far-reaching impact on the meaning of the monkey: the introduction of agriculture around 300 B.C. and the introduction of Buddhism in the sixth century.

Agriculture diffused to Kyūshū from the Asian continent via the Korean Peninsula, spread northeastward in three successive waves, and gradually replaced the hunting-gathering way of life throughout Japan. Archaeologically, we see an obvious end to the use of monkeys as food, as suggested by the presence of bone remains at sites of the Jōmon hunting-gathering period and the absence of monkey skeletons at sites dated to the agricultural Yayoi period (300 B.C.–A.D. 250) (Hirose 1979:6). While monkeys were a source of food for the hunting population, they were a menace to farmers because they stole crops.

The fundamental change in the ecological relationship between the Japanese and monkeys did not transform the latter into enemies. Since the historical records I have mentioned date to the periods well after the introduction of agriculture around B.C., we may conclude that even when monkeys stole crops, the Japanese assigned them a semi-deified status and the positive role of mediation between humans and deities. Had they taken a functional attitude, the Japanese would have made monkeys simply negative figures, such as evil deities or demons, instead of viewing them with ambivalence.

The advoidance of monkey meat may also infer that these agriculturalists saw proximity between monkeys and themselves. As pointed out in a well-known article by Leach (1968), people do not eat the meat of animals that they perceive to be close to humans.

In short, then, the belief in the monkey as a deified animal and an animal close to humans seems to date to the Yayoi agricultural period.

The old hunting culture survived in some areas, especially in the mountainous regions of northeastern Japan. Hunters continued to hunt monkeys and to supply farmers and warriors with skulls, hides, and other parts of the body for various purposes (Chiba 1977:452–53). Even today, in the regions northeast of the Hakusan Mountain Range in the Ishikawa Prefecture, hunters observe no taboo in regard to monkey hunting, while those in the regions southwest of the mountain range observe numerous taboos (Chiba 1975; Hirose 1979:47–48).

The impact of the second historical event, the introduction of Buddhism during the sixth century, is difficult to assess. The Buddhist doctrine of a humane attitude toward all living beings might have had a major impact on the Japanese attitude toward the monkey. We might speculate, for example, that the farming population's elevation of the monkey to a sacred mediator, in the face of a changing ecological relationship with the monkey as it became a menace to crops rather than a food source for the farmers, might have been influenced by Buddhism. My guess, however, is that the Japanese attitude toward the monkey during these early periods derives primarily from the Japanese world view prior to the introduction of Buddhism, whose impact upon the thought structure of the people was negligible for some time.[9]

[9] Hirose (1978) emphasizes that the deification of the monkey occurred in the process of Buddhism's gaining hegemony over Shintoism, during the Muromachi period. I still believe that the meaning of the monkey during the Muromachi and subsequent Early Modern periods was as messenger from the powerful Mountain Deity of Shintoism. Moreover, the monkey as a semi-deified messenger is already found in the *Kojiki* and the *Nihongi*—the two earliest myth-histories of Japan (both compiled in the eighth century A.D.) which portrayed the early Japanese world view that provided the basis of early Shintoism.

As I noted in the text, Buddhistic thought seems at first to have had little effect on the meaning of the monkey in popular culture; its impact was felt only later. For example, in A.D. 676, the government under the reign of Emperor Tenmu issued a law prohibiting fishing, hunting, and trapping,

Transitional Period

A major transformation in the dominant meaning of the monkey took place sometime during the three or four hundred years between the latter half of the Medieval period and the beginning of the Early Modern period. Although it is almost meaningless to try to cite exact dates for the transition, we might place it roughly between the mid–thirteenth century and the beginning of the seventeenth century. During this period, the dominant meaning of the monkey shifted gradually from that of a sacred mediator between humans and deities to that of a metaphor for human scapegoats, that is, undesirable humans or human qualities. In particular, the monkey came to represent Japanese who both engaged in silly imitations of others and, during the Early Modern period, tried to achieve beyond their capacity, or more specifically, beyond their ascribed status in their rigidly stratified society.

The simultaneous existence of both meanings of the monkey during this period may be illustrated by a pamphlet posted in the streets of Kyoto in 1591 (Elison 1981:244).

Masse to was	The end of the world
Bechi ni wa araji	Is nothing but this:
Ki no shita no	Watching the
	monkey

---

as well as the consumption of cows, horses, dogs, monkeys, and chickens. Violators of the regulation were punished. The implementation of the regulation indicates that these animals had been eaten previously. The regulation, however, did not seem to have been too effective (Iida 1973:54, 63–64).

In regard to monkey meat specifically, although its consumption never died out entirely, even after the pressure from Buddhism, it was practiced by only a small number of people throughout history. By the Early Modern period, not only monkey meat but even deer and wild boar meat were sold by only a restricted number of stores that specialized in the meat of wild animals (Hirose 1979:89).

58

| *Saru Kanpaku o* | Regent |
| *Miru ni Tsuketemo* | Under the tree |

As Elison explains, the poster was a satirical commentary on Hideyoshi, the commoner who became a regent (*kanpaku*). As we saw earlier, Hideyoshi strove to identify himself with the Monkey Deity, and the people nicknamed him "Monkey Regent" (*Saru Kanpaku*). "Under the tree" is a reference to Hideyoshi's alleged original family name, Kinoshita, which means literally "under a tree." The satirical comment in the poster laments the approach of the end of the world, when a commoner can be a regent, and worse yet, when a monkey is governing humans.

During this period, then, the monkey continued to be a semi-deified mediator, as is evident both in Hideyoshi's eagerness to identify himself with the monkey and in Ieyasu's choice of the monkey as the guardian of peace in the nation. In addition, the monkey took on an additional role in the transitional period: blessing the harvest through dancing. At the same time, however, the monkey's meaning turned increasingly negative, and the poster succinctly expresses the simultaneous existence of the positive and negative meanings.

THE MONKEY AS SCAPEGOAT AND TRICKSTER IN LATER HISTORY

The Monkey as Scapegoat

Gradually, the monkey as sacred mediator lost prominence, and as the Early Modern period progressed, the monkey became increasingly a scapegoat in the Japanese system of meaning. We recall that the meaning of the monkey as scapegoat is succinctly expressed in the Japanese saying that the monkey is "a human minus three pieces of hair." The literal meaning of this saying is that the monkey is a lowly animal trying to be a human and therefore is to be laughed at. However, the saying is understood by the Japanese to portray the monkey as representing undesirable humans that are to be ridiculed.

It should be noted here that during the Early Modern period Buddhism continued to be influential in Japan. Yet, even the Buddhistic teaching calling for mercy for all living things was not extended to cover "metaphorical cruelty" expressed in the notion of monkey as scapegoat.[10]

Before I begin a description of the monkey as scapegoat, I wish to reiterate here that although the dominant meaning of the monkey shifted, its role as mediator continued to exist, as, for example, it was expressed in the kōshin belief, which continued to be held during the Early Modern period. However, references to the monkey as mediator were much less frequent during the later periods in history than they had been during the earlier periods. Conversely, the meanings of the monkey both as scapegoat and as trickster were present early in history, but they gained dominance only during the later periods in history.

A tale from the transitional period portrays the scapegoat image of the monkey. The *Saru Genjizōshi* ("A Tale of the Monkey Genji") dated to the Muromachi period (Ichiko

---

[10] Buddhistic influence during this period may be seen in a law, notorious among the Japanese, first issued in 1685 by the fifth shogun, Tokugawa Tsunayoshi, and several times thereafter until his death in 1709. Called *Shōrui awaremi no rei* (a law requiring mercy toward all living things), the law prohibited placing dogs and cats on a leash but later was expanded to protect hawks, eagles, pigeons, cormorants, and deer. It also prohibted fishing and the selling of live fish and birds. Tsunayoshi's official reason for issuing the law was to require mercy toward all living things—the Buddhistic philosophy. However, it stemmed, in fact, from his personal desire to produce offspring: he believed that his acts of cruelty to living things in his previous life had caused the death of his child, and he hoped that the enforcement of these rules might somehow improve his chances of producing an heir (Hirono 1968). The impact of Tsunayoshi's rules on the people seemed negligible. They ridiculed the law, even though they were afraid of punishment.

1958a:13) is so titled because a fish peddler tries to pass as a feudal lord and, in courting a courtesan, acts like the prince in *The Tale of Genji* (the tale reproduced in Ichiko 1958b:165–86). Obviously, during this period the monkey stood for someone who engages in a superficial imitation of others and by so doing tries in vain to achieve a status beyond his own.

Folktales illustrate well the monkey as a scapegoat who tries unsuccessfully to imitate or to become a human. For example, *Saru Muko Iri* is about the foiled attempt by a monkey to marry a human.

Once upon a time a man and a woman lived with three daughters. The man went to the field to harvest *gobō* roots, when a monkey came to watch him. The man felt very tired and offered to give one of his daughters as a bride to the monkey if the monkey would help him. The monkey immediately agreed and harvested the root crops for him. After returning home, the man started to feel very sorry about what he had done and went to bed. The daughters took their turn in coming to his bedside to ask how he felt. [As he disclosed the story], the two oldest were enraged and flatly refused to marry the monkey. The youngest, however, readily agreed. The next day, the monkey, dressed as a groom, came and took the daughter away. In the following March, the monkey and his wife pounded rice to make rice cakes to take to the wife's parents as the custom required. When the monkey was about to put the rice cakes into a wooden bucket, his wife said they would catch the smell of the bucket. When he wanted to put them in a pan, she said that the cakes would catch the smell of the pan. Therefore, the monkey carried the mortar on his back with the rice cakes in it and they set out to visit her parents. Along the road, she spotted some pretty cherry blossoms on a branch hanging over a cliff. She asked the monkey to break off the branch in order to bring it to her parents as a gift. In order to climb the tree, the monkey put the mortar on the ground, whereupon she told him that her father would not like the rice cakes if they caught the smell of the dirt. So the monkey climbed the tree with the mortar on his back. She urged him to climb higher and higher up the tree [to reach the best-looking blossoms] until he fell into the river below [from the weight of the mortar and himself on a thin branch]. Although the mortar floated, the monkey was drowned. (Yanagita 1951:242, 1982b:451–63)

There are a number of variations of this story, depending upon the historical period and region. In many versions, the marriage between the monkey and the daughter never takes place, and the drowning incident occurs as the monkey brings the woman to the mountain.

While the monkey is the target of ridicule in the tale because it tries to be human, the moral of the story is intended for humans: one must not try to achieve beyond one's means, lest misfortune strike. In other words, the monkey reflects negative aspects of humans who hope for more than they have. The message is also found in a well-known poem belonging to the *dōka* genre of moral poems of the Shingaku school of philosophy-ethics during the Early Modern period. The poem reads: *Michi naranu mono o hoshigari/yamazaru no kokorogara to ya fuchi ni shizuman* (Going after things beyond its reach/a mountain monkey falls into a pool of water) (dōka cited in Ouwehand 1964:48; translation mine).

The same moral message is succinctly expressed in a well-known Japanese proverb: *Tōrō ga ono, enkō ga tsuki* (The axes of a praying mantis are like the moon for a monkey). A praying mantis trying to crush the wheel of a cart with its forelegs (the axes) is portrayed as being as ridiculous as a monkey mistaking the reflection of the moon in the water for the moon itself and trying to capture it. Although the proverb originated in a Chinese story called *Sōshiritsu*, its widespread use during the sixteenth century is evidenced by a famous painting entitled *Enkō sakugetsu* (Monkey Capturing the Moon) by Hasegawa Tōhaku (1539–1610).[11]

Another expression of the same theme is found on a lacquer-ware stationery container made by an anonymous artist during the nineteenth century and now housed in the Freer Gallery at the Smithsonian. On the cover of the box, three macaques, all wearing glasses, are opening a scroll while night falcons hover over them. The picture is meant to convey a moral—"Do not attempt things beyond your capacity"—although no written message accompanies the picture. The monkeys, of course, do not have the ability to read—an ability which, to the Japanese, distinguishes humans from animals. While the monkeys are attempting the impossible, they are risking their lives by letting their chief enemies, night falcons, approach them; a night falcon (*yodaka*) is also a euphemism for a prostitute or a night stalker.

In short, the theme of the monkey as "a human minus three pieces of hair" is repeatedly expressed in a number of mediums.

During the late Medieval period and the beginning of the Early Modern period, the meaning of the monkey seems to have been generalized from an undesirable "copycat" to all types of undesirables. In *Shinchōki*, a biography of warlord, Oda Nobunaga (1534–1582), by Oze Hoan, a beggar is referred to as a monkey (Minakata 1972:415). Minakata interprets the use of the term for monkey in the book to suggest that some *senmin* ("base people") who were physically disabled and who resorted to begging were referred to as monkeys. During the Early Modern period, the expression "the

[11] The "monkey" in this painting is a gibbon, not a macaque. As noted in Chapter 2, a clear-cut division between gibbons and macaques no longer existed by this time.

monkey in the kitchen" (*zensho no saru*) was commonly used to refer to beggars (Hirose 1978:303). Moreover, Minakata (1972:407, 414–15) cites a number of publications from the early eighteenth century in which prostitutes and various other "undesirables" were referred to as monkeys.

The monkey as scapegoat is also depicted, though perhaps less negatively, in a well-known painting of Ōtsu-e, a genre of folk paintings by anonymous artists that flourished from the late seventeenth to the early eighteenth century. In this painting, a monkey tries to subdue a catfish with a gourd. This seemingly simple painting may be interpreted on several levels. The catfish is slippery and so is the gourd. At the simplest level, then, the monkey who tries to subdue a catfish with an equally slippery gourd is a fool who tries to do the impossible. During this period, however, the catfish was believed to be the causal agent of earthquakes (Ouwehand 1964). Therefore, the painting caricatures a monkey trying to perform the impossible task of controlling an earthquake. Either way, the monkey is depicted as a fool. At another level, the painting expresses a Zen teaching: the impossibility of achieving *satori* (enlightenment) if one makes a voluntary effort to achieve it.[12] In Chapter 6, I discuss this painting further by pointing out yet another meaning within the reflexive structure of the Japanese.

In rendering the monkey as a caricature of undesirable human beings, the Japanese made the monkey into a scapegoat figure during the Early Modern period. Even more specific examples of this treatment of the monkey are seen in the seventeenth-century belief and associated practice of making the monkey a scapegoat for human victims of smallpox. It was believed that the monkeys kept at the Sakamoto Sannō Shrine suffered from smallpox when the em-

[12] Professor Herman Ooms of the University of Illinois, Chicago Circle, kindly pointed out to me the Buddhistic meaning of this painting.

perors fell victim to the disease. In one instance, Emperor Gokōmei (who reigned between 1648 and 1664) died of smallpox and the monkeys became better, while Emperor Higashiyama (who reigned between 1688 and 1713) recovered from smallpox when the monkeys died from it (Minakata 1972:378–79).

It seems that the role of the monkey as scapegoat has persisted for centuries. The belief in the monkey as a scapegoat for a human victim of disease has continued even until recently. For example, around 1900 it was reported that people with eye diseases prayed at the Tennōji Shrine in the belief that the monkeys in the compound would become victims of eye diseases and the human victims would recover from it (Minakata 1972:378–79).[13]

The monkey as scapegoat continues to be the dominant meaning of the monkey in contemporary Japan. The monkey continues to project the negative side of humans, although the strong Confucisn moral message, which was influential in the Early Modern period and was used by the government for social control, is no longer present. Rather than conveying an order in the form of "Thou shalt not . . . , lest . . . ," most contemporary sayings simply ridi-

[13] The Japanese usually explain that the association during the late nineteenth and early twentieth centuries of the monkey with smallpox derives from the play on words: *saru* (monkey) is a homonym of the word for "to go away" (*saru*), and an illness "leaves" the patient's body (cf. Ema 1932:14). Even today, monkeys made of porcelain and brick are sold at temples and shrines specializing in the curing of illnesses (Ohnuki-Tierney 1984a:135–36). I think, however, that the play on words is a secondary explanation which originated at a later date; the auspicious meaning already had been assigned to the monkey. Since the word *saru* does not specify what leaves, the monkey at time turns into a taboo because of the idea that good luck can also leave. Thus, it can be taboo at weddings—a bride may leave. A contemporary monkey trainer recalls that in the early 1930s, he and his monkey were sometimes chased away from houses by those believing that their visit would cause good luck to leave the household, although at most households they were welcomed, since their visit meant the departure of bad luck (Maruoka 1975b:134).

cule people with the use of the monkey metaphor. Some examples of such expressions and their applications follow.

saru mane (monkey imitation)—superficial imitation of others (copycat).

saru jie (monkey wisdom)—shortsighted cleverness.

saru rikō (monkey cleverness)—clever but not wise.

sarugoshi (monkey hip)—poor imitation of others, such as the quadrupedal monkey imitating the bipedal posture.

sarumen kanja (monkey face)—a face funny and ugly like that of a monkey.

saru no ebōshi (fancy hat for a monkey)—behavior not appropriate for the person; *ebōshi* is a special hat worn in the past by aristocrats and warriors. The monkey wears this hat during the monkey performance (see the hat worn by the monkey in Photo 1).

saru no shiri warai (monkey laughing at someone's butt)— laughing at someone's weakness while disregarding one's own weakness.

saru no tsura warai (monkey laughing at someone's face)— laughing at someone's ugliness when one is ugly oneself; laughing at someone's weakness while disregarding one's own.

saru me (monkey eyes)—eyes that are deep-set and ugly.

sarumawashi no saru (monkey of the monkey performance)—someone who is under control by someone else and therefore has no freedom.

Of all the expressions, *saru mane* (monkey imitation) is most frequently used. Newspaper editorials, for example, often excoriate the Japanese for copying Western customs and admonish them not to engage in "monkey imitation" of the West.

庚申年春二月庚申日戯筆

祖仙

Photo 1. A monkey dancing *Sanbasō*, by Mori Sosen (1747–1821). Sanbasō was usually danced on happy occasions. The painting is dated to 1800—on the first day of the year of the monkey. (From *The Harari Collection of Japanese Paintings and Drawings*. 1973. London: Lund Humphries)

Three Monkeys: A Self-Designated Scapegoat

No discussion of the monkey can be complete without reference to the three-monkey theme found in a great many cultures, including those of Africa, Egypt, India, and China. My discussion, however, is confined to the meanings of the three monkeys in Japan alone.

The meaning of the three-monkey theme varied greatly in the different historical periods. Furthermore, intellectuals and folk assigned different meanings to it. After a brief discussion of these intra-cultural variations, I shall focus on the common people during the Early Modern period, who saw themselves as scapegoats for the society governed by the shogun, and who thus projected, as an implicit satire, their own image onto the three monkeys.

The Japanese expression for the three monkeys—*mizaru, kikazaru, iwazaru*—means "no see, no hear, no say," without specifying what the monkeys do not see, hear, or say. In other words, the expression should not immediately be translated as "see no evil, hear no evil, and speak no evil." The saying originated as a translation of the Chinese moral code of *santai*, or the three *tai* (close identifications), that is, the philosophy that espoused the use of the three senses in making close observations of the observable world (Iida 1973:158). Only later was the moral-philosophical code linked with the three monkeys. The idea of propagating the moral code through an icon of three monkeys is said to have been conceived by Denkyō Daishi (known also as Saichō) (?–822), who founded the Tendai sect of Buddhism during the Heian period (794–1185) (Iida 1983:72–85). The association between the moral code and the three monkeys was easily established, since *zaru* (a negative case in Japanese), which appears three times in the moral code, and the word for monkey, *saru*, which becomes *zaru* when combined with certain words, are homonyms. By the Kamakura period (1185–1392), the three-monkey theme had become very popular among the common people (Iida 1983:27–30).

The meanings of the three-monkey theme were complex; moreover, as stated above, its meanings for the intellectual and the folk differed profoundly. Among the intellectual elite, a highly abstract philosophy underlay the three-monkey theme. The aforementioned moral-philosophical code of santai, which called upon the person to examine closely or identify objects and phenomena in life through the use of the three senses, is one example of the meaning of the three monkeys. An even more abstract interpretation of the three-monkey theme is that it expresses the state of "undifferentiatedness" in which the senses are not yet activated, that is, "the ineffable undifferentiatedness of the primeval chaos" (Ooms 1985:407–8).

While these philosophical/epistemological meanings were assigned to the three-monkey theme by the intellectuals, to the folk, the moral-philosophical code of santai became three tai, whose meaning is "to give up" (most characters have more than one meaning); that is, the three monkeys meant that one should give up fighting the system; one should neither see nor hear injustice, and one should not express one's dissatisfaction (Iida 1983:23–24, 78). The three monkeys stood for a recommended code of conduct during the Early Modern period. Even today, this is what the three monkeys mean to the common people, although contemporary Japanese may not hold it as a personal belief. At shrines, for example, three-monkey figures are sold in the belief that they will maintain the buyer's health: if one does not see, hear, or speak about the weaknesses of others and evil in the world, one can maintain both peace of mind and physical health (Ohnuki-Tierney 1984a:133–34).

Perhaps the most famous iconic representation of the three-monkey theme is the one carved in a panel on the façade of the sacred stable at Tōshōgū in Nikkō. The stable has eight façades, with a total of sixteen monkeys carved on them (Iida 1983:32). The Nikkō Tōshōgū Temple was built as the mausoleum of Tokugawa Ieyasu (1542–1616), the first shogun of the regime in Edo, and it was completed in 1634 (Okawa 1975:16, 28). Since Nikkō represents Ieyasu, who held the utmost power and authority at the time, one might be tempted to think that the three monkeys represented Ieyasu, who in turn represented the power and authority of the military government. It is well established, however, that the choices regarding the design and style of the mausoleum were not closely supervised at the time of its construction. As Okawa (1975:29) notes, "Apparently the shogunal authorities were unconcerned where the details of architectural styles were at issue."[14] There is sufficient evidence to infer that, in the absence of shogunal supervision of the details of construction, the architect and craftsmen built into the shrine an implicit but definite anti-establishment theme. We may therefore interpret the three monkeys of Nikkō Tōshōgū to represent the self-projection of the folk during the Early Modern period, a time when they were resigned to neither see, hear, nor speak the evils of a society imposed on them by the *okami* (the shogunal government). It likely was a sarcastic jibe aimed at both the shogun and

---

[14] The distinctive style in the main sanctuary is called *gongen zukuri*, an appellation that derives from Ieyasu's posthumous title, Dai Gongen. Despite its name, however, this style was actually the one used for the mausoleum built for Hideyoshi, who controlled the nation before Ieyasu came into power and from whose conventions Ieyasu attempted to depart. The gongen zukuri style was also used in constructing the Kitano Tenjin Shrine in Kyoto, built for worshipping the martyred scholar-statesman Sugawara no Michizane (845–903) (Okawa 1975:28–29). The use of the gongen zukuri style for Kitano Tenjin is especially intriguing: Kitano Tenjin was one of the most common motifs in paintings by the Tosa family (Kita n.d.), who played a central role among the machishū, a group of townsmen in the Kyoto area who became artists toward the end of the Medieval period, and who resisted the power and control of the shogunal government (see Chapter 2).

themselves, since they did not have enough courage to stand up to the oppression of the shogun.

The Monkey as Trickster

Although the dominant meaning of the monkey since the seventeenth century has been as scapegoat, its variant, the monkey as trickster, has also been present. For example, in a story by Takizawa Bakin, published in 1807, a pet monkey attempts to rape a woman and, when punished, kills her (Takizawa Bakin 1958:102–114; for the English translation, see Leutner n.d.:44–60).

According to Ishida (1966) and Yanagita (1982e), the *kappa*, a mythical water creature in Japanese folk tales, is the other side of the monkey. Its prototype appears in a nineteenth-century collection of tales called *Suiko Kōryaku* (Yanagita 1981:341–42). The morphological and behavioral characteristics assigned to the kappa, together with its relationship to the monkey, have been transformed through time, and a great deal of regional variation still exists in the kappa's conceptualization. There are, however, characteristics common to most of these descriptions, including the kappa's portrayal as a childlike figure; a head that is concave at the top and filled with water (when the water spills, the creature dies); arms that are flexible, stretchable, or otherwise abnormal; and behavior that is mischievous and, at times, malevolent. Dorson summarizes the features attributed to the creature.

[The *kappa* is] an ugly child with greenish-yellow skin, webbed fingers and toes, resembling a monkey with his long nose and round eyes, wearing a shell-like tortoise, fishy smelling, naked. He is said to live in the water and come out evenings to steal melons and cucumbers. He likes to wrestle, will rape women, sucks the blood of cows and horses through their anuses, and drags men and women into the water to pluck out their livers through their anuses. The trick on meeting a kappa is to make him spill the water in his concave head, whereupon he loses his strength. (Dorson 1962:59)

In some regions the kappa is said to be the chief enemy of the monkey. Nevertheless, based upon the work of Ishida and Yanagita, Ouwehand (1964:203–20) painstakingly demonstrates that the monkey and the kappa may be seen as structural opposites, one being a transformation of the other. When they are paired, the monkey represents the positive side of the trickster, and the negative side is expressed by the kappa.[15]

In addition to tales involving the kappa there are a number of folktales in which the monkey is portrayed as a trickster figure who cheats others by his clever wit.[16]

CONTEMPORARY DEVELOPMENTS

While the monkey continues to be a scapegoat in contemporary Japan, two new meanings have emerged recently. First is the appearance of *bunkazaru*, or cultured monkeys (Miyaji 1973). Sold as souvenirs at parks and elsewhere, these figurines have carved on them exaggerated gestures of the monkeys "to say, to see, and to hear." Sometimes called "*Shōwa sanzaru*" (the three monkeys of the Showa period, the period of the current emperor's reign), or "*sakasa-*

---

[15] See Ouwehand (1979:309–14, 326–27); for the monkey-kappa relationship, see Ishida (1966); Yanagita (1951:111); and Yanagita (1951:111; 1982e:49–110).

[16] These folktales include "A Badger, a Monkey and an Otter (*Mujina to saru to kawauso*)"; "A Monkey and a Toad Go on a Trip (*Saru to kaeru no ryokō*)"; "A Rice Cake Contest between a Monkey and a Crab (*Saru kani mochi kyōsō*)"; "Stealing of a Rice Cake by a Monkey and a Toad (*Saru to gama no mochi dorobō*)"; and "The Joint Cultivation of a Rice Paddy by a Monkey and a Toad (*Saru to gama no yoriaida*)" (Seki 1979:68–70, 90–92, 108–18, 119–27, 127–30, respectively).

zaru" (inverted monkeys), they endorse the attitude "speak out, examine, and listen"—the attitude considered to represent the "modern," "progressive" stance of new Japan.

Second, a new form of monkey performance has emerged recently. Thus, the monkey performance, once discontinued, has been revived, and the trainers who perform in Tokyo have developed the performance into a clowning act, jointly enacted by trainer and monkey. The clowning is aimed both at assumptions of humans' superiority over animals and at the principle of hierarchy in Japanese society, as we will discuss in detail in Chapter 8.

These developments seem indicative of the spirit of dynamism and transition characterizing contemporary Japan. The present is often compared with the gekokujō (the below conquering the above) era of the late Medieval period, when those who were able could capitalize on cultural fluidity to surpass those above them.

The continued viability of the monkey metaphor among contemporary Japanese is quite intriguing, since they no longer see "monkeys in nature." Japanese unfamiliarity with monkeys is seen, for example, in their drawings of monkeys with long tails when Japanese macaques have only very short tails, and in the question of a kindergartner who saw a monkey performance and asked if the animal was a stuffed monkey with remote control. Elsewhere (Ohnuki-Tierney 1981b), I have pointed out that the Japanese, most of whom have never seen a catfish, feel they know the fish, just as many Americans who have never seen a bald eagle feel they know the bird. Mu-Ch'i's monkey, discussed in Chapter 2, is another example of "knowing" an animal without actually having seen one. In all these cases, the culturally construed visual image, as well as the characterization, constitutes practically the exclusive source of information that feeds into the people. Yet, monkeys remain culturally important animals in Japan and they serve as powerful metaphors in that culture.

In this chapter I have tried to trace the transformations of the dominant meanings of the monkey throughout Japanese history. We saw that from the time of the earliest records in the eighth century the monkey has been a culturally important animal. As we will see in Chapter 6, all the meanings assigned to the monkey—mediator, scapegoat, clown—are intimately involved in the Japanese structure of reflexivity. In other words, the monkey has sensitively expressed the changing notion of the self and other in Japanese culture; thus, by tracing the meanings of the monkey, we are able to trace the transformations of the Japanese structure of thought. Even today, when the animal is no longer seen in a natural setting, new meanings are emerging, reaffirming the animal's centrality in the Japanese structure of reflexivity.

4

The Special Status People in Japanese Society: Historical Transformations of Their Meaning

JAPANESE monkey trainers belong to a group of people who I refer to in this book as "special status people," and who have occupied a special position—sometimes positively defined and other times negatively defined—in Japanese society. Collectively, these people have been assigned various meanings at different times in history. My research into these meanings suggest curious parallels not only between the meanings assigned to the monkey and the meanings assigned to these people, but also between the historical transformations of the two sets of meanings. It should be noted here that the monkey has rarely been used as a direct metaphor for these people, except during the Early Modern period, as we saw earlier. In order to demonstrate what I see as parallels, I present in this chapter a brief history of the meanings assigned to these people.

The stereotypical image of special status people that was held until recently by the dominant Japanese was that of people engaged only in occupations deemed culturally "defiled" and "defiling." But a closer look at the history of special status people shows that their ancestors were heterogeneous people with diverse occupations, some of which the dominant Japanese would no longer associate with special status people today. Furthermore, there is no clear-cut linear descent linking the people from one historical period to those of another (Harada 1978a, 1978b; Noguchi 1978; Ueda 1978a, 1978b). Most important, the meaning and cultural valuation assigned to the occupations and the people who held them have gone through significant transformations over time.

Perhaps the only common denominator of special status people throughout history is that in a society that has been predominantly agrarian until quite recently, these people have engaged in non-agrarian occupations, including religious, artistic, and artisan specializations. Since they have not been a monolithic group cloistered from the rest of the Japanese throughout history, no single label, even in Japanese, is either appropriate or actually in use to refer to them. I adopted Susan Tax Freeman's suggestion to use the designation "special status" people,[1] since it is neutral in value and can be both positive and negative, just as the values assigned to these people have been positive or negative at different historical times. I also use other designations, such as senmin ("base people") and *burakumin* ("settlement people"), as they have been called at different periods in Japanese history, including the present. I do not use these terms in any derogatory sense. Likewise, I use the term "outcaste" or, sometimes, "former outcaste" only to refer to the historical fact that, during the Early Modern period, the designated status of these people was below the four "castes" that were believed to constitute Japanese society.

---

[1] Professor Freeman feels strongly that the designation should be "special status *group*." I use "people" most of the time in this book primarily to avoid the inference that these people constitute a well-delineated social group that has existed throughout history. The use of "people" also enables me to avoid long phrases such as "members of (individuals from) the special status group."

At present, the official-legal desgnation for these people is *hisabetsu burakumin*, which literally means "the people of settlements who are subjected to discrimination." The term burakumin is preferred by the people themselves.

ANCIENT PERIOD
(300 B.C.–TWELFTH CENTURY)

Stratification and Senmin

Archaeological records indicate that Japanese society has been stratified since prehistoric times, and the earliest historical documents testify that society was hierarchically ordered, with slaves at the bottom of society (for a description of stratification during these periods, see Ninomiya 1933:60–64). Not until the Taika Reform of A.D. 645, however, did the society become legally stratified. This reform divided the population into *ryōmin* ("good people") and senmin ("base people"). The senmin constituted 10 percent of the total population, which was five to six million at the time (Ueda 1978b:80), and they were divided into five clearly delineated types: the *ryōko*, who guarded and maintained the mausoleums of the Imperial family; the *kanko*, who cultivated the official land for the government; the *kenin*, who were servants of individuals, and of shrines and temples; the *kunuhi*, who were "public slaves" owned by the government and ordered to perform miscellaneous labor; and the *shinuhi*, who were slaves of private individuals (Ninomiya 1933:70–71).

Since some of the senmin specialized in advanced metallurgy and other crafts, there are scholars who argue that some of them must have been Korean artisans and craftsmen who came to Japan during the Tomb period (A.D. 250–A.D. 646), introducing skills in various crafts unknown to

77

the Japanese (see Ninomiya 1933:69). Others (e.g., Ueda 1978b:77–78) strongly argue against this line of interpretation. Emphasizing that the special status people during the Medieval period were not direct descendants of the senmin during the ancient period, Nagahara (1979:394) explains why the "Korean descent theory" cannot be accepted. According to him, the concentration of the special status people in the Kansai region, and especially Kyoto and Nara where the nation's first and second capitals were located, derives from the fact that purification was of utmost importance to the emperor, the court, the nobles, and large temples. These institutions and people employed the special status people to purify their surroundings regularly.

Special Status People as Artistic/Religious Specialists

Akima (1972, 1982) presents a revealing interpretation of one of the occupations held by these people during the ancient period—attendants at the funerals of emperors. His argument about the nature of such funerals and the people who tended them is based on the two earliest myth-histories, the *Kojiki* and the *Nihongi*, compiled in A.D. 712 and 720, respectively, and on the *Ryō no Shūge*, a late ninth-century work chronicling earlier events. Akima points to a passage in the *Ryō no Shūge* relating why special funeral services began to be performed. According to this account, Prince Tsuburane, an illegitimate son of Emperor Ikume, married into the Hijikiwake family, which had performed such services. He thus performed a special funeral service at the time of the emperor's death, and his descendants continued to conduct funeral services for later emperors (Kuroita 1966:966–67).[2]

---

[2] Historical data about the special status people suggest both practical and symbolic relationships to emperors. As already noted, the special status people were closely related to emperors, whose residences and funer-

Equally revealing is that the funeral attendants described in the *Ryō no Shūge* were shamans who sang "the songs of the dead" during their possession trance and also played music during the funeral rites. They were called *asobi-be*.[3]

By piecing together the information in the *Kojiki*, the *Nihongi*, and the *Ryō no Shūge*, we are able to reconstruct a picture of asobi-be, whose literal meaning in contemporary Japanese is "the play people." They were shamans who tended the corpses of emperors by performing funeral services that included music, dancing, and spirit possession. Additional support of this interpretation of the asobi-be is

als required purification rituals. The *Ryō no Shūge* even suggests a marriage between an illegitimate son of an emperor and a daughter from the special status group.

Symbolic opposition between emperors and the special status people has also been suggested. K. Inoue (1967) first proposed that emperors and special status people constituted polar opposites in terms of symbolic valuation in Japanese culture. Yamaguchi (1977; also Yamaguchi in H. Inoue et al. 1978:154) draws on K. Inoue's interpretation to advance a highly provocative hypothesis that states that both Japanese emperors and special status people are symbolic descendants of *marebito*, the stranger-deity (this deity will be discussed in Chapter 6). According to Yamaguchi, the emperor is a stranger-deity who became settled, whereas a stranger-deity who never settled became the special status people. Both Inoue's and Yamaguchi's interpretations are suggestive of Dumont's proposition about the symbolic opposition between the Brahmans and the Untouchables in India. These lines of interpretation remain tenuous—although provocative—without a detailed historical and ethnographic study.

[3] Akima (1972, 1982:498–500) convincingly argues that the term *asobi*, whose literal meaning today is "play," meant music making rather than playing in general. During this early period in history, the term referred to merrymaking, including singing, dancing, and drinking.

On the basis of etymology, Akima further asserts that the two members of the Hijikiwake family—the original family of asobi-be—who entered the funeral house were called Negi and Yoshi. Negi is a noun form for *negu*, which means "to propitiate." *Yoshi* is a noun form for *yosu*, which means "to cause [a god or a spirit] to come near," or "to be divinely possessed" (Akima 1982:500–501).

Similarly, Origuchi (1976a:62) points out that during ancient times the term asobi (play) referred to the dance performed to placate the soul of the guardian deity of the nation or the household.

found in the description of Ame-no-Uzume-no-Mikoto, a shaman-deity in the *Kojiki*. When the Sun Goddess hid in a cave, an act interpreted as the symbolic interring of her corpse, Ame-no-Uzume-no-Mikoto, being possessed, sang and danced seminude in front of the cave, thereby placing the departed soul of the Sun Goddess back into her body. The act of reviving a holy person or a deity by placing the departed soul of the dead back into the corpse is called *musubi* in Japanese. Since musubi can be achieved only through ritual performance, we see that the performative arts in ancient Japan were first and foremost religious in nature (cf. Ikeda 1974:289).

In summary, information about the asobi-be reveals three major characteristics of at least some of the senmin during the Ancient periods: 1) there was proximity between the center of power, that is, the emperor, and the periphery, that is, the senmin; 2) the occupation that involved dealing with corpses, which were considered to be defiling, was held by artistic-cum-religious (shamanistic) specialists; and 3) the performing arts, that is, music and dancing, had religious significance.

Besides the information about the asobi-be discussed above, other evidence testifies to the artistic involvement of the senmin during the Ancient period. Kakinomoto-no Hitomaro, one of the most celebrated poets of the *Manyōshū*—the first collection of poems in Japan, compiled in the mid–eighth century—is believed to have been an itinerant poet of senmin status, as indicated by the inclusion in his name of the morpheme *maro*, a title used for senmin members (Origuchi 1976b:464).

In addition to those who were clearly defined as senmin, there were non-sedentary people of various occupations, including diviners, healers, itinerant priests, artisans, and entertainers. It should be noted here that the labels of these occupations are misleading: often the same individual was a diviner-priest who cured illnesses through a ritual performance, which was simultaneously a form of entertainment and a religious ritual (as we shall see in Chapter 5, the same is true of the monkey performance). All of these occupations were religious in nature, and when these people visited a village periodically, they invoked sacred power during their rituals for the village inhabitants. Not only could they harness sacred power, but they could also *refuse* to harness it, whereupon the life in the settlement could become stagnant or, worse yet, subject to calamities (Yamaguchi 1977).

In short, some senmin during the Ancient period were mediators between deities and humans, and without them villagers risked suffering the capricious power of the deities. The power of the senmin, therefore, must have been considerable.

MEDIEVAL PERIOD
(TWELFTH–SIXTEENTH CENTURIES)

We have more detailed records of the special status people during the Medieval period. Both the general dynamics and increasing rigidity in certain aspects of society and culture during the latter half of the period are vividly expressed in the lives of the special status people during this time. During the first half of the period, their occupations were quite varied, and they were not clearly demarcated from other occupations, indicating beyond doubt that the special status people did not constitute a well-defined and separate group within the society. Furthermore, the values assigned to these people and to their occupations were often ambiguous, having both positive and negative meanings and power. During the latter half, while the general dynamics continued to be at work, certain occupations of the special status people became subject to the notion of impurity, which by then had come to receive increasing negativity, losing its positive power.

81

Occupational Diversity in Medieval Society

Medieval society was characterized by increasing occupational specialization, and the occupations of the special status people were no exceptions. For example, funeral attendants, who during the Ancient period were simultaneously religious and artistic specialists, may have been transformed during the Medieval period into several types of worker: cleaners of temples, shrines, and their compounds, who also cared for the dead; itinerant priests, diviners, and entertainers, whose performances were believed to have religious power; and the *jinin*, ritual specialists at important shrines who were responsible for performing rituals at these shrines, and in turn were exempt from taxes and granted the privilege of conducting cross-regional trade (Amino 1984).

If we combine the categories of occupation proposed by Ninomiya (1933:74–76, 85–86) and Noguchi (1978:91), the following were the occupations of the special status people during this period: 1) cleaners of temples, shrines, and their compounds, whose job was also to care for the dead; 2) landscape architects, as well as general construction workers; 3) plasterers, carpenters, and arms manufacturers; 4) butchers, tanners, and makers of leather goods; 5) dyers and manufacturers of bamboo articles; 6) entertainers, prostitutes, and diviners; and 7) undertakers and tomb caretakers.[4]

A document, dated to A.D. 1180, provided by the leader of the people, Danzaemon Yorikane, is another source of information about the occupation of the special status people at this time. It lists twenty-eight occupations held by the

---

[4] Of these categories, the first three are proposed by Noguchi, while the other four are proposed by Ninomiya, who specifies that these occupations were held by the special status people during the Kamakura (1185–1392) and the Muromachi (1392–1603) periods.

special status people (then loosely called *eta hinin*), including, in addition to those listed by Ninomiya and Noguchi,
the *saru hiki* (monkey trainer/performers); the *onmyōji* (diviners); the *sarugaku* (*sarugaku* performers); and the *shishimai* (lion dancers of the New Year).[5]

Danzaemon's list clearly testifies that the codification of
the outcaste occupations was not rigid. Thus, the occupations listed by Danzaemon as those of eta hinin overlap
with the occupations we know were held by the *shokunin*
(professionals) (Morita 1978).[6] As we shall see shortly, the
shokunin were primarily craftsmen-cum-traders, and they
constituted a non-agrarian segment of the population. The
overlap attests to the fact that neither the people who engaged in these occupations nor the occupations themselves
were clearly delineated. Consequently, various other occupations that were not included in the lists for shokunin or
eta hinin are identified in other sources to be the occupations of the special status people.[7] In short, during much of
the Medieval period, people apparently were not concerned with precise identification of the special status peo-

[5] The list of occupations is reproduced in Takayanagi (1981:14–15). The
document is said to have been prepared at the order of Minamoto-no-Yoritomo, then the shogun. There is some controversy over the authenticity
of the document and its date of publication; some scholars consider it to be
a composite of various documents over the years, therefore including occupations that emerged after the Kamakura period (1185–1392). Nevertheless, we can be fairly certain that the list tells of the occupations held by
these people toward the end of the Medieval period.

[6] Their occupations are illustrated in a number of picture scrolls called
shokunin utaawase, which is the term for the singing contest between people of various shokunin occupations.

[7] For example, falconry had previously been a sport of the elite. The department of falconry was abolished under Buddhist pressure in A.D. 860,
and the falconers are said to have joined the special status people as butchers by the Medieval period (Price 1966; see also Noguchi 1978:88). Although less well documented, cormorant fishing followed a similar route,
becoming an outcaste occupation of the special status people (Kitahara
1975).

ple, and therefore there was no single label applied to these people (as will be discussed in more detail below).

Special Status People as Nonresidents

The ambiguity that characterized the special status people during the Medieval period is often attributed to the structure of the society at large, which consisted of two systems: one governing "residents" and the other governing "nonresidents." Called the *heimin* (common people), residents were full-fledged members of society, were free in that they were not owned by other individuals, and were allowed to be armed and to move freely. They were, however, under obligation to pay taxes. The other class of residents, called the *genin* and *shojū*, were owned by other individuals and did not have "the right to be taxed" (Amino 1980:22–23).

"Nonresidents" also comprised two major categories: the shokunin (the aforementioned professionals) and the special status people, or eta hinin. (Since both terms, *shokunin* and *eta hinin*, were used loosely, there were also a number of nonresident occupations that were not classified in either category.) The shokunin enjoyed the legally and socially sanctioned privilege of being exempt from taxes, either partially or entirely. The use of the term shokunin as the designation for craftsmen and other "professionals" is first recorded in 1367 (Amino 1980:105–8, 1983:186–99), indicating the consolidation of these people as a social group by the mid–fourteenth century. In addition to having the right *not* to pay regular taxes, some of the shokunin were able to freely cross regional boundaries without being checked or assessed taxes, as the heimin were. Therefore, they were able to engage in the cross-regional trade of their crafts. It was the emperor himself who granted these privileges to the shokunin in western Japan, since it was he who directly controlled all boundary areas, while regional lords governed their own territories. In eastern Japan, although some of the shokunin received these privileges from the emperor, many received them from Minamoto-no-Yoritomo, the shogun (Amino 1980:133–45).[8] We have less information about other types of shokunin who did not enjoy this status and privilege; indeed, there seems to have been a wide range and variety of shokunin at this time.[9]

The eta hinin constituted the other group of nonresidents. While many special status people were without permanent residence, those who resided in a settlement did so at its boundaries, such as along river banks, under bridges, or near slopes. Since rivers, hills, and mountains were natural demarcations between settlements, these locations represented places away from the central or main part of the settlement. During the Medieval period, therefore, the term *kawaramono* ("people of the river banks") was applied to people who resided at these places where no tax was assessed (Yokoi 1982:335–39). Another term, *sansho*, referred both to these marginal areas and to the people who occupied them. The term *sansho* literally means "the scattered place"; it contrasts with the term *honsho*, which means either "central place" or "real place" (Yokoi 1982:337–39). Hayashiya (1980:130–31) maintains that the term *sansho* means "nontaxable." The sansho people held no land, and no land tax was levied against them (Noguchi 1978:89). In the Japanese society of the time, "nontaxable" also meant "marginal" or other than normal, since tax was levied against land and earnings. Thus, sansho expressed spatial marginality, which in turn was applied to the special status

[8] As mentioned in note 5, above, this is the shogun who ordered Danzaemon, the leader of the special status people at that time, to compile the list of their occupations.

[9] Amino (1984) points to two categories of shokunin: the *kugonin*, encompassing certain categories of shokunin, including blacksmiths, and the jinin, who, as noted previously, were religious-cum-artistic specialists providing religious services at shrines but also engaged in cross-regional trading. Some kugonin were simultaneously jinin and vice versa.

people who lived on untaxed land, and yet it did not carry a negative meaning. [10]

In addition to the shokunin and kawaramono, a number of other categories of people loosely included in the special status group, made up the nonresident population. These included *mooto* (outsiders), *kojiki* (beggars), *hijiri* (saints), and the *hinin*. A brief account of the hinin during this period succinctly illustrates the nature of the special status people at the time—marginal without being negative in valuation. A group of people called the hinin first appeared during the early phase of the Heian period (794–1185) and became more visible in cities only after the mid-Heian period (Takayanagi 1981:11–13). Although the literal meaning of *hinin* is "nonhuman," during the Medieval period the term referred to those individuals who voluntarily abandoned their society (Morita 1978:79–80). The hinin included a small number of criminals who were expelled by the society and plain beggars who begged purely for economic rather than religious reasons. But many hinin were hijiri (saints) who, primarily for religious reasons, decided to leave society (*shukke*) and to reject the demands and responsibilities of their secular life as citizens, such as paying taxes (Kuroda 1972; Morinaga 1967; Takayanagi 1981). [11] As outsiders of the system, the hijiri stood for an anti-establishment element in that their abandonment of society symbolically represented a critical stance against the institutional-

[10] There has been controversy over the residential pattern of the special status people. Many scholars claim that they did not have permanent settlements but traveled from village to village. However, Ochiai (1972:66–67), citing Yanagita, emphatically states that many were not outsiders but rather members of a community. I suggest that the special status people in the artistic/religious category were temporary visitors to farming communities, as noted in the text, but that those who engaged in occupations concerned with removing impurity were permanent members of settled communities, occupying spatially peripheral areas.

[11] Kuroda (1972) does not include the hijiri in the hinin category, but discusses the fact that various types of special status people were lumped together under labels such as "hijiri-kojiki" or "kojiki-hinin."

ized religions that were increasingly identified with political power (Kuroda 1972:44–45).

Multiple Structures of Stratification and Social Mobility

As seen above, Medieval society was characterized by multiple systems of stratification in which there were two dominant systems: one governing the residents and the other governing the nonresidents. That which governed the residents consisted primarily of warriors and farmers—the system that has often been thought of as the only stratification in Medieval Japan. Equally important, however, was the other system, that governing nonresidents, some of whom in the west were directly governed by the emperor. The two systems coexisted side by side without any hierarchical relationship between the two.

Since the special status people belonged to the nonresidential group, we see that they were quite distinct from the slaves (genin and shojū), who belonged to the social structure of the residents. It follows, then, that the special status people during the Medieval period were not the linear descendants of the senmin of the Ancient period who were owned by other individuals (cf. Kuroda 1972:48).

In addition to the multiple structures of stratification, the Medieval society was characterized by the existence of institutionalized means whereby individuals with religious or artistic distinction could rid themselves of their ascribed status. The institution of the *tonseisha* (hermit) provided the opportunity for artists and religious specialists with unusual talents to remove themselves physically from the community and live in the mountains, where they continued their religious or artistic pursuits. Although physically removed from society, they often advanced their social ranking through their reputations. *Amigō* was a similar institution. It referred to a special title given to disinguished artists. Graced with this title, artists enjoyed prestige and respect regardless of their ascribed status.[12]

The institutionalized means of getting out of one's ascribed status and the multiple system of stratification together provided opportunities whereby talented members of the special status people gained direct access to centers of symbolic, religious, and political power. Renowned artists and architect-gardeners came under the special tutelage of the Imperial Court and the powerful warlords. Even those whose occupations dealt with the impurity of individuals in power held a special position because their services were vital. Thus, sweepers were under the special protection of shrines and temples. Falconers served aristocrats. Tanners and makers of leather goods were close to the center of military power, since they alone could supply hides for armor. As we shall see in detail in Chapter 5, monkey trainers were in close proximity both to the Imperial Court and to the Shogunal Palace; in their case, the relationship lasted well into the Early Modern period. Although less is known of the history of cormorant fishermen, they too maintained a close relationship with the Imperial Court (Kitahara 1975). Proximity to the centers of power was not available to all special status people, however—only to the powerful among them.

The activity of these early migrant entertainers and craftsmen undoubtedly seeded the ground for the later efflorescence of folk arts during the latter half of the Medieval period. The established arts of architecture and gardening

---

[12] See Hayashiya 1980:134–40 (for tonseisha) and 161–86 (for amigō); Noguchi 1978:95 (for amigō); and Yokoi 1982:14, 70, 336, 351 (for amigō) and 35, 228–30, 284 (for tonseisha). Although this book does not engage in comparisons between the special status people in Japan and "outcastes" and "untouchables" elsewhere in Asia, it should be noted here that, as Kailasapathy (1968:95) documents, the minstrels (the *pāṇar*) in India were one of the four noble clans and were held in high esteem until Medieval times, when the caste system was formed and the word *pāṇar* came to mean a lower caste.

and the performing arts of *kabuki*, *nō*, and *kyōgen* owe much to such people. Biographies of many of the artists and architects during this period recorded their "humble origin," that is, their belonging to the special status group. Examples include Zen-ami (1393–1490?), who designed the Fushimi Castle for Hideyoshi; Kan-ami (?–1384) and Zeami (?–1443), the father-son pair who developed the *sarugaku* (the forerunner of the noh play); and Nōami (1397–1471) and other masters of the tea ceremony (Noguchi 1978:94–95; for an exhaustive treatment of artists during this period, see Hayashiya 1981).

In short, the complex nature of the special status people during the Medieval period cannot be understood without placing it in the broader context of the Medieval social structure. While we cannot generalize about the special status people, who did not constitute a tightly defined social group and who were of diverse occupations and social ranking, the information presented above indicates that together with other types of nonresidents, some of the special status people had certain freedoms and privileges not accorded the resident population, at least until halfway through the Medieval period. As craftsmen and religious and artistic specialists, these people constituted the non-agrarian population, who often moved from settlemnent to settlement as their occupations required. Furthermore, the elite members of the group were in close proximity to the centers of sociopolitical power. Above all, there is no question how much the performing arts of Japan owes to talented individuals who belonged to the special status group, however loosely it may have been defined.

Emergence of Impurity as Radical Negativity

Flexibility and dynamics in culture and society were not the only characteristics of the Medieval period. Its other side was the gradual development of occupational specialization, which significantly affected the culturally defined meaning assigned to special status people. Some of the occupations of special status people that were concerned with culturally defined "impurity" became separated from other types of occupations, and the practitioners of these defiling occupations were subjected to increasing devaluation.

Indicative of the basic transformation of the meaning of the people in these occupations was the steady decrease in the status of and increasing prejudice against the aforementioned ryōko, caretakers of the Imperial mausoleums, who claimed the highest status among the senmin during the Ancient period. They became the lowest in social rank during the Medieval period. The tendency was already under way by the end of the Heian period (794–1185) (Ninomiya 1933:71), but it became more and more formalized throughout the Medieval period. The degradation process is attributed to the intensification of the notion of defilement assigned to corpses and, by extension, to those who handled them (Ninomiya 1933:71).

It should be noted here that the concept of the impurity of corpses had always been in the value system of the Japanese. Already clearly delineated in some of the oldest written records of the *Kojiki*, dated A.D. 712, and the *Norito*, dated A.D. 927, killing, handling of corpses, and illnesses were all defined not only as impure but as sins (for details, see Ohnuki-Tierney 1984a:35–38). During the Medieval period, with the influence of Buddhism, impurity was extended from human deaths and corpses to dead animals and all activities associated with them. Consequently, many of the occupations of the special status people came to be regarded as defiling (Yokoi 1982:267–94).

The "defiling occupations" included butchers, falconers, tanners, makers of leather goods, cormorant fishermen, undertakers, caretakers of tombs, executioners, *tatami* floor mat makers, and sweepers. All of these occupations involved dealings with culturally defined impurity which derived from death and "dirt." Butchers and falconers handled the bodies of dead animals. Tanners and makers of leather goods handled the hides of dead animals. Undertakers, caretakers of tombs, and executioners were associated with human corpses. The tatami straw mat floor is culturally defined as impure, since it is touched by the most defiled part of the human body, feet, which in turn are in contact with the ground, that is, with "dirt" in a cultural sense. Thus, the tatami makers as well as makers of footgear of all types were associated with culturally defined dirt. Sweepers removed dirt (for details, see Ohnuki-Tierney 1984a:19–50). The special status people who engaged in these occupations were "the specialists in impurity," as Dumont (1970:48) put it; they specialized in removing impurity and thereby spared others the inevitable problems of dealing with culturally defined dirt and impurity. Nevertheless, they were seen to be defiled themselves.

A brief history of the term *eta*, frequently used for the special status people from the thirteenth cenrtury to the present, illustrates the process whereby these occupations and the people who engaged in them became devalued. Although the interpretation of *eta* in different periods of history has been quite controversial among scholars, many agree that the term appeared for the first time in the *Chiribukuro* ("A Dust Bag"), a document dated A.D. 1280 (Morita 1978:86; Noguchi 1978:88). Here, *eta*, written in the *kana* (syllabary) and not in characters, referred to the *kiyome* ("purifiers," i.e., sweepers) and did not then have a derogatory connotation.

By the latter half of the fourteenth century, the pronunciation had changed to *etta*. It had already acquired a derogatory connotation and referred to various people, including sweepers, who resided on river banks and in other peripheral areas. Significantly, in the *Ainoshō*, a manuscript dated A.D. 1446, two characters were superimposed upon the term previously used only orally: the character for "impurity" was assigned to the sound type *e*, and the character for "many/much" to *ta*. In other words, the term *eta*, which referred without disparagement to sweepers during the thirteenth century, had become *etta*, written in two characters that, by the mid–fifteenth century, denoted "excessive impurity" (Morita 1978:88–89). In short, by the end of the Medieval period, the meaning of the special status people engaged in "defiling" occupations was firmly and negatively embedded in the value structure of Japanese culture. Similarly, all the terms associated with these people and their occupations, including sansho and kiyome, had likewise gone through a transformation of meaning, receiving strong negative value by the end of the Medieval period (Amino 1980:9–11).

To RECAPITULATE, the position and meaning assigned to special status people in Medieval Japanese society were quite complex and have gone through a series of transformations. The factors that correlate closely with the changing position and nature of the special status people during the Medieval period include structural features of social stratification, mobility, and occupational specializations, on the one hand, and the system of values, on the other.

During the early phases on the Medieval period, the flexibility and dynamics of Medieval society made it possible for many of the special status people to enjoy freedom of movement and even the opportunity to rise above ascribed status through individual abilities in trade, religion, and art. As the Medieval period progressed, we discern increased social and occupational complexity within the group. Most important, occupational specialization resulted in the separation of those occupations dealing with culturally defined dirt and impurity from others. The former type met a different fate, as it were, from the latter, since it was assigned increasing cultural devaluation. As impurity came to receive the value of radical negativity, the special status people engaged in defiling occupations were firmly placed at the margin of society.

EARLY MODERN PERIOD (1603–1868)

The establishment of the Tokugawa society at the beginning of the seventeenth century signaled major changes in Japanese culture and society that took place over the next three hundred years. Externally, the government enforced the closure of the nation by restricting trade and closing ports to most foreigners. It tried to eliminate influences from the outside, as manifested in the effective proscription of Christianity. Internally, the Early Modern period witnessed the development of a "caste society,"[13] divided into four castes (warriors, farmers, craftsmen or manufacturers, and merchants, in descending order in the hierarchy), plus two social categories outside the system—the emperor at the top and the outcastes at the bottom.

The attempt by the military to take control of the entire nation, partly accomplished through forced settlement of the population for census purposes, had been underway since the latter half of the thirteenth century (Yokoi, in H. Inoue et al. 1978:169–70). However, this effort reached its height at the end of the sixteenth century under the rule of Hideyoshi. In 1582 he recognized land tenure among the special status people and, at the same time, created two legally defined categories of special status people. Thus, while the special status people had been loosely called eta hinin some of them, including those who were previously called sansho and kiyome, became legally defined as kawata, while others fell into the category called hinin (Ueda 1978c:100–101). The *kawata-eta* alone were defined as having permanent, hereditary status. Legally, the hinin were placed lower than the kawata-eta, although they were able

---

[13] For a scholarly controversy about the concept of "caste," see Dumont (1970).

to move up to the farmer, craftsman, or merchant class under rigidly specified circumstances. Later, a number of rules were issued that were intended to place the special status people under the strict political control of the military government and to regulate their occupations (Ueda 1978c).

Furthermore, both the local and the central governments deliberately tried to create antagonism between the special status group and the rest of the population, on the one hand, and betweeen the two categories within the special status group, on the other. Some of the means they used to create antagonism were (1) placing the special status people's community in the midst of a farming community to enhance farmers' antagonism toward the special status people; (2) assigning the role of executioner of criminals to members of the special status group to intensify hatred of them by the rest of the population; and (3) deliberately elevating some hinin to the rank of farmers to wedge rivalry between the hinin and the kawata-eta (Irokawa 1983:21–22). In short, during this period the special status people were turned literally into scapegoats.

In 1710, the actors of kabuki, nō, and kyōgen were legally freed from their outcaste status. However, other artistic and religious specializations, especially those called *zatsugei* (miscellaneous arts) and *daidōgei* (street performances), were no longer recognized as forms of art or religion. Thus, these occupations, including monkey performances on the street, became increasingly devalued culturally (cf. Murasaki 1983:10).[14]

The marginalization of the emperor and the outcastes by their placement outside of society clearly established a social structure basically different from that of the Medieval period. Thus, instead of having multiple structures of strat-

---

[14] A curious exception to this rule was the *gōmune*, a type of religious street entertainer, whose status was that of the common people and remained as such (Takayanagi 1981:208–12).

ification in which the emperor-professionals (shokunin) constituted a separate structure, the emperor and the special status people—including some of the professionals of the Medieval period—belonged to a system that was in a subordinate position to the structure considered to be the core of Japanese society. Many scholars (e.g., Harada 1978a; Price 1966:23; Yokoi 1982:336) believe that the extreme legal and social discrimination against the special status people that has persisted until today originated during this period.[15]

Other significant movements during the Early Modern period were a rapid increase in the population of the special status people and the establishment of hierarchy among them, although this development had already been foreshadowed during the Medieval period. For example, Danzaemon in Edo, a descendant of the aforementioned Danzaemon, controlled the special status people in several regions besides his own district in Edo of 46,210 square meters (55,328 square yards) with 232 families; his compound was 8,593 square meters (10,215 square yards). His power and wealth were said to be equal to those of a feudal lord (Harada 1971:428; Takayanagi 1981:37–57).

Outside their own society, all the outcaste members, including Danzaemon, suffered extreme discrimination. For example, Danzaemon frequented one of the most exclusive restaurants in Edo, where there was a special room used solely by him. If for some reason he was fed in a room used by other guests, the owners removed the tatami straw mat floor after he left and replaced it with a new one so that the "polluted" tatami floor would not contaminate other guests (Harada 1971:428).

It is noteworthy that in contrast to the inflexible defini-

---

[15] See, for example, Bloch (1961) and Dumont (1970) for scholarly controversies over the term *feudal* and debates about whether the Japanese system was truly a "feudal" one.

tion of the special status people during this period, there was considerable mobility across the castes/classes of warror, farmer, craftsman, and merchant. Some individuals even voluntarily moved down the social ladder. For example, Ishida Baigan, the founder of the *Shingaku* school of thought, which had a profound effect upon the morality of the common people during the Early Modern period, was of farmer class but entered the merchant class before he became a full-time preacher/lecturer (Bellah 1970:134).

The crucial question here is which of the professionals (shokunin) and religious/artistic specialists (jinin) of the Medieval period came to be included in 1) the craftsmen (*kō*) class; 2) the kawata-eta category and the hinin category; and 3) the miscellaneous groups of nonresidents who were not lumped into the two categories of special status people, and who enjoyed freedom and mobility. Put the other way, the question is why only certain groups of people became the special status people.

The "fate" of the special status people undoubtedly must have been connected with the changing nature of the social stratification. As noted above, by the beginning of the Early Modern period, the warrior class had seized power from the emperor. The system of stratification consisting of the emperor and the professionals therefore was no longer viable. Both the emperor and the special status people were placed outside of the society governed by the warriors.

The changing nature of the special status people during the Early Modern period also was closely tied to the development of a value system that stressed the "productivity" of the people. As the functional ethic, which Bellah (1970:114) calls "economic rationalization" and likens to the Protestant ethic, came to govern the moral system of the period, the occupations that were "nonproductive" in the agrarian sense became devalued. Yet it should be noted that the interpretation of "productive" was not a simple matter.

While some people devalued merchants and, to a certain degree artisans, because they were "nonproductive" in the agrarian sense, others, including prominent Kokugakuha scholars such as Ishida Baigan (1685–1744) and Motoori Nobunaga (1730–1801), considered merchants "productive." The interpretation rested upon whether merchants were seen to profit only themselves or to deliver services to others and for the benefit of the economy of the nation at large. At any rate, this value system, which bestowed moral sanction on agrarian productivity, may have further contributed to the devaluation of the occupations of the special status people who were "not productive."

At any rate, the "naturalization" process whereby the special status people and their occupations came to be viewed as impure and morally inferior was firmly established during the Early Modern period and has persisted until today.

MODERN PERIOD (1868–PRESENT)

When Japanese feudal society came to an end in 1868, the Meiji government passed a series of legal reforms, including "emancipation" of the burakumin, the term most often used during the Modern period to refer to the special status people. The government abolished the law forcing them to wear special clothing and removed restrictions that had confined them to traditional occupations. Noteworthy in recent history was the vigorous liberation movement in the 1920s, known as the *Suiheisha* movement, through which the special status people attempted to achieve equality in Japanese society. Their effort to gain liberation was severely handicapped by Japan's involvement in wars, and the movement came to an end in 1942 (Akisada 1978).

Despite these efforts, both the people themselves and, at least to some extent, by the government, the burakumin have remained victims of social discrimination. DeVos and Wagatsuma referred to them as "Japan's invisible race" (DeVos and Wagatsuma 1966); they are invisible because there are no physical characteristics that distinguish them from other Japanese.

Today a minority group in Japan, the burakumin are estimated to number 3,000,000 people, localized in 6,000 communities. More accurate figures for the population are difficult to come by. The government census is probably inaccurate; its 1973 figure of 1,048,566 (Ueda 1978a:3–6), for example, is probably too small. The burakumin communities are found primarily in western Japan, with the highest concentration in the Kinki district. Many burakumin are employed in small factories connected with their traditional occupations, such as butchering and leather and fur processing. Others are farmers, fishermen, and unskilled laborers. Although many individuals have become economically or socially prominent, the average standard of living is far below that of the non-burakumin. In the main, the burakumin have remained endogamous; marriages with non-burakumin are infrequent due to intense prejudice on the part of the non-burakumin. The most common feature of prejudice against the burakumin is the attribution of "uncleanliness" (Donoghue 1966:138). The Japanese government has made some effort to provide them with special funds for housing and has prohibited job discrimination against them; moreover, Japanese society, as we noted in Chapter 1, is going through fundamental changes. Whether these changes have affected or will affect the basic symbolic structure of the Japanese, and whether the prejudice against them will consequently ease, if not be eliminated, it is too early to tell.[16]

---

[16] For publications on the contemporary situation, see Buraku Kaihō Kenkyūsho (1978a, 1978b). See also several articles in DeVos and Wagatsuma (1966). None, however, deals with the most recent scene.

Summary and Interpretation

Since the special status people have not constituted a well-delineated group unilinearly linked throughout history, any generalization may not apply to all those who were considered to be the special status people in each historical period. However, we can safely say that most of them have been non-agrarian and their status has always been low. In terms of values, some of the special status people and their occupations have always been regarded as impure. These are the constant features that have characterized the special status people in Japanese society throughout history. However, the precise nature and intensity of these features have undergone changes, and these changes have paralleled the transformations in the social position and cultural meaning of the special status people. During the Ancient period, the structure of the society was fairly inflexible. Despite the negative value assigned to impurity, such tasks as handling corpses and arranging funeral rites were imbued with religious meaning as well as with aesthetics. During the Medieval period, flexibility in the sociocultural systems provided the special status people, both as a group and as individuals, with considerable freedom. As nonresidents, they were exempt from taxes and other obligations. At least some of them received special privileges from the emperor and could travel across the political-geographical boundaries of the areas controlled by regional lords. Furthermore, individuals who excelled in religious or artistic matters were able to free themselves from their ascribed status.

On the other hand, the negative value assigned to impurity continued to intensify as the Medieval period progressed, and occupations dealing with impurity became separated from other religious and artistic occupations. Thus, impurity as radical negativity facilitated a process whereby "naturalization" of impurity as a moral evil became firmly established.

It was during the Early Modern period that the dominant Japanese view of the special status people as "naturally" impure and hence morally inferior was firmly established. Intense aversion to impurity "justified" the devaluation of the special status people and the occupations dealing with culturally defined impurity or dirt, and rigid social stratification placed them as outcastes at the bottom or figuratively outside of society. In short, they were turned into scapegoats. Increasing occupational specialization elevated some religious and artistic occupations relieving those who engaged in them from their outcaste status, but leaving behind street entertainers and others in the "little" tradition. In short, both occupational specialization and stratification among the special status people themselves added to the complexity of this group.

Despite some dramatic events during the Modern period, both the nature of social stratification as it affects the special status people and the symbolic structure of purity and impurity for the most part have remained unchanged. Only now do we finally see some signs of change. In Chapter 3 we saw that new meanings of the monkey have emerged, suggesting transformations in the reflexive structure of the Japanese. How basic or permanent these changes are cannot be answered for some time yet. More specifically, it is difficult to determine at the moment if these transformations in contemporary Japan include changes in the attitude of the dominant Japanese toward the special status people.

5

The Monkey Performance: Historical Transformations of Its Meaning

A DISTINCT form of monkey performance developed in Japan is that in which a trained monkey dances to the tune of its trainer's singing, to the *shamisen* (three-string musical instrument), or to the beat of a drum (cf. Ishii 1963:39). Based on the belief that the monkey is the guardian of horses, it started as a ritual performed at stables for the purpose of healing sick horses and improving their welfare in general. Later in history it was performed also on the street and at the doorway of individual homes. Until recently, all of these forms of the monkey performance were religious in nature. The dance performance by the monkey, the messenger from the Mountain Deity to humans, symbolized the Mountain Deity's visit to the people in order to bless them with health and prosperity. Throughout history, the monkey performance has been a male occupation, although in some representations, such as paintings or porcelain dolls, trainers are depicted as women, following the Japanese artistic tradition of depicting beautiful women in male occupations (Photo 2).

Two types of historical records describe the monkey performance: written sources and paintings. The latter often appeared in picture scrolls that were popular forms of publication in the past. Although such sources are by no means

君をためしに春の松うら

重ねてん

かさ名のん

やれしま

千年と

影うま

源氏

鈴木春信画

Photo 2. Monkey performance, by Suzuki Harunobu (1725–1770), a well-known *ukiyo-e* artist. Note that a woman is depicted as a monkey trainer when monkey training was a male profession. Portraying beautiful women in male professions was a common practice of artists when they wanted to highlight the beauty of women. (From *Ukiyo-e 1: Moronobu Harunobu. Nihon Hanga Bijutsu Zenshū* [A Collection of the Japanese Art of Woodblock Printings]. Vol. 2. 1961. Tokyo: Kōdansha)

abundant, these records do enable us to trace the development of the monkey performance. On the other hand, most historical records are extremely sketchy about the performance itself.[1] Leaving an extensive analysis of the symbolic content of the monkey performance to Chapters 7 and 8, I will trace in this chapter the historical development of this performing art—both as a ritual dance performed by the monkey at stables and as a street entertainment in which, while maintaining its religious meaning, the monkey performed dances and tricks—by placing it against the wider background of the nature and development of Japanese performing arts in general. Historical records of monkey performances also offer important insight into the complex cultural meanings assigned to trainers and the special status people in general, and how these meanings have changed through time. Therefore, in this chapter I also attempt to understand the meaning assigned to the monkey performance in different historical periods by situating the monkey performance in the broader contexts of the performing arts and the history of the special status people.

ANCIENT AND MEDIEVAL PERIODS (300 B.C.–SIXTEENTH CENTURY)

Historical Developments

Just as the monkey has been a dominant symbol in India, China, and elsewhere, so too has the monkey performance been widespread in Asia. In fact, the idea of the monkey performance may have been introduced to Japan from the Asian continent. Like many other cultural institutions of foreign origin, however, the monkey performance became

[1] For a brief history of the monkey performance, see Miyaji (1981) and Oda (1967a, 1967b, 1967c, 1968a, 1968b, 1968c, 1968d, 1968e, 1968f, 1968g).

deeply embedded within Japanese culture (Yanagita 1982e:esp. 90–93; see also Ishida 1966).

An early—possibly the earliest—record of the monkey performance is found in a pictorial representation of a monkey and a trainer in the *Nenjū Gyōji Emaki* (Picture Scrolls of Annual Events) (Kadokawa Shoten Henshūbu 1968: no page number). Waving a fan and wearing tattered clothes, the trainer is barefoot, suggesting his humble status. The monkey has a rope tied to its neck, is not clothed, and is walking on all fours. Although probably published during the mid–thirteenth century, the scrolls depict annual events of the late Heian period (794–1185) (Fukuyama 1968).[2]

Another early reference to the monkey performance is found in the *Ryōjin Hishō* (1169–1179). Here, a monkey is described as leaving the stable to "play" (*asobu*), which, according to Yanagita (1982e:336–37), means "to dance." We saw earlier that the term *asobu* (to play) once meant to dance in order to placate deities. I therefore interpret this passage in the *Ryōjin Hishō* as a portrayal of the monkey acting like a shaman—dancing to appease the spirits and deities so that these supernatural beings will exercise beneficial power over horses.

The first account of an unmistakably identifiable monkey performance appears in the *Azuma Kagami*, dated 1245, in which a monkey is described as dancing like a human. The same episode is recorded in greater detail in the *Kokon Chomonshū*, dated 1254, in which the term *mau* (to dance) is

[2] Ema (1932:14) points to the *Shin Sarugakuki* ("Description of the New Sarugaku") as the earliest publication in which the monkey is depicted as "performing." The *sarugaku* was then a new form of entertainment introduced from China. Said to be authored by Akihira Fujiwara (989?–1066), the *Shin Sarugakuki* is considered to have been published toward the end of his life, around the mid–eleventh century. It describes various sarugaku performances and the lives of individuals in the audience (Fujiwara 1979: 133–52). I have found no specific description of the monkey performance in the *Shin Sarugakuki*.

used four times, leaving no doubt that monkeys indeed "danced" (Tachibana 1966:535–36). The passage describes the monkey's clothing, including the ebōshi, a type of hat worn by aristocrats and warriors at the time, which has become a trademark for performing monkeys. The passage also describes the monkey collecting payment after each performance. Following the performance, according to the *Kokon Chomonshū*, the monkey was tied to a stable where it was later bitten by a horse and died. The type of clothing, the dance, the collection after each performance, and the tying of the monkey to the stable, as described in this passage, constitute the major features that define the monkey performance during subsequent periods, from which we have more detailed records. In both the *Azuma Kagami* and the *Kokon Chomonshū*, however, the audience is described as watching the performance in amazement; perhaps they were amazed by the skill with which the monkey danced like a human. The passages in these publications seem to indicate that the monkey performance became established as a folk performing art by the mid–thirteenth century, although its prototype may have been created as early as the beginning of the Medieval period (cf. Miyamoto 1981:82; Oda 1967b:49, 1978:15).

Records from the *Azuma Kagami* and the *Kokon Chomonshū* are also significant because they demonstrate that, during the mid–thirteenth century, the dance at the horse stables and the street performance were so nearly identical that the same monkey performed both.

It should be noted, however, that not all the monkey performances during this period took the same form. Some street performances were much simpler. For example, the *Yūzū Nenbutsu Engi Emaki* ("The Origin of the Yūzū Nenbutsu Sect of Buddhism"), dated 1391 (Umezu 1972), contains a picture in which a monkey and its trainer are watched by a few spectators (painting reproduced in Suō Sarumawashinokai Jimukyoku 1978). The monkey, tied to a leash, is unclothed and stands on its hind legs, holding a pole. The trainer wears no special clothing and is barefoot.

Monkey training (saru hiki) is similarly depicted as one of thirty-two professions in another picture scroll, called *Sanjū Niban Shokunin Uta Awase* ("Poetry Contest among Thirty-Two Tradesmen") (Kadokawa Shoten Henshūbu 1969), which appeared during the late Muromachi period (1392–1603). In the picture, the barefoot trainer wears a skirt-shaped garment apparently made of straw, although he carries a long sword, like a warrior, and a stick to give signs to the monkey. The monkey, with a leash tied to its neck, is unclothed and is walking on all fours (see also Hanawa 1940:39, 44).

Several other paintings dated to the sixteenth century depict a relatively simple monkey performance as a door-to-door entertainment. In a painting by Sesshū (?–1506), a monkey in simple attire is dancing in someone's yard, while three men are playing musical instruments. The trainer holds a leash and a stick (Toda et al. 1982: Plate 6). In a painting by Kanō Motonobu (?–1559), a monkey carries on its shoulder a stick with a bucket hanging at each end. The trainer holds a leash and a stick. The scene depicts an entire family looking at the dancing monkey (Toda et al. 1982: Plate 88).

These records, in both writing and painting, tell us that two types of monkey performance—as a ritual at horse stables and as a form of street entertainment—had likely been in practice during most of the Medieval period and had definitely been in practice since the mid-thirteenth century. But while the monkey performance appears to have persisted as a form of street entertainment, the performance of dances at horse stables declined after reaching its zenith during the Muromachi period—the period characterized by continuous warfare among regional lords, which made the welfare of horses vital to warriors and farmers, all of whom were engaged in these wars.

Toward the very end of the Medieval period and the early part of the Early Modern period, a new role was assigned to the monkey performance. It became a part of the ritual of rice harvesting, as depicted in several paintings from this period, such as one by Iwasa Katsumochi Matabei (1578–1650) and one by Kusumi Morikage (1620–1690); curiously, however, there is no written record of this new role.[3]

The new role of the monkey—blessing the rice harvest—is a logical extension of the monkey's role as messenger from the Mountain Deity. The Mountain Deity is believed to be the same deity as the Deity of the Rice Paddy: he goes back to the mountains in the fall after overseeing the rice growing during the warm season (Ouwehand 1964; Yanagita 1951:642). In other words, the monkey as messenger from the Mountain Deity exercises the sacred power of its master to promote not only the welfare of horses but also the growth of the new crop of rice. It is important to note here that in Matabei's painting the monkey seems to be performing in front of a house, and in Morikage's painting it is definitely performing at the doorway of a house; the major motif of both paintings is rice harvesting. The monkey performance at the doorways of individual houses was an important form of monkey performance in the recent past,

[3] I am most grateful to Professor Jan Vansina of the University of Wisconsin who brought back to me a photocopy of Morikage's painting from Museum für Ostasiatische Kunst of Staatliche Museen Preußischer Kulturbesitz of West Berlin, which subsequently sent me a photograph of the original painting, entitled "The Dancing Monkey; Details from the Screen [Rice Growing and Harvesting]." I had not encountered in any of the written sources the monkey performance as part of the rice harvesting ritual. Professor Sandy Kita, of the Department of Art History at the University of Wisconsin, kindly told me that he had seen a painting by a Chinese painter, Liang Kai, which provided the model for Morikage's painting, although the figures are Chinese. Professor Kita also pointed out that despite the Chinese model for Morikage's work, other paintings of the same period, such as the one by Matabei, attest to the fact that the monkey performance had become associated with rice harvesting by this time. I am grateful to Professor Kita for bringing to my attention the Matabei painting (reproduced in Tsuji 1981: Photo no. 62).

and these paintings suggest that it may have begun as early as the late Medieval period.

Little is known about the position of monkey trainers during the Medieval period. With the trend toward occupational specialization, artists and artisans began to settle down and form their own separate communities toward the end of the period. Monkey trainers, too, formed their own communities, from which they traveled in groups of several people when they performed (Oda 1967b:52, 1967c:43). Paintings from this period also provide us with insights into the position of monkey trainers in Medieval society. Thus, we see in the *Sanjū Niban Shokunin Uta Awase* a trainer carrying a sword, as noted earlier. Since the common people (heimin) were allowed to bear arms (Amino 1980:22–23), the sword carried by the trainer seems to signify that monkey trainers were close to the common people, who as a group were above the special status people in the social stratification of the time. This is plausible since, as discussed in Chapter 4, the position of the special status people was both flexible and diversified, and their lives were relatively free of restrictions.

The Meaning of the Monkey Performance

We saw in Chapter 4 that in ancient Japan performing arts were religious in nature, and we saw earlier in this chapter that the monkey performance was no exception. In this section, I will trace the historical development of the Japanese performing arts in order to shed further light on the cultural meanings assigned to the monkey performance.

Pointing to passages in the *Kojiki* (712) and the *Nihongi* (720), T. Kitagawa (1972:4–9) emphasizes that *monomane* (imitation, mimicry) was seen by the Japanese during their early history as the basic feature of the performing arts. I might speculate that there is at least a conceptual association between the monkey, whose major characterization in

Japanese culture lies in its ability to imitate humans, and the basic nature of the performing arts as seen by the ancient Japanese.

During the reign of Prince Shōtoku (?–621), Japan imported cultural institutions en masse from China. In addition to many beliefs and practices related to the monkey, several forms of the performing arts were introduced, of which the *sangaku* is particularly relevant here. The sangaku consisted of miracle or trick performances (cf. Fujiwara 1979). A commonly accepted interpretation by scholars is that the sangaku eventually evolved into the *sarugō* or the *sarugaku* (*saru* = monkey; *gō* or *gaku* = music), which became a popular form of folk performance during the Medieval period. Hayashiya (1979:17–18) suggests that since a monkey jumping through a ring was a featured event in the sangaku, the label for the stage performance included the term *saru* (monkey). We see here a close association between the use of a monkey in performance and the development of Japanese performing arts.

The Imperial Court maintained a department of sangaku (*sangakuko*), where a number of sangaku performers were employed. The department was abolished in 782 because the popularity of sangaku among the people made the Imperial Court's protection unnecessary. Released from the Court, some sangaku performers sought the protection of temples and shrines, where they performed; others became itinerant priest-performers and traveling entertainers, whose performance was of a religious nature (Hayashiya 1979:21–28, 107–25).

In short, while some of these performers no doubt contributed to the eventual growth of the sangaku into the sarugaku, which in turn developed into the nō play (Hayashiya 1979:21), many became *shomoji*, itinerant priest-diviner-entertainers of low social rank. Yanagita (1982c: 434–44) points to the multiple roles that the shomoji filled. They were diviners, primarily of the Taoist tradition, who also were entertainers. Their performances, called *manzai*, were considered to have healing power. On New Year's, they visited from house to house, reciting prayers for happy occasions and performing comical acts and dances (Yanagita 1951:548).

During the Muromachi period (1392–1603) and later, when horses were vital to warriors, the shomoji performed the manzai at warriors' stables at the beginning of the New Year—fulfilling the same role as that served by monkey performances. Only certain families held this occupation, although they were located in various parts of Japan. One such group, located in the Echizen district (Fukui Prefecture), whose descendants continued to follow the same occupation until recently, maintained in family lore that the family occupation originated when an ancestor's prayer cured a favorite horse of a prince, possibly Prince Shōtoku (?–621) (Yanagita 1982c:437–38). They called their annual spring dance performance an *utsubo-mai* (quiver dance); as noted earlier, warriors covered their quivers (*utsubo*) with monkey hides, which were believed to protect their horses. On the basis of these facts, Yanagita (1982c:437–38) suggests a strong relationship between the aforementioned manzai performed by these shomoji and the monkey dance performance at horse stables. Elsewhere, Yanagita (1951:241–42) suggests that human diviners originally prayed for horses but began to combine their religious service with entertainment by using the performing monkey. Noguchi (1978:94–95) is more explicit: he lists the monkey performance as one of the *zatsugei*, a label for miscellaneous performing arts performed by the shomoji.

Not only can the connection between monkey trainers and the shomoji be established on the basis of similar meanings attached to and roles fulfilled by both occupations, but also there is clear historical evidence that the Ono family, ancestors of the monkey trainers, established a longstanding affinal relationship with the Sarume family, ancestors of the shomoji. Thus, many of the families that specialized in monkey training and performance during the early twentieth century traced their ancestry to the Ono family in Ōmi, although many of the descendants had by then spread from Ōmi to other parts of Japan. The Ono family specialized in singing and other performing arts of a religious nature (Takasaki 1956:15; Yanagita 1982e:336–40). Yanagita further argues that the Ono family was related to Sarumaru Dayū, who was named as the author of a well-known collection of poems of the late ninth century (Inada and Ōshima 1977:395–96; Ueda et al. 1937:20). As noted in Chapter 3, some consider Sarumaru Tayū to be a single poet, but others claim that the name Sarumaru Tayū, which bears the term *saru* (monkey), was given to a group of itinerant priest-poets. If so, poets who formed this professional group were related to the Ono family, ancestors of monkey trainers.

As for the shomoji ancestry, some of them, including the family in Echizen, claimed their ancestry from Sarume (monkey woman). A prominent figure in the *Kojiki*, Sarume claims that she is the daughter born of the union between Saruta Biko, the monkey deity who led the grandson of the Sun Goddess on his descent to earth, and Ame-no-Uzume-no-Mikoto, the divine shamaness who danced seminude in front of a cave when the Sun Goddess hid herself in it (Inada and Ōshima 1977:28; Kurano and Takeda 1958:129–31). The Sarume family, who traced descent through women, provided dancing women for the Imperial Court during the Ancient period (Inada and Ōshima 1977:535; Yanagita 1982e:338) and was one of the families who specialized in the recitation of oral traditions (Takasaki 1956:15). It is relevant to note here that Hieda-no-Are, the narrator of the *Kojiki*, is also said to be a descendant of Ame-no-Uzume-no-Mikoto (Inada and Ōshima 1977:28; Yanagita 1982c:207–19). In short, both the court narrator-historian and the court dancers were women who descended from Ame-no-

Uzume-no-Mikoto, who represents the shaman-dancers of ancient Japan. It should also be noted that despite their proximity to the Imperial Court and their possession of magico-religious powers, the descendants of Ame-no-Uzume-no-Mikoto were of low social status in the formalized hierarchy of the early Medieval period (Yanagita 1982c:212). In other words, Ono males married Sarume women, despite the fact that during the early Medieval period the Ono family enjoyed a much higher status than did the Sarume family, who nevertheless could provide the Ono family with access to the Imperial Court (Yanagita 1982e:336–40).

The historical information presented above suggests that various cultural phenomena were woven into the rich texture of the monkey performance, which eventually became established both as a stable ritual and as a street entertainment—an entertainment which itself maintained strong religious implications. These religious/artistic strands included: (1) the training of the monkey to perform tricks and dances; (2) the belief in the healing power of the monkey; (3) the special relationship established between the monkey and the horse; (4) the human entertainers who were also diviner-healers; and (5) a close relationship between monkey trainers and specialists in oral tradition, including poets and narrators of myth-history. The interweaving of these strands makes it apparent that to understand the meaning of the monkey performance, we need to view it in this larger historical context—a context in which entertainment, literature, oral tradition, and healing were inseparable and all were imbued with religious meaning.

There is enough of a basis, therefore, to support Yanagita's (1982e:339) assumption that the monkey performance started as a religious performance at the Imperial Court and later became a ritual conducted at stables to promote the well-being of horses. We can be sure at least that the monkey performance originally was a performing art with religious significance, and that it was performed by people of low social status who were in close proximity to the Imperial Court—and, as we saw in Chapter 4, this was in fact characteristic of the special status people in general, at least up to the mid–Medieval period.

Toward the end of the Medieval period, while the religious significance of the monkey performance persisted, both the monkey and the monkey performance took on a negative meaning, as is well illustrated in a play from *kyōgen* (a genre of comic interlude) entitled *Utsubozaru* ("Quiver Monkey"). An analysis of the play with its text in translation is the focus of Chapter 7, but it is well to briefly point out here that in this play both the monkey and the trainer are ambiguously characterized. At the onset of the play, a feudal lord wants to kill the monkey for its fur, thereby acknowledging the supernatural power of monkey fur. Yet, when the trainer begs him not to do so, the lord is ready to shoot both the monkey and the trainer with one arrow, indicating that the monkey and the trainer are identical in the lord's mind, and that they are scapegoats whose lives may be cut off at the lord's will. Yet the play ends with the lord's being mesmerized by the spell, as it were, of the monkey's dance. In other words, in this play, written toward the end of the Medieval period, both the monkey and the trainer are assigned both positive and negative meanings and power.

EARLY MODERN PERIOD (1603–1868)

During the Early Modern period, the monkey performance both at horse stables and on the street persisted, although a gradual change in meaning, foreshadowed in the play from the late Medieval period that was discussed above, seems to have taken place. In effect, we see an increasingly ambivalent attitude toward the monkey performance during this period.

With the establishment of lasting peace, horses lost their significance for warriors, and as a result, at least in part, the monkey performance conducted to maintain the health of horses became a highly specialized profession restricted to certain individuals. By contrast, the monkey performance on the street developed fully as a form of entertainment for the common people (cf. Takayanagi 1981:131), although it continued to have a religious meaning.

The monkey dance that was performed for horses became part of the solemn ritual enacted at the beginning of the New Year, both at the Imperial Court in Kyoto and at the Shogunal Court in Edo (Tokyo) (Iida 1973:147–53; Yanagita 1982e:99, 336). The adoption of the monkey performance at the Shogunal Court originated from a well-known incident in which Ieyasu summoned Takiguchi Chōtayū from Shimousa (Chiba) because three of his horses became ill. When the horses recovered, Ieyasu rewarded Chōtayū by providing him with a piece of land and a fixed income; in exchange, Chōtayū conducted the monkey performance at Ieyasu's stable three times a year (Takayanagi 1981:133–34). The privilege of performing with a trained monkey on these occasions was held exclusively by certain families: by Tatsui Hyōgo for the Imperial Court, and by Ogawa Montayū and Takiguchi Chōtayū for the Shogunal Court (Ema 1932:15; Murasaki 1983:10–19).

According to Ema's description (1932:15–16), the repertoire of dances performed at the Imperial Court seems to have consisted of traditional pieces such as the *sanbasō* and the *shishimai*, whereas the repertoire at the Shogunal Court included folk dances such as the *wakashū odori* and the *kagoshima odori*, as well as trick performances. The ritual at the Shogunal Court placed strong emphasis on purifying the stables. Such an emphasis is not reported to have been present at the Imperial Court, where, until 1870, the monkey performance continued to be practiced at the beginning of the New Year (Ema 1932:15–16; Iwabashi 1920:328).

The monkey trainers performed the purification ritual not only at the Shogunal Court but also for the local lords stationed in Edo. Ogawa Montayū, one of the two leaders of the monkey trainers, had 689 clients; it took him three months to finish his rounds for the New Year (Murasaki 1983:18).

While the monkey performance continued to be conducted as a ritual at horse stables during the Early Modern period, the monkey performance as a form of entertainment with definitely religious overtones became increasingly important. It was performed at three sites: on the street, at the doorways of individual homes, and in makeshift theaters. As during the Medieval period, then, the monkey performance was held on the street as well as on the grounds of temples and shrines, especially during festivals. Monkeys also performed at the doorways of individual homes on auspicious occasions, such as the New Year or the day on which a marriage ceremony was held or a house or a piece of land was purchased.[4] In Edo and Osaka, it was performed also on inauspicious occasions, such as funerals and annual memorial days for the deceased.[5]

The third type of monkey performance as entertainment, which took place in small makeshift theaters, was a new development during the Early Modern period. It was quite popular, as shown in the *Kii-no-kuni Meisho Zuroku* (Oda 1978). In 1785, a clothed monkey wearing a wig performed a piece from kyōgen, and its success established a tradition

---

[4] The auspicious meaning attached to the monkey performance is also seen, for example, in the *Oshun Denbei Chicagoro Kawarano Tatehiki*, a famous piece of *jōruri* (a type of ballad) published in 1785. In this ballad, the monkey performance is described repeatedly as *medetayana* (auspicious) (Nihon Meicho Zenshū Kankōkai 1929:935, 936).

[5] For more discussion of the monkey performance as street entertainment during this period, see M. Kitagawa (1981:206). See also Asakura et al. (1969:220); Ema, Nishioka, and Hamada (1967:528–29); Ishii (1963:38–39); and Takayanagi (1981:132).

of monkey performance in these roadside theaters (Iida 1973:152), at least by the 1830s (Hirose 1979:161).

In short, during the Early Modern period, the monkey performance took two forms: the ritual at horse stables and the entertainment at the three different sites. Each type of performance became more elaborate as a cultural institution than it had been during the previous periods. The monkey dance performed for entertainment continued to carry its magico-religious meaning, but it was distinctly more secular and lighthearted than the ritual performed at stables, although the monkey performance at the doorways of individual houses at the beginning of the New Year continued to maintain its religious function of blessing the household. Moreover, the performance at horse stables became confined to a smaller segment of the population, whereas the performance for entertainment became much more widespread among the folk than it had been during the previous periods. The shift in emphasis from a ritual at stables to entertainment may in part be explained by the decreasing importance of horses to the warriors, resulting from both the introduction of guns and a long period of peace (Iida 1973:145–46). The growing popularity of the monkey performance as entertainment may also be seen as part of the efflorescence of folk culture during the same period, and as part of the secularization process, as I will discuss in Chapter 9.

During the Early Modern period, monkey trainers were reported to have worked in various regions of northeastern, eastern, and central Japan, and as far west as Osaka. Of all the regions, Edo had by far the most trainers. Danzaemon, the leader of the special status people in Edo, had under his control forty-six families of monkey trainers in various regions of eastern Japan, including fifteen families in Edo itself.[6]

---

[6] Kitamura (1970:643) claims that there were only twelve families in Edo,

As noted in Chapter 4, special status people of the Early Modern period were subjected to intense legal and social discrimination in society at large, while their own society, at least in Edo, also became highly stratified. This stratification is reflected in how the audience paid for the monkey performance. For door-to door-performances, people in Osaka paid the leader (*zatō*) of the group on both auspicious and inauspicious occasions but paid the trainers only on auspicious occasions; in Edo, however, they did not pay the trainers on either type of occasion and paid the leader on both types of occasion (M. Kitagawa 1981:206).

In general, the station of monkey trainers was low during this period, but they were accorded a somewhat special status. It was defined to lie between the two categories of special status people during this period (Takayanagi 1982:110). Officially, they were lower than the kawata-eta and grouped with the hinin, who were at the bottom of the hierarchy, legally bound to their hereditary status and subjected to the most intense legal and social discrimination. Yet the monkey trainers enjoyed privileges not accorded to the hinin.

During this period monkey trainers often were caricatured as trying in vain to become samurai, the ideal in Japanese society. Many of the trainers wore attire resembling but not identical to that worn by warriors. Leaders of the special status people, too, wore the quasi-samurai outfit, especially when they visited warriors and the shogunal government. However, their attire was marked by a broad hem at the bottom of the hakama, an ankle-length skirt-like garment which warriors wore without the hem (Ishii 1963:318–19). Monkey trainers in samurai attire often ap-

---

while Murasaki (1983:10–11) notes that the number was reduced from fifteen to twelve toward the end of the Early Modern period. There were also six trainers in Kyoto, six in Fushimi, and some in Akita, Kai, Suruga, Owari, Kii, and Osaka (Iida 1973:151; see also Ema 1932:16; Harada 1971:428; and Takayanagi 1981:132; 1982:93–94, 108).

pear in woodblock prints (*ukiyo-e*), such as those by Toyo-
kuni, Hokusai, and Harunobu. To point to but one example, a print by an anonymous artist of the Early Modern
period, now housed at the Freer Gallery in Washington,
D.C., shows a trainer wearing a samurai outfit with a pair
of swords. Unlike a samurai, however, he is barefoot, a
characteristic of people of lower status at the time. Footgear, while a must in contemporary Japan for walking outside, was used only by upper-class and wealthy Japanese
during this period (Ushioda 1973:223–24). This print is
meant to depict the mid–seventeenth-century satirical
maxim "The long sword of a monkey trainer is something
the world can do without" (*Yononaka ni iranu mono sarumawashi no chōtō*). We recall that during the Medieval period
the sword carried by monkey trainers signified their freedom and somewhat privileged status. The same sword during the Early Modern period signified an unnecessary item,
or even more appropriately, the negative side of humans
that causes them to try in vain to imitate those superior to
them, as defined in the ideological structure of the dominant Japanese.

MODERN PERIOD (1868–PRESENT)

The fall of the Tokugawa shogunal government and the return of the emperor to power inaugurated the beginning of
the Meiji period. The transfer of power had an immediate
impact on the monkey performance. It no longer found pa-
tronage at the shogunal stables, and the warrior class that
had patronized the monkey trainers also disappeared. The
last monkey performance at the emperor's stables was conducted in 1871 (Oda 1968e:35) in Kyoto, although the emperor had already moved to Tokyo. The stable ritual continued to be conducted in rural areas, such as in Shinshū
(Matsuyama 1941), but it became increasingly limited as the
nation grew more industrialized. It should also be noted

THE MONKEY PERFORMANCE

that monkeys started to perform for oxen, a vitally important animal for farmers, although we have no record indicating when such performances began (cf. Oda 1980:18).
While the stable ritual lost its significance for the Japanese during the Meiji period, the religious meaning of the
monkey and the monkey performance did not disappear altogether. As Yanagita (1982f:163) notes, monkey trainers
had been protected at Nikkō, where Ieyasu's mausoleum is
located, because of the religious significance of the monkeys. The practice at Nikkō lasted until "recently," according to Yanagita, who originally published his article in 1955.

Throughout the Meiji period, the monkey performance
as entertainment on the street, at the doorways of individual households, and in makeshift theaters seems to have
continued. At the height of its popularity during the Meiji
and the Taishō periods (1912–1925), there were 150 trained
monkeys and an equal number of trainers (Murasaki
1980:13–30).

There is little information about monkey performances
elsewhere in Japan.[7] However, we do have some information about trainers and their activities in the Yamaguchi Prefecture since the middle of the Meiji period.[8] According to
these studies, trainers during the latter half of the Meiji period all originated from the settlements of special status
people located in the southeastern part of the Yamaguchi
Prefecture (see also Gonda 1971:317). They journeyed all
over Japan to perform but returned to these settlements
when they completed the journey. It is not altogether clear
whether trainers did not exist elsewhere in Japan during
these periods. We also do not know how the trainers in Yamaguchi Prefecture came to be concentrated there, and

[7] Nakada (1970) is an exception, but it does not provide us with detailed
information.
[8] See Maruoka (1975a, 1975b, 1975c, 1976a, 1976b, 1976c, 1976d, 1977a,
1977b); Murasaki (1983); and Yamaguchiken Kyōiku Iinkai Bunkaka (1980).

119

how they were related to trainers in Edo, Osaka, and elsewhere during the Early Modern period.

In any event, the trainers from Yamaguchi Prefecture traveled east and west on a journey known as the *jōgeyuki* (upward and downward travel). These trainers were always accompanied by women, many of whom were their wives. Organized as a group by a male leader and his wife, they visited various cities and towns throughout Japan. The women sold camellia oil, considered in Japan to be the best hair oil, while the trainers earned their living by performing on the street or at the doorways of individual households. In most cases, except among very experienced trainers, their earnings were unpredictable and meager, and their way of life was made possible only by the income of the women. In addition, the trainers and some younger men who were not experienced in the art earned their living by performing divinations and various other tasks (Yamaguchiken Kyōiku Iinkai Bunkaka 1980:10). These men and women were bound to the leader through the indenture system, which frequently led to his abuse of them. Murasaki views the hierarchy within the trainer's organization as being similar to that which characterized the society of the special status people during the Early Modern period under Danzaemon, their autocratic leader.

It is quite important here to bring in historical information in order to properly understand the women's job of selling hair oil. We recall in Chapter 4 that some of the professionals (shokunin) and ritual specialists (jinin) during the Medieval period were governed directly by the emperor. One of the occupations of these people was selling oil. It is recorded that during the Nanbokuchō period (1336–1392) the ritual specialists at Ishikiyomizu Hachimangū peddled oil in various regions while they were under the protection of the Imperial Court. Amino (1984:202) believes that the relationship between these ritual specialists and the Court began some time during the Heian period (794–

1185) and lasted until the end of the Medieval period. In other words, there seems to be a definite historical connection between the traders of oil during the Medieval period and the women who sold hair oil while accompanying the monkey trainers during the Meiji period.

Some of these trainers recollect how they were received by people (in Maruoka 1975a, 1975b, 1975c, 1976a, 1976b, 1976c, 1976d, 1977a, 1977b). One trainer recalls a generally negative attitude that stemmed from the identification of the monkey performance as one of the traditional occupations of special status people. The attitude was demeaning, and the trainers were regarded as analogous to beggars (Maruoka 1976b:64). On the other hand, another trainer recalls how farmers invited him to perform for the welfare of their oxen and rewarded him generously (Maruoka 1975b:135). Yet another trainer reports how some families welcomed him while others treated him badly, sometimes even chasing him off and tossing out salt at the doorway to purify the area defiled by his presence (Maruoka 1975b:134).

With the aforementioned development in the 1920s of the burakumin liberation movement, called the *Suiheisha*, the leaders' inhumane treatment of their people came under attack, despite their efforts to prevent employees from getting involved in the movement. Police arrests of these bosses, as well as other movements challenging the power structure of special status groups, led to a sudden decrease in and eventual disappearance of the jōgeyuki in the 1920s (Murasaki 1983:161–62). During this period, many special status people wished to eradicate any trace of their identity, including "traditional" occupations. This attitude also contributed to the discontinuity of the monkey performance.

One of the rare published recollections of a monkey performance by a spectator is that of Ozawa (1978). He remembers that during his childhood trainers often came to a grass field in his neighborhood to perform. A particularly memorable repertoire was entitled "The Three Brave Heroes as Human Cannons (*Nikudan San Yūshi*)." A monkey dressed in military uniform and carrying a toy torpedo would pose at attention, salute to the spectators, and then make a mock dash into enemy territory—an act simulating kamikaze pilots. The monkey, however, always dropped the torpedo midway to the supposed enemy territory. Ozawa recalls how spectators burst into laughter every time a monkey performed this act.

If we consider what "The Three Brave Heroes" stood for during that time, the profound significance of this monkey performance emerges. "The Three Brave Heroes" refers to three Japanese soldiers who gave their lives carrying a land torpedo into a barbed-wire barricade in order to blast a way through it. Their act facilitated the advance of their unit against formidable Chinese resistance. The Japanese attribute this event to the so-called Manchurian incident of 1931, although in fact it took place some time after the Manchurian incident and during the Japanese assault on Shanghai (Smith and Wiswell 1982:232). Until the end of World War II, the three brave heroes were celebrated and ingrained in the minds of the Japanese as the supreme models of patriotic self-sacrifice, to be emulated by every Japanese.

"The Three Brave Heroes as Human Cannons" therefore represented a "sacred" theme to the wartime Japanese. Yet the monkey was able to turn it into a comic act. The monkey (that is, the trainer) could make fun of a very serious act—a function only a clown could perform. The monkey in Ozawa's description is a clown who becomes a fool and makes spectators laugh, while implicitly scoffing at a society that has turned military doctrines into a "religion." This clowning has been an important element of the monkey performance throughout history—an implicit aspect from the time of the earliest performances but more pronounced in the contemporary monkey performances at parks in Tokyo, as we will see in detail in Chapter 8.

Since the 1920s, the monkey performance was virtually absent[9] until 1977–1978, when a group of young burakumin revived it. Unlike other burakumin, who believed that the eradication of all traces of their past was essential in achieving equality and removing prejudice, these people felt that knowledge of their past was essential in asserting their own identity in Japanese society (Murasaki 1980:39–43, 1983:32; Suō Sarumawashinokai Jimukyoku 1978:2, 17).

My first observation of the monkey performance was in 1980 in Hikari City, Yamaguchi Prefecture. There, I observed the training of the monkeys in the backyard of the Murasaki family. I engaged in extensive discussions with the trainers, their families, and their friends. They had named the monkeys with the first names of humans. For example, the trainer Tarō's monkey was named Jirō. Tarō is a common first name for the oldest son in a family, and Jirō is a common name for the second oldest son in the family. Thus, this trainer and his monkey were "posing" as brothers. The trainers talked and interacted with the monkeys as if they were their own children. On the other hand, they repeatedly emphasized that the initial process in the training of these monkeys was almost a life-and-death struggle. They stressed the ferocity of the "beast," which could instantly rip off one's nose, ears, or fingers—a fierceness to which some of the scars on their arms testified. The trainers discussed two important steps in the training: first, establishing the authority of the trainer over the monkey, and second, teaching the monkey the bipedal posture, which required almost endless trial and error (Murasaki 1980). I was impressed by the trainers' dedication to the difficult task of training and performing with monkeys as a way of asserting their own identity, since there must be other ways

---

[9] In 1947, shortly after the end of the war, women resumed traveling to peddle their oil, but the monkey performance was not at first revived. One couple in Tokyo revived the monkey performance after the war, but they soon discontinued it.

of asserting their burakumin identity that are easier to undertake.

Thus in those early years of revival, the progress was slow and tough going. In a preliminary interpretation of the monkey performance based on my observation in 1980 (Ohnuki-Tierney 1984b), I had even predicted its eventual disappearance, since there are too many cars on the road now to encourage street entertainment of any sort, and since the profusion of television, video, and other forms of entertainment provide so much competition for the monkey performance. Luckily, I was wrong. When I returned to visit in 1984, I found the monkey performance thriving in the post-industrial urban setting.

The original group of monkey trainers I had observed, consisting of two Murasaki brothers, their families, and others, had split into two groups shortly after I visited them. The division of the original group was due to a philosophical difference about the nature of the relationship between humans and monkeys.

Shūji Murasaki, the younger of the two brothers, disagreed with the philosophy that the trainers must establish dominance over monkeys. He maintained that humans and monkeys must be in a harmonious and egalitarian relationship with each other. He and those who held a similar view formed the Sarumaiza (Monkey-Dance Company), and they have tried to revive the traditional monkey performance as accurately as possible. Their first performance was in August 1982 (Maruoka, Murasaki, and Kataoka 1982). When I visited them in 1984, the group had formed two parties, each performing in different parts of Hokkaido, although they perform in other parts of Japan as well. The trainers sing songs that were sung during monkey performances in the past, and they engage in only a limited amount of improvisation and narration. The monkeys, clothed in the traditional Japanese attire of the kimono and the hakama, dance to music consisting of the trainers' songs and

124

drumming. The major emphasis of their performances are the fine movements of the monkeys, especially their lower limbs (Photo 3).

The other group, headed by Yoshimasa Murasaki, the older of the two brothers, and his son Tarō, continues to believe that the establishment and maintenance of a "pecking order" is vital to the trainer's relationship with the monkey (see Ohnuki-Tierney 1984b). In sharp contrast to the first group, this group, called Sarumawashinokai (Monkey Performance Group), has adapted the monkey performance to

Photo 3. A contemporary monkey performance of the Sarumaiza group. The monkey is in traditional Japanese attire. (Courtesy of H. Sawada)

contemporary Japanese popular culture, reviving the monkey performance throughout Japan, as it were, by frequently appearing on television. Beginning in 1984, two parties, each consisting of a trainer, an assistant, and a monkey, have regularly performed in two parks in Tokyo. At Sukiyabashi Park, a very small park located next to a train station in the midst of a densely populated shopping district, they perform to a relatively small crowd of about thirty to forty people several times on Saturday and Sunday afternoons. This performance is similar to the one at Yoyogi Park, where the second pair perform to a very large crowd on Friday, Saturday, and Sunday afternoons.

Although a detailed description of these performances is presented in Chapter 8, it should be noted here that the major characteristic of the performance at Yoyogi Park is clowning. Its highlight is the regular repertoire during which the trainer stages the monkey's deliberate disobedience of an order, thereby implicitly challenging the human assumption of superiority over animals and, in addition, hierarchy in Japanese society in general.

SUMMARY

The monkey performance must be understood within the broader context of the performing arts, which in ancient Japan were religious in nature. In early history, the monkey performance symbolized a blessing by the Mountain Deity. It was a direct extension of the monkey's role as the messenger from the Mountain Deity. Thus, the monkey performance was held at stables to ensure the well-being of the horses, at rice harvest to ensure the blessing of the new crop by the Mountain Deity, and at the doorways of individual homes at the beginning of the New Year and on various other auspicious occasions.

While sketchy historical records on the monkey performance itself make it difficult to precisely determine its changing nature, it appears that since the late Medieval period the meaning of the monkey performance turned increasingly ambivalent. Thus, on the one hand, not only in stable rituals but also in street entertainment, its religious nature persisted, and yet, on the other hand, there are hints, such as the description of a performance in a play and the depiction of trainers in paintings and sayings, that suggest that negative meanings were assigned to trainers and, by extension, to the monkey performance itself.

As the Modern period progressed, the original idea of the monkey performance as a blessing from the Mountain Deity was lost. Some type of secularization evidently took place; that is, the monkey performance continued to be associated with auspicious occasions without the involvement of specific deities. Moreover, the monkey performance as strictly secular entertainment also seems to have emerged some time during the Modern period, as evidenced by the performance in which a monkey carried a toy torpedo and then dropped it. In this form of secular entertainment, we detect an element of clowning in the performance: the monkey, or the trainer represented by the monkey, becomes a trickster and a clown, while overtly presenting itself as a laughable scapegoat. This tendency has reached a new height in contemporary performances, whose major characteristic is clowning. Symbolic analyses of the monkey as trickster-clown will be presented in Chapters 7 and 8.

6

The Monkey and the Special Status
People in the Reflexive Structure
of the Japanese

CHAPTER 3 discussed the various meanings assigned to the monkey, as revealed in ethnographic and historical data on folk religions, visual and performing arts, and oral traditions. Although several meanings have persisted throughout Japanese history, the dominant meaning of the monkey in early historical times was as mediator; later, its meaning as scapegoat predominated. A parallel shift in the meaning of the special status people took place; many were mediators in early times but became scapegoats by the end of the Medieval period. As for the monkey performance, we noted that its meaning gradually became ambivalent toward the end of the Medieval period, and that during the Modern period clowning became an important element of the performance. In this chapter, I reexamine the meaning of the monkey and the special status people as mediators, scapegoats, and clowns within the broader framework of the reflexive structure—the concept of the collective self as defined in relation to the other—of the Japanese.[1]

[1] There is a long tradition of anthropological interest in the collective concepts of *self* and *other*. Lévi-Strauss (1967), Geertz (1973:360–411), and other contemporary anthropologists have pointed to the central place that

128

A predominant interpretation of Japanese deities among contemporary scholars is that from the earliest times they have been characterized by a dual nature and power, having both peaceful power (*nigitama*), which is good and creative, and violent power (*aratama*), which is evil and destructive. Origuchi (1965a:79–82, 1965b:33–35, 1976a:303–17) first called attention to this aspect of the deities, called *marebito*. According to him, the marebito was a god in ancient Japan who periodically visited the villages from the world located on the other side of the sea, where aging and death were unknown. The god visited the villagers to bring good luck, although he was also potentially dangerous. Since in the animistic religion of the Japanese the deities are beings of nature, the dual nature ascribed to deities is extended to Nature as well.[2]

This interpretation may be summarized in terms of basic symbolic oppositions providing order in the Japanese uni-

---

the concepts of the self and other and personhood occupy in the thought structure of most peoples. My concern here derives from this tradition, rather than from recent epistemological debates about reflexivity in fieldwork.

The term *reflexivity* is used here to refer to the capacity of the self "to become an object to itself, that is, to objectify the self" (Babcock 1980:2; see also Fernandez 1980:35). Therefore, whereas reflectiveness simply involves "isolated attentiveness toward oneself," reflexivity "pulls one toward the Other" and away from oneself (see Myerhoff and Ruby 1982:5).

[2] For further discussion of the marebito, see Higo (1942:103–4); Matsudaira (1977); Ouwehand (1958–1959); Suzuki (1974, 1979); and Yoshida (1981). For the continuity of the marebito concept into the present day, incisive analyses of folk festivals in contemporary Japan by Higo (1942) and Matsudaira (1977) are especially helpful.

Some scholars link the marebito deities to the figure of the "stranger," who is simultaneously both far and near, or belongs to and does not belong to the community in which he or she is in a position to exercise considerable power. The concept of the stranger, originally developed by Simmel (1950:402–8), is further developed in Shack and Skinner (1979). See also Berger and Luckmann (1967:122, 156); Schutz (1971:91–105); V. Turner (1975:esp. 231–71); van Gennep (1961:26, 27); and Yamaguchi (1978). For uses of the concept in ethnographic analysis, see Frankenberg (1957) and Myerhoff (1980).

verse. They are: humans:deities :: inside:outside :: culture
(human way):nature (the divine world).

DUALISTIC COSMOLOGY

The dual nature of the stranger-outsider deities is, I think,
a concrete expression of the basic Japanese cosmology,
which is dualistic.[3] The basically dualistic Japanese universe is a universe that constantly ebbs and flows between
two opposite principles: purity and impurity, good and
evil, order and its inversion. With opposing forces simultaneously present, it is a universe in which negative elements are as integral as positive elements. I posit here that
the dualism of the Japanese cosmology corresponds to the
cosmology represented by *yin* and *yang*. I further speculate
that although the yin-yang principle was introduced to Japan from China, a similar dualism had already characterized Japanese cosmology before the introduction of the yin-
yang, which nevertheless provided a formal expression of
native dualism.[4] I return to broader theoretical implications
of this topic at the end of this chapter. For now let me further elaborate on the dualistic cosmology.

Two significant features characterize this type of dualistic
universe: first; the complementarity of the two principles,
and second, the universe as a process or movement. Referring to the Chinese system of yin and yang, Freedman
(1969:7) remarked that "*yin-yang* is a system of complementary opposites, not (as was sometimes thought in the past)
a dualism of mutually antagonistic forces." As graphically
expressed in the iconographic representation of yin-yang
(Figure 2), the two small eyes (*upper right*) are of paramount

[3] I am indebted to Professor Jan Vansina of the University of Wisconsin,
whose insightful remarks on the yin-yang principle initially stimulated me
to examine the dualistic cosmology of the Japanese.

[4] For the Chinese yin-yang, see Porkert (1974). For the yin-yang in Japan,
see LaFleur (1983), Putzar (1963), and Yokoi (1980). For its contrast to the
original Chinese yin-yang, see Yoshino (1984).

importance because they indicate that yin always has a yang element, and vice versa. Yin and yang, therefore, represent relative proportions or degrees of significance, rather than yin representing a separate element antagonistic to yang. The two principles are complementary to each other, for neither is meaningful without the other.

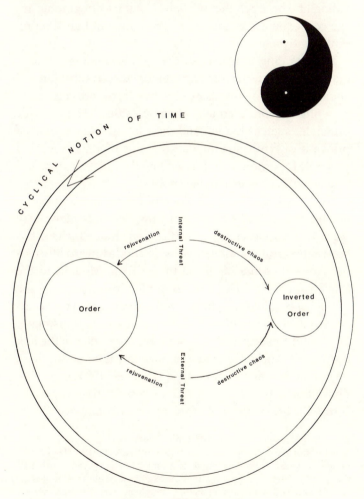

Figure 2. A dualistic universe.

The second important characteristic of this type of dualism is that the universe represents a process or movement in which one principle grows in time into the other, and vice versa. As illustrated in the yin-yang iconography, when the small eye of yang in yin grows large enough, it becomes yang with a small eye of yin in it. The curved dividing line between the two halves of the iconographic image consequently is not a permanent line; rather, it represents a movement.

The resulting universe consists of harmonious complementarity, a state in which neither force asserts absolute hegemony over the other, since the two forces are constantly in gentle motion, gradually changing sides.[5] The dualistic principle, such as the yin and the yang, is thus as much a principle of synthesis and an expression of totality as it is a principle for ordering and classifying the universe, which is conceived as an ever-moving process.

To characterize the cosmology of the Japanese throughout history in terms of the yin-yang principle alone may seem to be a sweeping generalization. Indeed, there has been a discernible shift in the basic attitude toward life from the Ancient to the Medieval to the Early Modern to the Modern period. LaFleur, for example, documents that the Medieval cosmology (which he calls "epistome") was characterized by the notions of karma and *rokudō* transmigration—Buddhistic principles that were unfamiliar to the folk during the Ancient period and have lost their strong hold on people in contemporary Japan (LaFleur 1983:30–31, 59). These Buddhistic principles, however, are basically in accord with the dualism of yin-yang described above. Thus,

---

[5] Seen in this light, the original Chinese characters *liang-i*, which denote dual but not separate meanings, are noteworthy. As Porkert (1974:13) reminds us, *liang-i* "is used metonymically for *t'ien-ti*, heaven and earth, i.e., the cosmos. Therefore, *yang* signifies the beginning, while *yin* denotes the completion, and a number of paired complementary concepts are expressed by *yin-yang*" (Porkert 1974:9–43; see also Granet 1977:48).

the rokudō, or "six courses," is characterized by "the belief that karmic reward or retribution for anterior acts pushed every kind of being up and down the ladder of the universe" (LaFleur 1983:27). This system of belief espoused relative rather than absolute hierarchy, and each person was individually responsible for his or her own future. The rokudō belief, therefore, is in accord with the yin-yang principle, which negates absolute hierarchy.

A development in Buddhism during the Kamakura period (1185–1392) also demonstrates that these Buddhistic doctrines are basically compatible with the yin-yang principle. A movement called *jikkai*, considered of critical importance by scholars of Buddhism, formalized the belief that "good and evil are not seen as absolutely opposite but, on the contrary, mutually dependent" (LaFleur 1983:53).

These examples of formal Buddhistic doctrines illustrate that in terms of basic concepts, the yin-yang principle discussed in this section underlies formal Buddhistic beliefs, just as it underlies the concept of the marebito deities that originated in the native Shinto religion.

In a deceivingly "modernized" and industrialized contemporary Japan, there is a profusion of what I call "urban magic," much of which operates along yin-yang and Taoistic principles. Details of these forms of urban magic and the symbolic world of today's urban, educated Japanese are presented in an earlier book (Ohnuki-Tierney 1984a).

Deities as Mirrors of Humans

I propose that from the perspective of reflexivity, the marebito, or stranger/outsider-deities who come from outside a settlement or outside Japan, constitute the semiotic other for the Japanese, which is symbolically equivalent to their transcendental self; that is, they represent objectification of the Japanese themselves as a semiotic sign. The transcendental self, therefore, is the self that is perceived at a higher level of abstraction than when one sees a reflective self; it represents the highest degree of reflexivity. The dual nature of marebito deities, as presented above, is therefore a projection of the dual qualities that the Japanese see in themselves. The Japanese who ritually harness the positive power (nigitama) of deities do so because they are very aware of the deities' negative side (aratama), which is also their own. My interpretation is illustrated in Figure 3.

That the marebito deities provide the basic model of the reflexive other becomes evident when we pursue further the symbolic relationships among purification, the rebirth of the self, and the reflexive process—all in the context of the metaphor of the mirror in Japanese culture. In the *Kojiki* and the *Nihongi*, the mirror plays a significant role. In the *Kojiki*, for example, the Sun Goddess (Amaterasu Ōmikami, or the "Heaven Illuminating God"), ancestress of the Japanese in the creation myth, came out of a cave because of a mirror. In protest against her brother's breach of a taboo

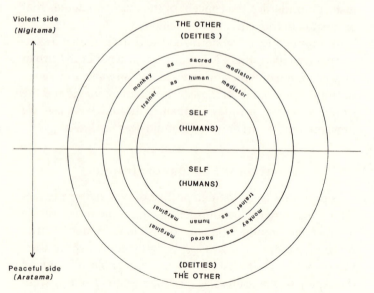

Figure 3. The monkey and the trainer as mediators and marginals.

involving a corpse, a most defiling object, she had hidden herself in a cave, depriving the universe of light. When other deities outside the cave told her that a superior deity awaited her, she opened the door slightly and peeked through. Upon seeing her own reflection in the eight-handed mirror (a long octagonal mirror), which the deities had hung from a tree branch in front of the cave, she mistook it as the image of a superior deity. At this point, the other deities grabbed her and forced her out of the cave. The Japanese universe was thus reborn with her light shining upon it (Kurano and Takeda 1958:81–83).[6] Scholars (e.g., Saigō 1967:78–87) suggest that the hiding and the subsequent emergence of the sun goddess symbolize her death and rebirth, the latter facilitated by a mirror. If she took her own image as that of a deity superior to her, the mirror represents, I think, her transcendental self.

The *Nihongi* also contains many passages that signify the symbolic equation of a mirror with a deity. For example, the Sun Goddess gives a mirror to a deity, remarking, "My child, when thou lookest upon this mirror, let it be as if thou wert looking on me" (Aston 1956:83). Elsewhere, two deities are described as being born out of white-copper mirrors (Aston 1956:20). Similarly, the divine Imperial Princess identifies with a divine mirror as she commits suicide: she buries the mirror and herself in the ground (Aston 1956:341).

Besides passages from the *Kojiki* and the *Nihongi*, other ethnographic data describe mirrors or reflections in water as the embodiments of deities. The belief that supernatural power can be harnessed by a mirror is illustrated by the figures on ancient Japanese tombs who hold mirrors on their chests. These figures, called *haniwa*, are considered to represent ancient shamans (Yanagita 1951:94). Even today, at a number of shrines, mirrors are installed as the embodiment

---

[6] For the English translation, see Philippi (1969:81–85).

(*goshintai*) of the deity enshrined there. Throughout Japan, a number of places, such as valleys, ponds, mountains, hills, and rocks, bear the term *kagami* (mirror) in their designations; these are sacred places where supernatural power is thought to reside (Yanagita 1951:94). Another example of mirror-deity symbolism is mirror rice cakes (*kagamimochi*)—double-layered rice cakes that are traditionally offered to the deities on New Year's Day. They consist of two, round—that is, mirror-shaped—rice cakes, one placed on top of the other. These cakes are believed to give power to those who consume them (Yanagita 1951:94–95), for supernatural power is thought to be embodied in the mirror rice cake, and the act of consuming it is analogous to the performance of ritual during which the beneficial power of deities is harnessed for human benefit.[7] Even today, this practice is observed by almost every household in Japan.

The most crucial dimension of the reflexive structure of the Japanese is that the dualism of the self and other is not a static one. Because the other is a transcendental self, the self must forever reach for the other. The act of reaching out for the other is not a theoretical abstraction in the symbolic exercise. At the level of individual behavior, the Japanese, even as children, are constantly reminded of the importance of self-improvement, as is well expressed in the motto of *kokki* (self-conquest). At the collective level, the desire to reach for the other has propelled the Japanese to emulate and then surpass the superior features of both Chinese and Western culture, be they their writing systems, their arts, their technology, or their scientific achievements. As detailed in a later section of this chapter, the Japanese have perceived foreigners as the symbolic equivalent of the stranger-deity.

---

[7] For ethnographic information on the mirror-deity relationship, see Ishibashi (1914); for ethnographic details of the equivalence of water with the mirror and with the deity, see Nakayama (1976).

PURITY AND IMPURITY IN THE JAPANESE ETHOS

While the dual nature of Japanese deities who represent strangers/outsiders is the dominant characteristic of the Japanese world view, the symbolic opposition of purity (*jō*) and impurity (*fujō* or *kegare*) is the major theme of the Japanese ethos throughout history. In this section, I will describe the symbolic opposition of purity and impurity, which I will relate in the following section to the Japanese concepts of sacred (*hare*) and secular (*ke*).

In two of the earliest records of Japanese history, the *Kojiki* and the *Norito*, there is clear evidence that the opposition of purity and impurity provided the basic structure of the ethos at that time. In the *Kojiki*, the most important deities of Japan are described as having been born out of purification rites (*misogi*) performed by their father (Izanagi-no-Mikoto), who had been defiled by seeing the corpse of his deceased wife (Izanami-no-Mikoto) covered with maggots in the underworld of the dead. According to theogony, when their father washed his left eye, Amaterasu-Ōmi-kami, the founding ancestress of the Imperial family, was born; her brother, Susanō-no-Mikoto, was born when their father washed his nose (Kurano and Takeda 1958:71; Philippi 1969:62–70). In other words, the major deities of the Japanese pantheon were born out of the dialectic between the two opposing values of purity and impurity, which are correlated with life and death. The two pairs of opposition are in turn correlated with the spatial classification of the universe into this world and the underworld. The world of the *Kojiki* therefore revolves around three oppositions: purity:impurity :: life:death :: above:below.

The *Norito* (the book of legal regulations of A.D. 927) spells out clearly what constituted sin in ancient Japan. Of paramount importance here is that record's definition of impurity as the gravest sin of all. Listed among the sins of impurity are "cutting living flesh; cutting dead flesh; white

137

leprosy; skin excrescences" (Philippi 1959:46–47). In other words, killing, handling corpses, and illness were considered sins of impurity (see Motoori 1971:119–21 for a detailed discussion of the sins). Also of interest is the manner by which these sins are purged. The sins are taken to the great ocean by a goddess who dwells "in the rapids of the rapid-running rivers." The sins are "swallowed with a gulp" by another goddess who dwells "in the wild brine in the ocean" at the *unasaka*, a slope at the farthest limit of the sea (Akima 1982:487). They are then blown away by another god into the underworld, where a goddess wanders off with them and loses them (Philippi 1959:47–48).

These passages from the *Norito* also equate impurity with below. Upon closer examination, however, we see that death is sent below only after purification with salt and water—two elements used for purification throughout Japanese history and even today. In other words, death sent below is not one which just took place. Furthermore, these passages establish the association between impurity and the state of liminality—the state that is betwixt and between (V. Turner 1967). The corpse, that is, the freshly dead, represents, as in most cultures, a state between life and death; he or she is no longer a living person but has not yet become an ancestor, the bona fide dead. The corpse is in a liminal state par excellence, as indicated by the almost universal existence of rites de passage such as elaborate funerals. Illness, too, represents a liminal state, because the body is out on a limb: one's health is in limbo. During illness a person hovers between life and death.

Numerous sources in Japanese attest to the continuity of the concepts of purity and impurity throughout Japanese history. For example, in an excellent ethnohistorical account of the folk culture during the Medieval period, Yokoi (1982) reports on notions of purity and impurity. Death continued to be the ultimate impurity. Yokoi (1982:267–94) points to documented cases of female servants being thrown out of their masters' houses, often into the river, before their death, so as not to defile the houses; the death of a woman was doubly polluting. Other phenomena considered impure during the Medieval period were birth, menstruation, miscarriage, pregnancy, and meat-eating. While meat-eating was impure because it involved the death of animals, the other phenomena all related to women and to their liminal states. Women were marginal members of Japanese society, unlike men who were full-fledged members. During the Medieval period, then, impurity was associated with marginal or liminal states, just as it was during the Ancient period.

In addition to these sources, historical continuity of the concepts of purity and impurity in Japanese culture is well documented in Umehara (1967), who traces these concepts from the beginning of history through the Meiji period.

The purity/impurity opposition remains important in various other forms in contemporary Japan. R. Smith (1974) calls our attention to the prolonged and elaborate funeral process, whereby the care of the dead in contemporary Japan aims at eliminating the pollution incurred by death (cf. Norbeck 1952). In my work on Japanese perceptions of illness and health care (Ohnuki-Tierney 1984a), I devoted a chapter to the importance of the concepts of purity and impurity both in daily hygienic behavior and in moral values. Although their efforts are couched in modern biomedical terms, the Japanese are systematically guided by their need to protect the purity of self and body. Similarly, the home—the spatial representation of the self—must be protected from contamination by impurity. This impurity is associated with margins, that is, the area between home and nature, the two spatial zones considered pure. In other words, dirt is located outside one's home but within society—on the streets and in public places.

Purity remains strong as a moral value in contemporary Japan and often appears as a motto of various institutions, such as schools and companies. In a high school in Kobe, the four mottoes intended as guides to character building are purity first, followed by justice, gentleness, and strength, and they are recited daily and posted on the walls almost everywhere (Ohnuki-Tierney 1984a). Likewise, according to Rohlen (1974:36–37), one of the nine mottoes of a certain bank is *seiketsu*, which means "cleanliness" of both body and mind. Rohlen translates the word as "purity" and explains it as "noble character and proper behavior."

In politics, which is by definition "dirty" in the view of many Japanese, political candidates woo "votes of purity" (*kiyoki ippyo*), implying that they seek only votes of purity because they themselves are pure. In 1983 Chikara Higashi, campaigning for a seat in the Diet, wore a pair of white gloves, symbolizing the purity of his character. White gloves are also used by taxi drivers, by attendants at bank entrances, by attendants of escalators and elevators at department stores, and by people at various other places as a symbolic expression of the purity of these places.[8]

I now turn to a discussion of how the concepts of purity and impurity relate to the concepts of sacred and secular.

The Sacred, the Secular, and the Impure

The Japanese concepts of sacred and secular, expressed by the pair of words *hare* and *ke*, have received much attention among scholars of Japanese religions. The term *hare* refers to space, time, objects, and phenomena out of the ordinary, as opposed to *ke*, which refers to mundane or day-to-day property. Celebrations and rituals in honor of deities mark the time as hare; people use hare space to perform rituals and wear special clothing for hare occasions. Extending my

[8] See Ohnuki-Tierney (1984a) for further discussion of the importance of purity and impurity in contemporary Japan. See also Benedict (1967); Lebra (1976); and H. Nakamura (1978).

interpretation in the previous sections of the structure of reflexivity of the Japanese, I propose that the hare, or the sacred, consists of dual qualities, as concretely expressed in the stranger-deities. Ke is the secular counterpart of hare. While both the other and the self consist of dual qualities, the other is the transcendental projection of the self.

If both the sacred and the secular consist of the dual qualities of life/death and creation/destruction, we must reconcile these dualisms with the dualism of purity and impurity. The relationship of hare and ke to a third concept, *kegare*, or impurity, has received much attention.[9] A major line of

[9] While the relationship between hare and ke is fairly straightforward, when we introduce the concept of impurity, kegare, and the act of avoidance, *imi*, the issue becomes highly complex. Yanagita's interpretation of avoidance (imi) (summarized in Yanagita 1951:165–67) has been accepted as orthodox for some time. For him, imi involves avoidance of both the sacred and the impurity incurred by death, childbirth, and menstruation. In a rare reference to Western scholarship, Yanagita, who championed the indigenous development of scholarship in Japan, points to the concept of taboo in Polynesia, as discussed in Western scholarly literature, as being somewhat similar to the concept of imi in Japanese culture. Yanagita's view is that hare opposes kegare, but that the two constitute a pair of qualities toward which the act of avoidance, imi, is directed. Takenaka (1977:16–17) supports Yanagita's interpretation on the basis of etymology; both the term *imu* (to avoid) and *iwau* (to celebrate) have in their roots the same word, which may be pronounced either *yu* or *i*.

Sakurai (1981) views these three concepts as having arisen out of agrarian life. Basing his argument on terms used by farmers, he proposes that *ke*, hitherto interpreted as secular and assumed to lack any power, refers to the vital energy in a seed that makes germination and growth possible. He explains that the daily life of farmers, as expressed in the term *ke*, is characterized by this mysterious and "animistic" (his term) power. When the productive power of ke decreases, events of hare must rejuvenate the state. The state of decreased ke, in his scheme, is kegare; *gare* comes from *kareru*, which means "to wane or wither." According to Sakurai, this scheme is opposed to the hitherto accepted interpretation that kegare represents the polar opposite of the purity of hare. Instead, he argues, we should view kegare as a state of waning ke.

Namihira (1979), who expounds on the importance of pollution and its relation to hare and ke, sees the concept of kegare (impurity) as constituting the third axis, thus creating a tripartite scheme. Although she does not spell out the exact nature of the relationship between the three, her main thinking has been that the sacred is equated with purity, since the term *hare* denotes a quality of clarity, such as a sky without clouds.

I propose that the hare purity is a state in which the positive force of life and creation become dominant through proper rituals, so that the negative force of destruction becomes the small eye (see Figure 2). The ideal state of hare is achieved through ritual during which the negative force of impurity is cleansed and controlled. Therefore, hare in my interpretation is neither a permanent state nor the property that exclusively defines the sacred. It must be constantly maintained through ritual. As Yamaguchi (1977) points out, ritual is assigned the critical role of harnessing positive power and preventing negative power from befalling villagers capriciously. Until about one hundred years ago, villagers periodically performed a ritual during which they constructed an effigy believed to embody the negative power of the deities, carried it around, and then finally either demolished or burned it at the edge of the village.

As a mirror image of the sacred, the secular (ke) too has both pure and impure qualities. However, purity has seldom been regarded as a quality of the secular. I think the failure to see the association between the secular and purity is due to a narrowly conceived notion of ritual, assigning it only to sacred phenomena. If we examine secular rituals, it becomes abundantly clear that the secular too is being kept pure through rituals. The hygienic behavior of the contemporary Japanese confirms the association of the secular with purity. As noted above, the contemporary Japanese constantly strive to keep their body and house—the spatial representation of the self—clean. The "purification ritual" in-

---

argument departs from Yanagita's in that she sees kegare as opposing both hare and ke.

Itoh's (1973) overview of these concepts is quite useful. Informative also is a lengthy scholarly debate on the subject published in book form (Sakurai et al. 1984).

cludes the removal of one's shoes, the washing of hands, the cleansing of the throat by gargling, and the changing of clothes—all done when one returns home from outside, which is defined as impure or dirty. Any spatial units equivalent to the inside of a house, such as the inside of a private car, are kept meticulously clean. For this reason, owners of Toyotas and Hondas flock to shrines and temples in order to have their cars purified on New Year's Day—the liminal period between the previous year and the new year. Their purpose is to rid their cars of defilements accumulated through constant exposure to the outside world during the previous year.

Hygienic practices in contemporary Japan, then, are secular rites of purification. Terminologically, however, the word *hare* is not applied to the purity of the secular. I suggest that while purity is a quality of both the sacred and the secular, *hare* refers to "sacred purity," that is, a higher form of purity that humans associate with deities. It is a transcendental purity which the Japanese constantly attempt to secure in the hope of transforming it into *their* purity.

Likewise, impurity characterizes both the sacred and the secular. It represents a state in which the positive force of life and creation wanes until it is taken over by the negative force of death and destruction. Impurity, then, is most clearly associated with the state of liminality. Thus, it finds expression in temporal liminality such as illness, corpses ("freshly dead"), pregnancy, and childbirth. Similarly, it is associated with the spatial liminality of village borders, where an effigy embodying the negative power of the deities was demolished or burned, and where the special status people were quartered.

Kegare (impurity), therefore, is a quality of both the sacred and the profane, and yet it must be kept in the background. For this reason, purification rituals, including funerals, are characterized by objects and behavior that are opposites of those involved both in the daily life of humans and in sacred rituals. Thus, special dishes for auspicious occasions are taboo for funerals. It once was taboo to cook for funerals on the same hearth on which daily meals were cooked; separate hearths had to be constructed (for other examples, see Namihira 1979, whose interpretation of these concepts differs from mine).

In short, the self, referred to as the ke (secular) and represented by the house and one's body, must be kept pure just as the hare (sacred) must be kept pure. Both, however, are subject to degeneration into the state of kegare (impurity). To reiterate, purity and impurity are structural principles of classification, rather than absolute properties. Thus, when the boundary is contrasted with the structure, the former receives the value of impurity, while the latter is assigned purity. However, if the deities as a category are contrasted with humans, the former are pure, while the latter are impure. When the deities are seen alone and not in contrast to any other category of beings, they are believed to have a dual nature and power, just as humans do.

Cosmological Principles and Classification of People

The stranger-deities representing the semiotic other for the Japanese self constitute the basic model by which the Japanese interpret and classify their universe. Thus, the symbolic equations of humans:deities :: we:they :: inside:outside, which are used to place deities and themselves in the cosmological structure, are extended to classify other people and events. The scheme is used both to identify certain foreigners with stranger-deities and to identify the "marginals," who are seen as neither insiders nor outsiders.

At this juncture, it is necessary to refer back to the monkey, a group animal, as a metaphor for the Japanese, who define the self in dialectic and dialogical relation to the other. This reflexive structure is the conceptual dimension of the pragmatic aspect of life in a community—be it the Japanese nation, an agrarian community, or one's kin group—in which people establish close mutual dependencies. These close relationships with each other, however, are coupled with the exclusion of outsiders, who are welcome only as passers-by, bringing in the positive forces from outside. They are prevented from becoming insiders; if they try to become so, they meet with harsh treatment and at best become marginals marked with negative value. Interdependence within and exclusion of without are well documented in regard to agrarian communities in the past (Irokawa 1981; Yonemura 1979). Furthermore, the principle has been applied to other social groups throughout history.

Since deities were thought to come either from outside a village or from outside Japan, there has been a tendency to equate foreigners with deities, therefore often assigning to foreigners dual—both beneficial and destructive—natures and power. Until fairly late in history, the Chinese were the predominant foreigners in Japan. They introduced items of material culture as well as many cultural institutions that the Japanese eagerly adopted, including some deities (discussed in Chapter 3), Buddhism (originally from India but arriving in Japan via Korea and China), the writing system, the medical system, city plans, the tea ceremony, metallurgy, and artistic traditions. The Chinese were gradually replaced as the principle foreigners by Westerners, beginning with the Portuguese, who introduced guns and Christianity to Japan in the mid–sixteenth century. Like the Chinese, Westerners, including the Dutch, Germans, and Americans, also introduced religion, technological skills in such areas as firearms and medicine, and various other cultural institutions to the Japanese.

The Japanese sought foreign customs and items with extraordinary zest, often aggressively visiting other countries by ship to bring back objects and ideas. This positive attitude toward foreigners has continued to the present, despite the bitter experiences of the Japanese in the wars. Their affluence permits the contemporary Japanese to tour the world, including the People's Republic of China. They continue to treat foreigners—especially Westerners—very well when they visit Japan.

While it is possible to argue that what the Chinese and the Westerners had to offer were "objectively" superior cultural institutions, I think a more appropriate reading is that these cultural institutions were eagerly sought because, to the Japanese, they represented the superior qualities of the other.

Good treatment of foreigners is conditional, however, on their remaining foreigners. They must be outsiders who are allowed to be inside only under prescribed circumstances, like the stranger-deities who are brought in only through rituals. Therefore, once foreigners attempt to become bona fide members of Japanese society, they encounter enormous personal and even legal difficulties. At the turn of the century, Hearn (1904:472) compared foreigners in this situation to an Antarctic explorer who seeks in vain some inlet through endless cliffs of everlasting ice. The situation has not changed much since then. Not until 1983, for example, were foreign nationals able to hold regular positions at national universities, and the status of foreign nationals teaching at lower levels remains unstable.

Foreigners are kept outside since they, like deities, may exercise their negative side at any moment. Drawing from illustrations in *The Tale of Genji*, dated to ca. 1010, Pollack (1983) describes how the Japanese viewed the Chinese as "worthy of emulation" but at the same time "threatening." The most dramatic expression of this mistrust of foreigners was the extended closure of the country to the outside world during the Early Modern period, although factors leading toward the closure of society were complex. Mistrust of foreigners even increased during this period. Another expression of this mistrust was the attribution of calamities to foreigners. During the cholera epidemic of 1879, for example, the Japanese government's policy of quarantining cholera victims in hospitals led some Japanese to publicly protest; they believed that the hospitals were keeping the families and relatives away from the victims so that the victims' livers could be removed and sold to Westerners for their consumption (Ono 1968:113).

The same attitude underlies the Japanese eagerness to visit other places. They enjoy foreign countries and people but only under prescribed circumstances. Seen from this perspective, tourism is a secular ritual through which the Japanese harness the positive power and quality of foreigners and foreign cultures (cf. Graburn 1977). The Japanese eagerness to be tourists, which has been noted throughout history (Tsurumi 1974), contrasts sharply with their reluctance to reside permanently in a foreign country. Unlike the Chinese, the Koreans, and even the British, most Japanese, including Japanese students in the United States, return to Japan; foreign countries remain more foreign to the Japanese than they do to other peoples. Only recently, some signs of change have begun to appear, although the extent and the nature of these changes are difficult to assess at this point.

Besides "insiders" and "outsiders," there are various groups of people who are neither insiders nor outsiders in the Japanese scheme of classification. While the Chinese used to be the strangers/outsiders, they, together with other Asians, became marginals—neither insiders nor outsiders—when Westerners took over as the strangers/outsiders. The Japanese attitude toward marginals is at best ambivalent and usually downright negative. Included among the marginals are the Japanese who were born or raised in foreign countries, such as Japanese Americans. They are supposedly Japanese, and yet they are regarded as falling short of a full-fledged Japanese identity because their upbringing and behavior show departures from those of the "fully Japanese." A recent addition to the category of marginals are the children of Japanese parents whose work required them to raise their children overseas. They are derogatorily labeled *han-japa* (half-Japanese, from *han* = half and *japa* = an abbreviation for Japanese), and they are clearly marked as such.[10] All people who lie "betwixt and between" in the conceptual scheme of the Japanese meet with prejudice and discrimination.

It is in this "betwixt and between" category that the special status people have been placed, especially since the Early Modern period. Those who had resided at the marginal areas of a settlement became clearly marked by impurity. Those who were migrants—itinerant priests, entertainers, and so forth—were forced to settle and became unwelcome marginals. While these people were migrants, they were thought to bring in the supernatural power of the deities to rejuvenate the community life, and thus they were treated well; in fact, they were treated like the mare-bito deities whose power they harnessed. However, once they became permanent settlers, they were subjected to intense prejudice and assigned a permanently marginal status.

This discussion has illustrated that the notion of the stranger-deity is not simply a myth. Had the stranger-deity appeared only in an ancient myth, we could not claim that it also served as a model of and for interpretation of historical processes. However, we have evidence that the model was a powerful tool used by the Japanese to interpret his-

---

[10] According to Roger Goodman, now writing his D.Phil. thesis on the "returnees" at the Institute of Social Anthropology, Oxford University, both the returnees themselves as well as other Japanese regularly attribute whatever problems the returnees encounter to the fact that they are returnees. Although returnees often meet with discrimination, they frequently use their returnee status to their advantage as well (personal communication).

torical events and classify people throughout history, thereby becoming a part of history.

MEDIATORS AND SCAPEGOATS AS REFLEXIVE AGENTS

This lengthy description of the reflexive structure of the Japanese enables us now to reexamine the meaning of mediator and scapegoat assigned to the monkey and the special status people within the broader context of the Japanese structure of reflexivity, as schematically shown in Figure 3.

Mediators as Reflexive Agents

We recall that until the end of the Medieval period, the monkey was a sacred mediator, while the special status people as religious artistic specialists were human mediators. As mediators, then, both served to harness in a ritually prescribed manner the positive power of deities to rejuvenate life in the village; they brought in the purity of the deities so that the lives of the humans became invigorated and purified.

The translation of the mediator role into a reflexive agent at a conceptual level is quite straightforward. In addition, there are more direct symbolic expressions of the mediator's reflexive role. For example, it is worth recalling in this connection that the aforementioned Saruta Biko, the Monkey Deity who led the grandson of the Sun Goddess in his descent from heaven, is depicted with eyeballs that glow like an eight-handed mirror and a light shining from his mouth and anus (Sakamoto et al. 1967:147–48; see also Minakata 1972:411). Thus, several of his physical features are associated with the mirror metaphor and its reflections. As a sacred mediator, he is endowed with a quality similar to the transcendental self of a deity as embodied in a mirror.

It is important to recognize here that the role assigned to ritual specialists in Japanese culture was quite complex. We recall that in early history the asobi-be were simultaneously specialists in impurity and performing artists of music and dance. Their role included the removal of impurity incurred by death—an act that ensured the rejuvenation of the lives of humans. But they did this by harnessing the purity of the deities. Similarly, the monkey was assigned the role of healing ill horses—an act of removing impurity from a sick body. The monkey was therefore a shaman to horses and performed the same dual role of removing impurity by harnessing the purity of the deities.

Scapegoats as Reflexive Agents

While in early history the specialists in impurity were mediators with positive cultural valuation, we find that since the latter half of the Medieval period they have been scapegoats. Scapegoats too serve as reflexive agents in the Japanese structure of the self and other, in which both the self and other are seen to have a dual nature and power and yet must be kept pure. Thus, in early history, the Japanese attempted to maintain purity by having mediators bring in purity from outside; later they did so by unburdening their impurity upon the structurally peripheral, that is, upon the monkey and the special status people, thereby rendering them scapegoats. Thus, the monkey and the special status people were assigned the negative semiotic sign of impurity; they became marked. As Burke (1955:407) points out in his discussion of scapegoats in the Hitlerite cult of anti-Semitism, the Japanese, like the Germans, "ritualistically cleanse themselves by loading the burden of their own iniquities upon" the special status people. Thus, the monkey and the special status people have always been assigned the role of keeping the Japanese pure; they did so as mediators by bringing in the pure and creative power of the deities, and they do so as scapegoats by shouldering the impurity of the dominant Japanese. Mediators and scapegoats therefore perform a similar function except in reverse.

The role of purification in the reflexive structure is deeply embedded in Japanese culture. We recall that both the Sun Goddess and her brother were born out of the dialectic between impurity (their father seeing the corpse of his deceased wife) and purity (washing his nose and eyes). In other words, purification has been equated with an act of rebirth, or more accurately, with the birth of the purified self.

The complex interrelationship between mediator, scapegoat, and purification is expressed in the motif of the monkey reaching for the moon reflected in water. At the surface level, the monkey is a scapegoat—a stupid animal that cannot tell between the moon itself and its reflection, and that strives for the unattainable; this is the interpretation presented in Chapter 3. There are two other readings at more abstract levels. First, the monkey is assigned the role of mediator, trying to harness the purity of the moon, as mirrored in water; water, we noted earlier, is often equated with a mirror in Japanese culture. Second, we can interpret the monkeys' reaching for the moon as striving to reach a transcendental self as symbolized in the mirror—that is, the moon. In other words, the motif of the monkey reaching for the moon reflected in water succinctly illustrates how the mediator and the scapegoat are two dimensions of the same phenomenon, and they ultimately serve as the reflexive agent reaching for a transcendental self.

CLOWNS AS REFLEXIVE AGENTS

In Chapter 3 I briefly introduced the fact that in contemporary Japan the monkey performance has taken on a clowning aspect. Rituals and most performances are reflexive processes during which performers achieve "the sense of distancing from self" (Fernandez 1980:28, 36). The reflexive nature of performance is particularly pronounced in a clown performance, since a clown must have this distance from self in order to offer himself as a target of laughter, that is, as a scapegoat. Through a reexamination of some of the monkey figures introduced in Chapters 3 and 4, I will illustrate in this section how a mediator/scapegoat is simultaneously a clown whose primary role is to offer critical commentaries about society and culture.

Saruta Biko (Monkey Deity) as Mediator/Clown

According to some scholars, Saruta Biko represents shaman-actors in ancient Japan (cf. Matsumura 1948:6–7, 32–36; 1954; see also Takasaki 1956). They argue that the unusual description of the physical appearance of Saruta Biko, with its long nose, mirror-like eyes, and so on, is a depiction of a shaman-actor donning a mask and a disguise. They consider the term *saru* to mean "to play" or "to perform a comic act causing laughter." In the view of these scholars, the incident in which Saruta Biko's hand is caught in a shell, recounted in Chapter 3, represents a comical performance which at the same time had magical power.

Whether we link Saruta Biko to a saru (monkey) whose primary characterization in Japanese culture is its ability to imitate—an act that constituted an important element of performance in ancient Japan (as seen in Chapter 4)—or whether we interpret Saruta Biko to be a shaman-actor in disguise, there seems to be a definite performative element in the meaning assigned to this mediator-deity. Seen in this light, Saruta Biko is a reflexive symbol par excellence, whose meaning is expressed through its various physical characteristics as well as through its roles as mediator-scapegoat-actor/clown. Saruta Biko therefore provides a concrete ethnographic case illustrating that mediator, scapegoat, and clown derive from the same structure of meaning.

Monkey Subduing a Catfish

While Saruta Biko serves as an intimate link between mediator and clown, the monkey trying to subdue a catfish in
the Ōtsu-e folk art represents a scapegoat turned clown. As
we saw in Chapter 2, the surface-level message of the folk
art is about the stupidity of a monkey trying to use a slippery gourd to subdue a slippery catfish, which was considered the causal agent of earthquakes during the Early Modern period. At a more abstract level, the painting depicts a
monkey attempting the impossible task of controlling evil
in the universe. Evil is an integral part of a dualistic universe, and therefore, as we saw in this chapter, it cannot be
eliminated. By being a foolish scapegoat, the monkey is simultaneously serving as a clown who causes people to
laugh at his folly; in this way, the monkey prods people to
contemplate the folly of such endeavors, and to accept the
centrality of ambiguity in a dualistic universe. In short, he
is reminding people of the presence of the small eye of yin.

Monkey as a Human Cannon

In Chapter 5 we saw that the monkey peformance in the
1930s included an act in which the monkey played the part
of a soldier hero who dashed into enemy territory with an
explosive. Since the monkey inevitably dropped the torpedo before it got there, it was in this act a silly animal who
could not measure up to the real Japanese war hero. It was
a scapegoat. At a more abstract level, however, the monkey
was indeed commenting satirically upon wartime Japan, a
society that consecrated the war. Dropping the torpedo was
the ultimate act of blasphemy that only a monkey could
perform. In Chapter 8 we will see a fuller development of
the clowning act in the contemporary monkey performance, in which the social hierarchy and the human-animal
distinction are the focuses of critical commentary.

These examples of the monkey in Japanese culture illustrate two important points. First, conceptually and ethnographically, mediator, scapegoat, and clown are all closely linked; they represent different facets of reflexive processes. Second, from the perspective of the hierarchy of meaning, clown represents a level higher than mediator and scapegoat, for as we discussed in Chapter 2, only when the scapegoat views himself in perspective and transcends the self as defined by the thought structure that rendered him a scapegoat can he offer himself as a target of laughter. The clown is truly a reflexive figure in that he is capable of distancing himself from the self, although all three are intimately involved in the reflexive structure of the Japanese. Chapters 7 and 8 will present more examples of the monkey as clown, but first I want to summarize this chapter by discussing the broader theoretical implications of the findings on the monkey as mediator, as scapegoat, and as clown.

Mediator, Scapegoat, and Clown in a Dualistic Universe: Theoretical Considerations

A mediator traverses across categories, a scapegoat is assigned a position at the margin of a structure, and a clown is funny and not exactly normal but often chides cherished cultural assumptions. All three are closely related to the concept of that which opposes structure and order.

If anthropologists are fascinated with culturally defined order and classification, they are equally fascinated by the fact that every culture gives significant symbolic prominence to the opposite—chaos, disorder, entropy, inverted order, anomaly, ambiguity, and the like. As Needham (1963:xl) puts it:

[I]f our first task as social anthropologists is to discern order and make it intelligible, our no less urgent duty is to make sense of those practically universal usages and beliefs by which people create disorder, i.e., turn their classifications upside down or disintegrate them entirely.

The long history of scholarly attention given this topic in myths and rituals testifies to its importance in anthropology. Seminal works include van Gennep (1961) on rites of passage and W. R. Smith (1972) on taboo and uncleanliness. These topics, together with associated phenomena such as ritual reversals, continue to attract the attention of numerous anthropologists, such as Leach, Needham, V. Turner, and Douglas.[11] Even Lévi-Strauss, whose concern is with "the science of the concrete" of *la pensée sauvage*, and who sees that "[a]ny classification is superior to chaos" (Lévi-Strauss 1966:15), has studied and written on mediators, tricksters, and the dual nature of gods (e.g. Lévi-Strauss 1967:224). Concern with this topic is shared by scholars in other disciplines. Most significant is Burke's (1955, 1966) notion of "the logic of negativity."

The most basic function of mediation is to transgress categorical boundaries in order to mediate. Its fundamental role, then, is to at least partially negate the classificatory system. By contrast, the fundamental role of taboo is to mark culturally produced discontinuous sections, as was well articulated by Leach (1963, 1968, 1971). Taboos, then, constitute a means whereby the systemic boundaries are

[11] An extremely short list from innumerable publications includes Babcock (1978); Barnes (1973); Beidelman (1980); Bulmer (1967); Douglas (1966, 1975); Eliade (e.g., 1971); Handelman (1981); Handelman and Kapferer (1980); Kapferer (1983); Leach (1963, 1967, 1968, 1976); Needham (1980); Steiner (1967); Tambiah (1969); and V. Turner (1967, 1969). Babcock (1978) represents an interdisciplinary approach to "symbolic inversion," and Needham (1980) represents his more recent and philosophical thinking. Particularly pertinent to my discussion on clowns is Babcock (1984); Bouissac (1976); Handelman (1981); Ortiz (1969); Peacock (1968); and Yamaguchi (1977, 1978). An extensive treatment of anomalous symbols and relevant theories on the topic is presented in Ohnuki-Tierney (1981a).

upheld. The same holds true for scapegoats—tabooed individuals.

Although this classical notion of taboo is applicable to Japanese culture, the emphasis that the Japanese place upon purification rituals compels further deliberation about the meaning of taboo. I propose that we recognize two types of taboo. There are certain taboos, like the incest taboos in many but not all societies, that must not be broken, lest severe punishment follow. However, I think there is another type of taboo. This type includes taboos to be violated, as long as restoration of the original state is accomplished through ritual. The violation of taboos does not negate the existence of taboos. When violated, taboos remain meaningful as long as the violator is required to undergo a culturally prescribed means of rectifying the breach—a purification ritual, for example. Taboos to be violated accommodate two apparently contradictory demands—demand for maintenance of boundaries and demand for inter-categorical traffic. They make separate but interacting categories possible.

I speculate that the existence and relative importance of mediation, absolute taboos, and breakable taboos in a given culture are directly related to the basic nature of the culture's cosmology. In a dualistic universe, such as one governed by the yin-yang principle, ambivalence, inversions, and the like are tolerated because dualism itself is based upon accommodation of opposites (Figure 2). Like breakable taboos, ambivalence, anomalies, and inversions may be semiotized and may hold a negative value, such as impurity, as they do in the Japanese cosmology. Yet, they are not excluded from the universe. Such a system is amenable to both mediation and breakable taboos.

The meaning of ambivalence in a dualistic universe may be further illustrated if we look briefly at a monolithic universe. Figure 4 shows a simplified model of a monolithic universe, such as the one espoused in the Western ration-

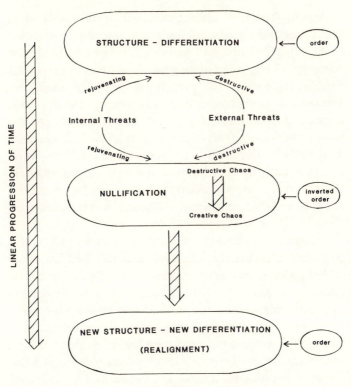

Figure 4. A monolithic universe.

alist tradition. It is a well-classified universe, in which classification and order are assigned the moral value of goodness. Both internal and external threats to order are assigned the moral value of evil. If anomalies and inversions are ritually celebrated, the *function* of these symbolic expressions is to strengthen and rejuvenate the existing structure (Douglas 1966, 1975; Eliade 1971:194; V. Turner 1967:97, 98). In the event that the structure deteriorates, chaos takes over the existing classificatory system, after which a new structure emerges. The dialectic between structure and anti-structure proceeds linearly through time.

157

Douglas (1966) articulates this type of universe and infers that order and chaos as defined in a monolithic universe such as this are universal. As evident in her 1966 book, the prototype of her vision of the universe derives from the Old Testament, in which God presides above both humans and animals and is the creator of a classificatory system whose basic dyad is culture (humans) and nature (animals). As the product of God, the classification or order is good, whereas its absence is blasphemy, a major sin against God, and thus evil. The basic dyad of humans and animals, therefore, is like two boxes, clearly separated by a sharp line of taboos not to be violated (for a detailed discussion of this topic, see Ohnuki-Tierney 1981a:108–11).

In contrast, a dualistic universe is characterized by the centrality of ambiguity. In such a universe, order and inverted order are not antithetical to each other. It should be pointed out here, however, that a dualistic universe neither lacks classification or order, nor fails to recognize inversions and anomalies as such. It has classificatory boundaries. However, boundary transgressions are encouraged so as to elicit meaningful interactions between categories; hence the presence of breakable taboos. The boundaries become well marked precisely because they are transgressed, since every transgression requires a purification ritual to restore and honor the boundaries and the classification system itself. Breakable taboos and scapegoats are ever-present in such a universe, while they are not tolerated in a monolithic universe. Seen in this light, mediation and taboo-scapegoats in a dualistic universe perform the like function of facilitating inter-categorical communication.

In short, a monolithic universe places emphasis on the separation of categories, whereas a dualistic universe emphasizes the synthesis of two opposing principles—yin and yang, the self and the other. Mediation and taboo-scapegoats take on a different meaning depending upon the type of cosmology. In a dualistic universe, meaningful inter-categorical communication is facilitated by mediators as well as by breakable taboos and scapegoats who are not expelled. The former carry a positive semiotic sign, while the latter guard the margins by signaling to others their impurity.

A question arises, however. Why mediator as opposed to breakable taboo? What is the historical context that encourages the presence of mediators, instead of breakable taboos, to facilitate inter-categorical traffic? A possible answer from the Japanese case seems to lie in the degree of rigidity of the system. We saw that the monkey and the special status people were mediators until the late Medieval period. During these early periods in Japanese history, the society and the structure of thought were fairly flexible. It was during the Early Modern period that the society became extremely rigid and so too did the thought structure. A system of such rigidity must opt for taboos and scapegoats to mark its boundaries while meeting the demands of boundary transgressions essential to the dualistic universe.

For the sake of illustration, I have chosen to contrast a monolithic universe with the yin-yang dualism of China and Japan.[12] I should note, however, that a dualistic universe is a fairly prevalent type of cosmology, seen in various parts of the Third World as well as in the folk conception of the universe in the West, both past and present.

[12] My contrast corresponds to Schwartz's contrast between what he refers to as an analytic conception of order and a synthetic conception of order. According to Schwartz (1975), the former characterizes various types of rationalism in ancient Greece, whereas the latter is represented by "Chinese rationalism."

Part Three

Basic Structure, Processual-Contextual Structure, and Multiple Structures of Meaning

7

The Monkey Performance of the Late
Medieval Period

IN CHAPTER 6, we reexamined the meaning of mediator, scapegoat, and clown from the perspective of the reflexive structure of the Japanese. In this chapter, I pursue the meaning of the monkey and the special status people through an interpretation of the monkey performance, first as stable ritual, and second, as street entertainment.

For analytical purposes, I will use the terms basic structure, processual structure, and contextual structure. *Basic structure* refers to the structure of meaning of the prototype monkey performance as it was originally developed to heal ill horses. Both the process of performance and the context of performance are crucial in determining the meaning of symbolic acts and objects, and these concepts will become significant as I attempt to examine the meaning of performance as street entertainment. The term *process* is used here to refer to the process involved in the ritual time during the performance.[1] The concept of *processual structure* is relevant

[1] Following Moore and Myerhoff (1977:7–8), I use the term *ritual* to refer to events characterized by the following properties: repetition; self-conscious acting; special stylization; ordered procedure; evocative presentational style, at least in intent; and collective meaning understood by the members of the social group. In my definition, then, the sacred/secular distinction is not a characteristic.

here because in some types of ritual performance, the structure of meaning is transformed during the course of the performance. This is the case with the monkey performance of the late Medieval period, as will be discussed shortly.

By the term *context*, I refer to both the historical context and the context of an actual performance. The three preceding chapters have illustrated how the meaning of the monkey, the special status people, and the monkey performance has been transformed through time. In addition to the historical context, we must also consider the "ritual context," by which I mean the ritual space of the performance, encompassing social relationships in transaction and the social activities of all the participants—the trainer and the spectators, in the case of the monkey performance. Most important for the contextual analysis is the differential perspectives of the participants—the trainer and the spectators—whose reading of the performance derives largely from the various structures of meaning that are simultaneously present at a given historical period.

In addition to these two conceptual frameworks, I also use the term *framing*, which refers to the definition or categorization of a given performance, for example, as "play," "ritual," and the like. The monkey performance is either a ritual at stables or a form of entertainment on the street. The framing is important in determining the structure of meaning of the performance.

BASIC STRUCTURE OF MEANING:
MONKEY PERFORMANCE AS STABLE RITUAL

The entire complex of the monkey performance is replete with symbolic expressions of nature: culture transformations. Let me first qualify my use of the currently unpopular terms *nature* and *culture*. The symbolic opposition of nature:culture as used by Lévi-Strauss should not be interpreted as *the* universal definition of nature and culture in terms of the *content* of these concepts. His emphasis is, first, on the oppositional relationship between nature and culture and, second, on the forms of these concepts and their relationship to each other, not on the empirical content. It is a classificatory principle at a very high level of abstraction. The universality lies not in any absolute properties of nature or culture, but in the use of this opposition as an abstract principle of classification in many societies.

We can contextualize the opposition, however, by applying it to a given culture under consideration, as I do in this book. I use the term *culture* to signify the human way of existence as defined in a given culture. The concept of *nature*, then, is something opposite to culture. In many religions of the world, including Japanese religions, in which deities are beings of nature (such as the sun, the moon, fauna, and flora), the sacred includes nature or segments of it. The sacred, however, is a culturalized nature, that is, nature as defined by the structure of meaning of that culture. Basically, then, both nature and culture are defined within the framework "culture," that is, the structure of meaning of a given culture; there is no "objective" world called nature sitting out there.

I now want to look at these concepts as they relate to the monkey performance. The initial step in the entire process is the capturing of a monkey, a fierce animal for its size. Whether a monkey is regarded as a messenger-deity or simply a beast, the capturing of a monkey involves humans dragging the deity-animal in nature into their cultural sphere. This act is followed by an even more explicit act of acculturation of the monkey: the establishment of a "social relationship" between trainer and monkey.

Socialization of the monkey is followed by instructing the monkey in the bipedal posture. While the evolutionary significance of the bipedal posture in the context of the monkey performance may not have been consciously recognized by the trainers of the past or, for that matter, by most Japanese, instructing the monkey in this posture embodies important meaning. Four-leggedness is, to the Japanese, the most distinctive characteristic of animals. In colloquial Japanese, the term *yotsuashi* (four-leggedness) is a synonym for *chikushō*, one of a few commonly used derogatory terms in Japanese. The teaching of the bipedal posture, which constitutes the most critical part of the training, is then, an effort, no matter how difficult, to culturalize or "Japanize" the monkey, although the process is exceedingly difficult and some trainers in the past have gone "insane" during this period (Murasaki 1980:148).

Indeed, the creation of a performing monkey succinctly symbolizes the creation of the Japanese religion. As I have elaborated elsewhere (Ohnuki-Tierney 1981a), unlike the Judeo-Christian tradition, in which God holds a commanding position above the basic dyad consisting of humans and animals, Japanese religion is similar to many so-called tribal religions in which nature constitutes the sacred. In such religions, the culturalization of nature is the very process by which deities are created. The basic dyad consists of deities and humans, that is, nature (sacred) and culture (profane). It is culturalized nature as the sacred that is symbolized in the performing monkey.

Furthermore, the ultimate goal of the training is to have the monkey perform dances to music, produced either by the *shamisen* (a three-stringed instrument) or by the trainer's singing or drumming. Dancing is an act in which the body, or nature, is transformed into culturalized movements. Like dancing, music creates patterned regularity. Thus, the two activities of the monkey performance represent the essence of culture (cf. Lévi-Strauss 1969). The monkey performance is therefore a process by which the human mediator (trainer) and the sacred mediator (monkey) conjoin to create one of the ultimate forms of culture: the art of dancing to music.

As noted in Chapter 6, a fundamental aspect of any performance is the performer's distancing of himself. The trainer distances himself from himself during the performance, thereby transforming the self into a sign. Similarly, as self becomes a sign, the trainer, although perhaps without articulating it in his mind, establishes an analogical relationship with the monkey. His monkey becomes a metaphor for him. This process represents the most basic human capacity to symbolize—the creation of a sign—which in turn is considered the most basic property of human culture.

The purpose of the monkey performance originally was to heal ill horses and maintain their health. The power to create culture, then, is equated with the power to cure illnesses. The act of healing represents a process by which human life and human ways—culture—are sustained against the threat of death, which, by returning the human body to nature, terminates culture. In other words, the culturalization symbolized during the ritual is an enactment of the function of healing for which the ritual is performed (cf. Ohnuki-Tierney 1981a:88–92).

In sum, the monkey performance enacts the transformation of a beast in "raw nature" into a deity, that is, into the transcendental self of humans—not simply a reflective self, which remains on the same level as humans, but the self objectified onto a higher level of abstraction.

This discussion of the basic structure of meaning of the monkey performance has been presented without reference to the context of an actual performance. Yet this is the structure of meaning of all the rituals at horse stables for which the monkey is by definition assigned the power to heal through its power of culturalization. In short, it is the framing of the monkey performance as stable ritual that is the sole determinant of the structure of meaning—a point to which I return shortly.

I also propose that the basic structure of meaning was the

only structure of meaning during the stable ritual. We know that the monkey performance at stables was an important ritual for both warriors and farmers during the Medieval period and, to some degree, during the Early Modern period. The transformation of nature into culture during the performance was the structure of meaning of all rituals at stables, no matter where they were held or from whose perspective we see them. Let us take as an example the monkey performance at the Imperial Court toward the end of the Medieval period, or at the Shogunal Palace during the Early Modern period. Since the emperor held symbolic power and the shogun political power, they epitomized the dominant Japanese over the special status people. However, when the monkey cured—or was believed to cure—the illnesses of horses and promoted their well-being, the emperor, the shogun, and the trainer must have shared the same structure of meaning.[2] In short, as stable ritual, the particular context of the performance was irrelevant and hence did not alter the structure of meaning.

PROCESSUAL AND CONTEXTUAL STRUCTURES
OF MEANING: MONKEY PERFORMANCE AS
STREET ENTERTAINMENT

In contrast to the stable ritual, which engenders one structure of meaning at all times for all participants, multiple structures of meaning seem to emerge in the case of the monkey performance as street entertainment. In this section, I will discuss the multiple structures of meaning and their determinants by interpreting the monkey performance during the late Medieval period as described in a play entitled the *Utsubozaru* ("Quiver Monkey"). As noted in Chapter 5, this is a well-known piece from kyōgen, a genre

[2] For theoretical discussions of whether the meaning is shared as an individual belief or as a collective representation, see Needham (1972:6); Ohnuki-Tierney (1981a:157–58); and Wittgenstein (1968:73).

of comic interlude staged between classical nō plays. *Utsubozaru* is thought to be a product of the Muromachi period (1392–1603) (Yanagita 1982e:339), and it vividly portrays the monkey performance as a highly developed street entertainment which nevertheless accorded a very low status to the trainer during the Muromachi and Early Modern periods.

First, a brief explanation of kyōgen and nō—two genres of performing arts developed during the Muromachi period—is in order.[3] Nō was created by the warrior class, which gained power over the emperors during a long and bitter struggle in the Nanbokuchō period (1336–1392). Nō reflects the perspectives on life of the new elite in Japanese society (Matsumoto 1981:192). Kyōgen, on the other hand, was created by and therefore reflects the attitudes of the lower-class warriors and the farmers, who were then finally freed from the old regime but were still under the newly created ruling class.

Both nō and kyōgen, then, were the products of people who had risen one notch or at times several notches above their assigned status. Yet, the two differ radically from each other in terms of philosophical content. Nō embodies the "great tradition," especially those traditions related to the institutionalized Buddhism at the time, including the highly sophisticated aesthetics (*yūgen*). It also represents and affirms the existing order and hierarchy of the society at the time. Conversely, typically set amidst the daily life of farmers, kyōgen are often full of anti-establishment satirical commentaries voiced from below (Hayashiya 1981:204–6; Koyama 1960:13). Therefore, many pieces of kyōgen include characters who are basically tricksters or clowns, such as Tarōkaja. Tarōkaja is a servant, yet through his comical behavior he controls his master and is free to mock him and

---

[3] Although both are products of the Muromachi period, kyōgen and nō are independent in origin, contrary to a widespread misconception that the two have a common origin (see Hayashiya 1981 and Matsumoto 1981).

the social structure that the lord represents. Other heroes in kyōgen achieve fame and fortune through their own abilities—through wisdom, courage, quick thinking, cunning, and even violence (Satake 1970:110).[4]

The following piece from kyōgen exemplifies the spirit of this literary genre, although in this kyōgen, the clowning role is assigned to the monkey. We now turn to *Utsobozaru*, which portrays a monkey performance as street entertainment during the latter part of the Muromachi period. The version presented below is from Nonomura (1968:158–66).

Utsubozaru ("Quiver Monkey"): A Synopsis

The story starts with a *daimyō* (feudal lord) announcing in the morning to his servant Tarōkaja that he plans to go hunting. As they set out, they immediately encounter a monkey trainer with his monkey. The lord is impressed by the beautiful fur of the monkey and decides to ask the trainer for the monkey in order to cover his quiver with its hide. The trainer begs the lord to spare the monkey, since it is his only means of livelihood. The lord then asks to borrow the monkey, and the trainer again begs for it to be

---

[4] Lest kyōgen be taken as proletariat literature, I must make clear that its perspectives are certainly not completely proletarian, as some Marxian scholars have understood them. As LaFleur (1983) argues, kyōgen ridicules not only "the above" but also "the below" who could not rise above the lowly status assigned to them. It is abundantly seasoned with black humor: those who are not clever enough to succeed during the late Medieval period when the below could rise above the above (Chapter 1) are lampooned (Satake 1970:110). These targets include the coward, the sucker, the country hick, the physically handicapped, and the person in trouble. Even the aged and the naively pious are ruthlessly ridiculed. For example, in one well-known kyōgen, called *Saru zatō*, a monkey trainer talks the beautiful wife of a blind man into leaving him and joining the trainer; he substitutes his monkey for the woman (Nonomura and Andō 1974). In the play, the cleverness of the monkey trainer is acclaimed and the blind man is the target of ruthless ridicule. Here, a member of the special status people is praised not because of his challenge to the establishment but because of his "cleverness" in fooling the blind.

spared. The lord, becoming enraged, decides to shoot both the trainer and the monkey with one arrow. But the trainer points out that if the monkey is shot, the scar from the arrow will ruin the hide. He then volunteers to batter the monkey with a stick; he knows how to kill a monkey with one stroke. In tears, he begs forgiveness of the monkey for what he is about to do, but he keeps stalling. The lord and his servant become impatient and order the trainer to take immediate action. As the trainer is about to hit, the monkey snatches the stick and starts to perform part of the repertoire—rowing a boat, which he has been trained to perform since he was a baby. The trainer, breaking into tears, laments, "It is a sad fate for a creature when it cannot tell that its life is in immediate danger." Observing this scene, the lord too breaks into tears and the two—the trainer and the lord—cry in unison. The lord tells the trainer not to hit the monkey. Overjoyed, the trainer has the monkey perform a dance in gratitude for the lord's mercy. As the monkey starts to dance, the lord, impressed by its dance, offers his fan as a gift. As the monkey continues to dance, the lord joins it in dance and offers even his sword and his jacket. *Utsubozaru* ends with the lord's servant begging the monkey to stop dancing so that his master will also stop.

While *Utsubozaru* is not a record of an ethnographic observation of the monkey performance during the late Medieval period, it presents unique data, since both the text of the performance and the context of the performance are written down. Furthermore, both the text and the context are authored by the writer of the play. In some sense, of course, it is an artificially construed monkey performance, but, on the other hand, it is a uniquely rich source of information about both the performance and its context. For the play to be successful and capable of becoming a classic, as it did, it must have had sufficient credibility with the Medieval audience; therefore, the portrayal of the monkey performance in the play must have been in accord with the general perspective of the actual performance at the time.

Processual Structure of Meaning

As with the monkey performance at stables, the nature:culture transformation is also a dominant theme in *Utsubozaru*, but it becomes extraordinarily complex when we take into account the processual and contextual structures. The play begins with the lord's viewing both the trainer and the monkey as animals; the lord's threat to kill the trainer and the monkey with one arrow reveals the lord's equating of the trainer with the monkey. In the dominant ideology of the Japanese at the time, the special status people and the monkey received the same meaning—nonhumans. At the beginning of the play, the trainer also views the monkey as an animal, one that cannot even tell when its own death is approaching; in contrast to humans like the trainer himself and the lord, it cannot understand language, the epitome of culture.

Despite the identification of the monkey as a lowly beast, the very reason for the lord's wish to acquire the monkey's hide is his acknowledgment of the supernatural power of the hide which, if placed on the quiver, will protect his horse from illnesses and injuries. At the outset of the play, the monkey appears as a polyseme: overtly a beast, covertly a sacred messenger.

As the story progresses, the monkey upstages both the trainer and the lord in one sense, while in another sense, the monkey and the trainer jointly trick the lord. This is done through the power of culturalization entrusted in the monkey. Thus, during the performance, the monkey's identity is transformed from that of a "beast" to that of an artist who transforms his body (nature) into the rhythmically controlled movements of a performing art (Figure 5).

We should note here that the capacity to create culture

BASIC STRUCTURE

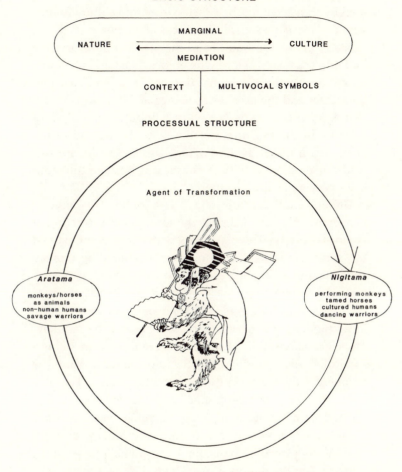

Figure 5. Transformations during a monkey performance.

out of nature characterizes not only the monkey performance but also other occupations held by the special status
people. For example, architects and gardeners in the rock
garden transform raw nature into culturally construed nature. Similarly, kabuki actors, who also used to belong to
the special status group (Yanagita 1982c:417), transcend the

biological givens of age and sex during their performances, thereby transforming their own nature into culturally construed personalities, including those of women. Additionally, the trainer and the monkey transform the lord into the peaceful lord who enjoys dancing. This transformation, then, reveals that the lord, who had regarded the trainer and the monkey as beings of nature, was in fact also a being of nature—a savage without appreciation of culture—in the beginning of the play. At the end of the play, we learn that the lord in fact has been analogous to a wild horse who has to be domesticated through the monkey's power of culturalization.

There is another dimension in *Utsubozaru*. This piece of kyōgen is a play that satirizes the sociopolitical structure of Japanese society. The play starts with a lord accompanied by a servant, Tarōkaja, who together encounter the monkey and its trainer. Although each pair constitutes a master/subordinate relationship, the four are hierarchically ranked, within the broader context of the Japanese universe, as follows: the lord, the servant, the trainer, and the monkey. Thus, at the onset of the play, we have three pairs of hierarchically ordered individuals: the lord and his servant, the trainer and the monkey, the lord and the trainer. The play ends, however, with the monkey's upstaging everyone and taking command of the Japanese universe, which consists of the sacred, represented by the monkey, and the three hierarchically placed humans. First, the animal proves to the humans that it has power over them, just as the Japanese nature deities have power over humans. Second, the monkey, who starts out at the bottom of the hierarchy and is an easy victim of the power of the lord, controls the whole scene at the end; neither the trainer nor Tarōkaja can terminate the magnetic spell cast over the lord by the monkey's dancing. Tarōkaja is forced to beg the monkey to stop dancing. Thus, as illustrated in Figure 6, as the ritual time progresses during the play, the normal hierarchy becomes totally inverted.

The inverted structure at the end of *Utsubozaru* forces the spectators to contemplate the fragility of the hierarchy taken to be so important in their society. The monkey, who represents the special status people, is the trickster in the play. He tricks the spectators, unaware of how the play will

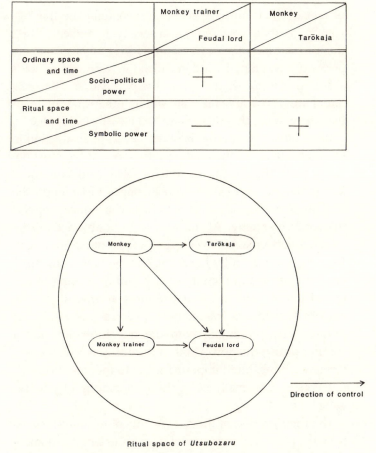

	Monkey trainer / Feudal lord	Monkey / Tarōkaja
Ordinary space and time / Socio-political power	$+$	$-$
Ritual space and time / Symbolic power	$-$	$+$

Ritual space of *Utsubozaru*

Figure 6. The structure of power and its transformation in *Utsubozaru*.

unfold, so that at the end of the play they find themselves comtemplating, albeit vaguely, the meaning of the structure of their society.

As illustrated in Figure 5, the nature to culture transformation and counter-transformation, and the social structure and its inversion, constitute the *processual structure* of meaning of the play *Utsubozaru*. Most important, the simultaneous presence of transformation and counter-transformation produces yet a higher level of meaning, that of reflexivity. It forces spectators to contemplate their assumptions about cosmology and society: it implicitly urges them to question the universe in which humans claim superiority over animals, and in which the warrior class holds absolute power over the rest of the population. The spectators are forced to realize, although perhaps not in an articulate manner, that this universe can easily be toppled.

In summary, we recognize three levels of abstraction in the message of the monkey performance. At the most obvious level, the message is anti-establishment—the monkey is the trickster-clown who manages to lampoon the lord, his servant, and even the trainer. The monkey topples the social hierarchy. At the next level of abstraction, the monkey performance inverts the process of nature to culture transformation by heralding the monkey as the epitome of culture and identifying the lord as a being of untamed nature. However, at the most abstract level, the performance moves ambiguity to a central position in the universe. By presenting both the transformation and a counter-transformation of both culture and society, the performance brings fluid impermanency to the fore. In short, it serves as the small eye in the iconography of yin and yang.

The fluid process of the movements of meaning derives from the polysemic structure of the meaning of the monkey in the late Medieval period, as discussed in Chapter 3.

Contextual Structure of Meaning

The transformation and counter-transformation that characterize the processual structure seem to be simultaneously present when we examine the context of the performance through the perspectives of both the trainer and the spectators.

As members of Medieval society, the spectators' perspective is at least somewhat influenced by the structure of meaning at the time. Since we have no record of direct testimony by spectators of the late Medieval period, most of whom likely did not belong to the special status group, my interpretation is based on the portrayal of the lord by the author of *Utsubozaru*, and on the ethnographic information presented in Chapters 3, 4, and 5. I begin my interpretation of the contextual structure by reexamining the symbols in the monkey performance of the Medieval period.

In the play, the lord begins by equating both the monkey and the trainer as beings of nature. This view may have been held by at least some of the Medieval spectators who did not belong to the special status group. The entire complex of the monkey performance may have been seen as a process whereby the supreme forms of culture, dancing and music, are reduced to clumsy imitation by "a human minus three pieces of hair"—the negative definition of the monkey in Japanese culture. The attire of the monkey yields to this reading. Its headgear, the ebōshi (usually worn by aristocrats) is often seen in pictures depicting performing monkeys (see Figure 5). As noted in Chapter 3, "saru no ebōshi" (a monkey wearing an ebōshi) refers to behavior considered out of character; it is thus a sarcastic statement about people who pretend to be above their station in life: no matter how hard it tries, the monkey is after all a human minus three pieces of hair.

The trainer in turn may have been seen by the spectators as analogous to the monkey, since in the ideology of the dominant Japanese at the time the special status people were nonhumans among humans. We recall that some of the occupations of the special status people became increasingly degraded during the latter half of the Medieval period and during the Early Modern period. As discussed in Chapter 5, the leaders of the special status people and the high-ranking trainers wore an outfit similar to that of the samurai but without hems at the bottom of the skirt. The trainer's sword was a metaphor for unnecessary items in life. In the dominant ideological system, the trainer in samurai attire was equivalent to a monkey. Just as the monkey could not read and thus could not become human, neither could the trainer become a samurai.

The monkey and the trainer are not the only polysemic symbols open to multiple interpretations. Thus, the shamisen, the musical instrument most frequently used by monkey trainers in the past, is associated with the merchant class, which was the lowest of the four castes during the late Medieval and Early Modern periods. In contrast to the *koto*, a "noble" instrument associated with the aristocrats and warriors, the shamisen had a sensual tone which was associated with the lower class. Likewise, the type of drum used by trainers both past and present is associated with folk festivals; it is not the type that is used in nō plays and other forms of the "great tradition." Most important, both the shamisen and the drum are made in part with animal hide, providing the basis for their symbolic association with animals and death.

In short, one structure of meaning, the transformation of nature into culture, is maintained by the trainers, while the other, the transformation of culture into nature, is maintained by the dominant Japanese. The simultaneity of two transformations in opposite directions is therefore a construct made possible by three factors: (1) the presence of two distinct groups of Japanese; (2) the polysemic structure of the meaning of the monkey, the special status people, and the monkey performance; and (3) the framing of the monkey performance as street entertainment. As we saw in the previous section, the presence of two structures characterizes the processual structure as well. In the case of the processual structure, the two occur *sequentially*, whereas in the case of the contextual structure, they occur *simultaneously*.

FRAMING OF THE MONKEY PERFORMANCE

The simultaneous presence of the dominant Japanese as spectators and the trainers from the special status group as performers engenders a common structure of meaning for all the participants when the performance is a stable ritual, but it engenders a pair consisting of a structure and its inversion when the performance is a street entertainment.

The involvement of both groups of Japanese in both types of performance excludes the possibility that the difference in the contextual structure of meaning derives from intra-cultural variation, since in both types of performance two social groups within Japanese society, the dominant and the minority, are represented—as spectators and trainers, respectively. If the structure of meaning were determined by intra-cultural variation, it would be the same in both types of performance, since they both include two groups of Japanese.

It is therefore necessary to bring in the concept of "framing," that is, marking, defining, or classifying the performance as ritual, play, or game, for example.[5] The contrast in the contextual structure of meaning between the performance at the stable and the one on the street indicates that when symbols are polysemic, the framing is crucial in one type of performance but not in the other. At the stable, the

[5] My use of the analytical concept of "framing" is very general here, without closely following, for example, Goffman (1974), which represents an extensive use of this concept.

179

transformation from nature to culture is the structure, regardless of the specific context of the performance—the *framing* is the only determinant of the structure of meaning. By constrast, the framing of a performance as street entertainment does not determine the structure of meaning of the performance; determinants are other contextual factors, that is, the perspectives of the trainer and the spectators.[6]

The crucial difference, then, is that while the monkey performance at the stable is decisively a ritual, that on the street eludes any categorization. If we reject the neo-Tylorian distinction between the sacred and the secular and adopt instead a semiotic approach, and if we accept the minimum definition of *ritual* as "a culturally constructed system of symbolic communication" (Tambiah 1981:119; see also note 1, above), then the monkey performance both at the stable and on the street is a ritual, although it is not an ordinary form of "symbolic communication," because the trainer and the spectators "communicate" not directly but via the performing monkey. The monkey performance on the street, however, is clearly different from the one performed at the stable. It does not fit neatly into the categories of ritual, play or game. Play shares many features with ritual (Tambiah 1981:117–18; see also Huizinga 1970). However, in a more restricted definition of *ritual* than the semiotic one introduced above, the ritual frame is "sanctified" and is made "true and authentic." In this sense, the monkey performance at the stable is a ritual. In contrast, the meta-communication of *play* is "make-believe" and "untrue" (Bateson 1974:177–93; Handelman 1981:322, 357). In some sense, the monkey performance on the street does

---

[6] An analogous situation is pointed out by Kapferer, who sees a transformation of the meaning of the symbolic objects and actions of the Sinhalese demonic exorcism rites when the context of these rites moves from "the more clearly religious sequences, or episodes of marked supernatural reference, to those dominantly secular in context" (Kapferer 1977:91, 1983). Kapferer (1979:4) argues, therefore, that the "transformation of a context must involve a transformation of its constituent elements."

hold elements that are "make-believe" and "untrue." However, it is not unambiguously for fun, as play usually is, and hence the participants do not engage in it with passion or become excited (Huizinga 1970:esp. 19–22). Yet, as in play, it does manipulate images of reality in that the inversions of the cosmology and the social structure play havoc with the presumed reality in Japanese culture. Therefore, the monkey performance on the street does not entirely conform to the category of play, although it should be noted here that play is a very complex activity often eluding tight classification (cf. Huizinga 1970).

When we look at the two types of performance as symbolic communication, the framing creates a significant difference between them. In the case of the stable ritual, the framing as prescriptive ritual, underscored by the shared belief in the supernatural power of the monkey, renders the performance an event that unites trainers and spectators—from two different social groups—in the single goal of removing the impurity of illness in the cosmos. Therefore, when the ritual is completed, all the participants share a sense of accomplishment and embrace a cosmos that is rejuvenated and purified. By contrast, the monkey performance as street entertainment, framed as a quasi-play, lacks the power to conjoin the participants and symbolically transform them.

There is no need to elaborate upon the famous distinction between games and rituals made by Lévi-Strauss, who sees games as establishing a difference or inequality, while rituals "conjoin" initially separate groups of people and transform inequality and asymmetry into equality and symmetry (Lévi-Strauss 1966:esp. 32). In the case of at least some street performances, however, the ordinary hierarchy is never inverted. Instead, for those who view the monkey performance as a process of transforming culture into nature, the dominance of humans over monkeys and of the dominant Japanese over the special status people is in fact reinforced. The monkey performance as street entertainment is therefore neither a game nor a ritual. I might point out here that Lévi-Strauss's definition of ritual does not hold true even for the stable ritual. Like other rituals, the monkey performance at the stable brings together two hierarchically ranked groups of Japanese but never establishes equality between them. Instead, the trainer, who is ranked below the dominant Japanese in society, has symbolic power over the Japanese whose horses he attends. In other words, during the ritual space and time of the performance, the power hierarchy is inverted. In neither type of performance, therefore, is equality between the dominant Japanese and the special status people established even temporarily.

From the perspective of the meaning of the monkey, the monkey is a mediator in the stable ritual, harnessing the power of his master, the Mountain Deity, to protect the horses. In the street performance, he becomes at once a scapegoat in the structure in which culture is transformed into nature, and a trickster-clown in the inverted structure. I use the combined term *trickster-clown* to indicate that the monkey in *Utsubozaru* is a trickster whose tricks are not practical jokes but who plays tricks on the cosmological structure. In the next chapter, we will see the monkey as a fully developed clown.

8

The Monkey Performance in Contemporary Japan

IN THIS CHAPTER, I wish to examine the monkey performance as a form of entertainment in contemporary Japan. I will discuss two types of performance that I have observed: one type took place at a rural festival in western Japan in 1980 and the other took place at a large park in Tokyo in 1984. My objective is to analyze the contextual structure of these performances in order to compare it with the contextual structure of the Medieval monkey performance presented in Chapter 7; this analysis will serve as a vehicle for exploring further the possibility of multiple structures of perception in ritual as a general theoretical problem.

MONKEY PERFORMANCE AT A FESTIVAL IN 1980

Description

The following description is based on my observation of the monkey performances held at a shrine in the Yamaguchi Prefecture in western Japan. It was a shrine for Ebisu, a guardian deity of fishermen, who is closely associated with the monkey.

In the midst of the festival, while *sumō* was taking place

183

on the other side of the shrine compound, one of the three trainers whose monkeys were performing announced the beginning of the monkey performance by beating on a drum, which was later used to give signals to the monkey during the performance. Each set of performances by a monkey was preceded by his trainer's narration. The same story, presented below, was used by all the trainers.

One day I [the monkey] was happily swinging from tree branch to tree branch in the mountains with my family. I then heard the sound of a gun [here the trainer utters an onomatopoeia of a gun sound] and saw my father had fallen to the ground [the monkey falls to the ground on its back at the sound of the gunshot]. Without our father, we had no means of supporting ourselves. I left our mountain home and came to the city to earn money by performing so that I can send money back to my family. Here I begin [the monkey bows to the ground].

The audience always broke into smiles and laughter when the monkey fell to the ground at the sound of the onomatopoeia of a gunshot, and when the monkey bowed at the end of the trainer's narration.

Taking turns, each of the three trainers demonstrated several relatively simple stunts performed by his own monkey, including riding a bicycle, jumping through a hoop, walking on a pair of stilts, and walking on its head. These tasks emphasized the bipedal posture.

Interpretation

As seen in Chapter 7, the trainers strived to culturalize the "animal" through teaching the bipedal posture and through the establishment of a social relationship between trainer and monkey. The culturalization of the monkey was reinforced by teaching various tricks, all of which emphasized the "unnatural" posture of the monkey—riding a bike, walking on its head, and so on. The story told by the trainers at the beginning of the festival performances explains how the death—that is, nature—of the father monkey in the mountains gives birth to a performing—that is, culturalized—monkey.

While the transformation of nature into culture was the structure of meaning assigned to the performance by the trainers in my discussions with them, the view of the spectators at the festival seemed quite the opposite. The spectators consisted of men (many of whom were intoxicated), women, and children. Observing the monkey performance and the spectators' reactions at the same time, I experienced a somewhat vague but unsettling feeling that the lighthearted attitude of the spectators did not correspond to the attitude of the trainers. As I talked to a number of men, women, and children after the festival, I learned that although many of them thought the monkeys were cute (*kawaii*), they nevertheless interpreted them as creatures trying in vain to imitate humans.

In other words, the spectators, made up largely of fishermen and their families, saw the monkeys as "humans minus three pieces of hair." To them, the performance constituted an inept attempt by monkeys and their trainers to reduce art, that is, culture, to clumsy imitation. Their amusement and laughter did not derive from their perception that the transformation from nature into culture was successful. Instead, it derived from the monkeys' failed attempt at transformation which in turn assured the spectators that they alone were masterful in cultural ways. From the perspective of the spectators, then, the transformation went only in one direction: from culture into nature.

As with the case of the monkey performance as street entertainment during the late Medieval period, the contextual structure of meaning of the monkey performance at the festival consisted of a structure and an inverted structure, or a transformation of nature into culture as perceived by the trainers and its opposite as interpreted by the spectators.

After observing the monkey performance and the attitude of the spectators at the festival, and taking into account other factors, such as competing sources of entertainment from the mass media, I was prompted to predict that the monkey performance was not a viable performing art. Yet, when I returned to Japan in 1984 to do further work, I found that it had developed into two different forms, as I noted in Chapter 5. Here, I concentrate only on the performance at Yoyogi Park in Tokyo.

Monkey Performance at a Park in Tokyo in 1984: Monkey as Clown

In the previous chapter, we saw the monkey as trickster-clown in the Medieval play. The Medieval monkey was an implicit clown; the monkey in the contemporary performance in Tokyo has become a full-blown clown.

Description

The monkey performances at Yoyogi Park in Tokyo are staged by the trainer Murasaki Tarō and his monkey Jirō (Photo 4). Situated in an enormous open space and conveniently located in the Tokyo metropolitan area, this park, a center of youth culture in comtemporary Japan, attracts thousands of young people, many of whom are dating couples, and also older men and women, some with young children. On Friday, Saturday, and Sunday afternoons, Tarō and Jirō draw a crowd of up to four hundred people for each performance, even though they perform almost continuously.

Jirō the monkey wears a traditional jacket *(hanten)* worn

186

Photo 4. Monkey performance at Yoyogi Park, Tokyo, by Murasaki Tarō of Suō Sarumawashinokai. (Courtesy of Y. Azuma)

only by workmen. A drum is used to signal the beginning of the performance, drawing crowds from various parts of the park to the area where the performance takes place. The performance begins with the following narrative, whose setting derives from the genre of tales called *mukashibanashi* (stories of a long time ago), all of which start with an old man going to the mountains to fetch firewood and his wife going to a stream to wash clothes.

> I am Jirō, the monkey. When I was a little child, every-day I swung from tree branch to tree branch in the mountains with my family. One day, I heard the sound of a gun [the trainer utters an onomatopoeia of a gun sound] and saw my father had been killed. Since my parents died when I was little, I was brought up by my grandparents. Everyday, my grandfather went to the mountains to fetch firewood and my grandmother went to a river to wash our clothes. One day, I heard the sound of a gun and saw my grandfather fall to the ground. With the death of my grandfather, I had to help my grandmother. So, I left our mountain home and came to Yoyogi Park to earn money by performing so that I can send money back to my grandmother. Here I begin [the monkey bows, his head touching the ground].

The spectators break into laughter when the monkey imitates the motion of washing clothes with a washing board, and when he falls to the ground on his back at the sound of the onomatopoeia uttered by Tarō, who refers to himself as Jirō's older brother. The spectators also respond with laughter when the monkey bows at the end of this narration (Photo 5).

The monkey's repertoire does not emphasize dancing. Instead, it concentrates on activities that capitalize on the monkey's agility and fast movement, such as walking on

Photo 5. The beginning of the performance by Tarō, the trainer, and Jirō, the monkey. The monkey starts each performance by bowing to spectators, as a Japanese does. (Courtesy of Y. Azuma)

stilts (Photo 6) and jumping from block to block. Murasaki Tarō, the trainer, is a genius at recognizing every pulse of contemporary culture, especially those features proliferated by the younger generations. He does not sing, but he narrates with numerous references to current events and prominent figures in popular culture, many familiar to the spectators through television shows. These references almost always succeed in drawing laughter from the spectators. For example, as Jirō takes a certain sitting position, Tarō asks, "Are you Takamiyama?" Takamiyama is the most popular sumo wrestler, and Tarō's evocation of the posture, which Takamiyama takes at the ring just before a

189

Photo 6. A monkey on high stilts at Sukiyabashi Park, Tokyo. (Courtesy of Y. Azuma)

match and with which the spectators are very familiar through television, wins over the spectators and they break into laughter.[1]

Another example of Tarō's familiarity with popular culture is his impromptu comments when Jirō stalls near the audience or looks at individual spectators. Tarō calls Jirō the name of a popular television comedian whose trademark is being a clumsy womanizer, and he asks if he is losing concentration because of a good-looking woman.

Another act consists of Tarō's giving a tissue paper to Jirō to wipe his tears. Jirō puts the tissue paper on his head or some place other than over his eyes. Tarō chides, "You fool, where do you think your eyes are? Tears don't come out of your head." This act is part of the traditional repertoire and trainers in the past endeavored to teach their monkeys sixteen ways of crying. The Hokkaidō group also includes the crying scene as part of their regular repertoire. Tarō, however, emphasizes the monkey's clumsiness and turns the act into a comical scene. Similarly, when Jirō does not perform at Tarō's command, Tarō remarks, "If you don't know how to perform, you will be sent off for an animal experiment." Or, every now and then, Tarō tells Jirō, "Don't make a monkey face" ("a monkey face" is an ugly face in Japanese culture).

Jirō's cleverly staged disobedience to Tarō is even more successful in drawing laughter from the spectators. It comes as part of the act in which Jirō jumps from block to block (Photo 7). The performance starts with two blocks placed fairly close to each other. After Jirō successfully jumps from the ground to the first block and onto the next, Tarō moves one of the blocks farther away to create greater distance. This process is repeated, but at about the third or fourth jump, although Tarō seemingly shouts the same or-

---

[1] Tarō told me that he originally had started the scene by asking, "Are you a sumo wrestler?" but it had received no response from the audience.

Photo 7. A monkey jumps from block to block. (Courtesy of Y. Azuma)

der ("Go!"), Jirō leaps onto the first block and makes a miserable face (Photo 8), refusing to jump onto the next block. The difference between the signal with which Tarō commands Jirō to jump and the one with which Tarō "orders disobedience" is not at all apparent to the spectators. Every time this act is performed, the spectators break into prolonged laughter.[2]

Photo 8. Staged disobedience: the monkey jumps only to the first block and makes a miserable face.

[2] Tarō explained to me that the staged disobedience had begun as a natural act—Jirō had refused to perform. Tarō then cultivated Jirō's disobedience into a part of the repertoire.

193

Tarō's "dialogue" with Jirō is sprinkled with such remarks as "Iukoto o kike" (Listen and follow what I say); "Shūchū!" (Concentrate!); "Gyōgiyoku shiro" (Be well mannered), whereupon Jirō, sitting on a stool, pulls his two hind legs closer together; and "Kiotsuke!" (Attention!), whereupon Jirō stands at attention (Photo 10). These are cherished rules and manners which every Japanese is taught at home and at school, and with which the spectators are very familiar. When Jirō does not follow Tarō's order, usually spontaneously but at times as part of the act, as in the skit described above, or when Jirō's attempt to carry out Tarō's order is done in a clumsy way, Tarō immediately makes remarks that transform Jirō's act into a comical scene. Jirō's disobedience, however, is immediately followed by the act of *hansei* (self-examination and repentance), whereby Jirō puts his hand on Tarō's lap and lowers his head (Photo 9). At this moment, the spectators invariably roar with laughter. Hansei is a critically important form of moral behavior taught to the Japanese early on, and it continues to be reinforced throughout their lives.

After each performance, while the crowd lingers on, Tarō and Jirō sit together and sip a cup of barley tea, drawing smiles from the spectators, some of whom offer bananas and other goodies to Jirō.

Spectators' Reactions

The spectators' reactions to this performance were exceedingly varied. The majority of onlookers did not give it much thought afterward. Some older people came to see it because the performance brought back pleasant memories of their young days when they saw monkey performances during festivals at local shrines and temples. One man in his early forties said that he saw himself in the monkey, which was earning money for its master, just as he had been working every day to earn a living for his family.

Photo 9. After the disobedient act, the monkey repents (*hansei suru*). (Courtesy of Y. Azuma)

Photo 10. "Attention" (*Kiotsuke*). After the disobedience and repentance, the monkey resumes the act with this posture. (Courtesy of Y. Azuma)

The predominant reaction, however, was that the monkey was cute (kawaii) or great or admirable (*erai*) because it was clever and performed so many tasks *even though it was only a monkey*. In other words, the spectators put the monkey "in its place" as an animal and then praised it for its human-like abilities, although there was little disdain for or condemnation of the monkey.

This view is most clearly expressed in the short compositions written by the second graders who, with their parents, watched the performance of two monkeys and their trainers from the Tokyo group at an elementary school in Tokyo in 1983. In all but one of the twenty-two compositions, the comments centered on the human-monkey relationship; the exception simply described the performance at length. Eleven of them highly praised the monkeys on the basis of their adeptly performing tasks normally performed by humans—or by the Japanese—as the following excerpts reveal:

1. The monkeys have better manners than we boys [twice].
2. The monkeys know how to bow [like humans/Japanese].
3. The monkeys walk on a pair of high stilts when I [a boy] cannot [three times].
4. The monkeys are very clever in learning all these tricks [three times].
5. The monkey knows how to practice and *ganbaru* (persevere).

We can summarize these comments that they emphasize good manners, skills, wisdom, and the ability to work hard. Indeed, these are the focal points of the early education of children in Japan. The only other type of comment made frequently was about the dexterity of the monkeys' feet (I wish my feet were as dexterous as the monkeys').

Five of the comments stressed that even *monkeys* carried

out many tasks. In other words, the children praised the monkeys only because they were not supposed to be capable of these tasks that were expected only of humans. They added, therefore, that because of "a funny-looking face" and "a funny waddling," they could not help but laugh at them.

The responses of the parents of these children were directed to the value of the monkey performance as a school activity; thus, they did not focus on their reactions to the performance. These were nevertheless inserted between evaluations. One said that the monkeys had learned manners and tasks that human children should learn, and therefore the event was an educational experience. Two stressed that children should be *able* to learn, since even *monkeys* can learn as long as they try hard enough. Another wished that the children would learn the effectiveness of "teamwork," as demonstrated by the trainer and his monkey when they jointly succeeded in presenting good performances.

Relegating a fuller description of the contemporary monkey performance to a separate publication, I now move on to an analysis of the contextual structure of meaning underlying the monkey performance at Yoyogi Park.[3]

Interpretation

Contemporary Japan, or more precisely, Japan since the early 1970s, represents another dynamic period in the

[3] Many young spectators at the park had neither seen monkey performances before nor been aware that the trainers were from the special status group. Most older people were aware of the social identity of the trainers. The social climate in contemporary Japan is such that even academics never approach the subject of special status people. I felt that the social climate did not lend itself to a fruitful investigation of peoples' attitudes toward the special status people and thus did not press the matter in my discussion with spectators; I was concerned that I might somehow intervene superficially with the effort of the special status people to eliminate discrimination and achieve equality in Japanese society.

country's history, comparable to the latter half of the Medieval period, when the play *Utsubozaru*, discussed in Chapter 7, was written. It is certainly an overstatement to claim that the monkey performances at Yoyogi Park and on television represent contemporary Japanese culture in its entirety. However, they may be seen as an expression of a new and changing aspect of contemporary Japan. Or more appropriately, they are an index of the fact that a profound change is going on at the moment. It is perhaps for this reason that the monkey performance had been developed into a full-blown clowning act, playfully challenging the basic assumptions of Japanese society.

We should keep in mind that for most Japanese, monkeys are animals in zoos or in nature conservation parks specifically designed to protect macaques. We recall that a kindergartner once asked Tarō if the monkey was a stuffed animal with remote control. The inhabitants of this highly industrialized and urban nation have lived for a long time in the company of other humans and have had more and more contact with foreigners as well, but they have not lived alongside animals. Yet we see that the predominant reaction of the spectators, both at the park and at the elementary school, is to deliberate upon their own identity vis-à-vis that of the monkey. They cannot think of the monkey without reference to themselves and the question of who they are as humans. This is the case regardless of whether they look up to or down on the monkey. An integral part of their question about who they are is their search for a distinctly Japanese identity.

The spectators' deliberation upon the relationship between humans and monkeys is, I think, prompted by three factors. First, in an age when "nature" no longer provides any input into the human's perception of the monkey, the cultural input, namely, the culturally defined concept of the monkey as an animal close to humans, is responsible for urging the spectators to be reflexive. The second factor is that the spectators see in front of them a monkey that is capable of carrying out learned behaviors that they had identified as belonging exclusively to humans. Of paramount importance here is the monkey's attempt to imitate crying, or more specifically, the shedding of tears—part of the traditional repertoire of the monkey performance. Crying represents sorrow, an important human emotion. Emotions have always been highly valued in Japanese culture, and the shedding of tears has been considered an important and unique human behavior (for its importance in Medieval Japan, see LaFleur 1983:esp. 34–35). It should be noted here that Tarō's capitalization on the monkey's clumsy and unsuccessful attempt to shed tears causes spectators to ponder about human uniqueness without being seriously threatened. It is done in a playful atmosphere filled with laughter. Like the shedding of tears, laughter is not only universally and uniquely human, as Aristotle, Menippus, Rabelais, and many other Western intellectuals (cf. Bakhtin 1984; Boon 1984) have pointed out, but it also has been an important characteristic of humans in Japanese culture, in the great tradition of zen (Hyers 1973) as well as in the folk tradition which is rich in clowning.

Although the spectators' deliberation focuses upon the distinction between humans and monkeys, the behaviors enacted by the monkeys to impress the spectators are predominantly characteristic behaviors of the Japanese. They are manners and moral principles, such as concentration and hard work, that are central to defining the Japanese, not humans generally.[4]

The third factor that prompts the spectators to deliberate upon their identity as they watch the monkey performance is the hierarchical relationship between humans and monkeys which the trainer deliberatelly juggles. During the per-

---

[4] Neither the trainer nor the spectators, however, may articulate how Japanese these behaviors are.

formance, humans, represented by Tarō, the trainer, are alternately superior, inferior, and equal to animals, represented by Jirō the monkey. Tarō pokes fun at Jirō's inability to cry like humans, his "monkey face," his vulnerability to being used in experiments, and so forth, thereby defining the monkey as an animal below humans. On the other hand, albeit in a playful manner, Tarō is openly disobeyed by Jirō, who demonstrates that he is not going to be pushed around all the time. Instead, Jirō takes the commanding position during "the performance of disobedience." Although all these behaviors are deliberately staged by Tarō, they reinforce the spectators' observation that the monkey can carry out "human activities" as well as, or even better than, some humans, especially elementary school children. The play on the inverted hierarchy of the human and the monkey is most delightful to young spectators at the park. The present is a transitional period in Japan; it is the age of "the three cultured monkeys," who encourage people to examine, to listen, and to speak up (Chapter 3). These values, the opposite of traditional values, are embraced most enthusiastically by university students, who are accorded the maximum freedom in thought and behavior in Japanese society. The monkey represents young spectators who wish to challenge their parents, professors, government, or superiors at work. Perhaps the monkey does more than they manage to do.

In addition to taking superior and inferior positions, Tarō also assumes an equal relationship with Jirō. Thus, the two are named as brothers; as noted previously, the name Tarō is always given to the firstborn male in a Japanese family, and the name Jirō is given to the second-born male. The Japanese immediately recognize this declaration of brotherhood between Tarō and Jirō. Although in the traditional Japanese family the firstborn male child is definitely above the second-born in status, the names Tarō and Jirō for the trainer and the monkey capitalize on the closeness of the two, unlike the hierarchy that exists between two human brothers. This egalitarian stance is further enhanced through such behavior as the two drinking barley tea together. Needless to say, the equality between them is a variant of the inverted hierarchical relationship between humans and animals (Photo 11).

We recall from Chapter 5 that, historically, the monkey performance has always contained anti-establishment elements. What could be more anti-establishment than a monkey carrying a torpedo and "accidentally" dropping it—an act that would elicit severe punishment if done by a human in an era when military patriotism went unquestioned? It was a sacrilegious act par excellence which only a "monkey, the clown" could get away with without capital punishment. It was a superb clowning act containing a profound philosophical commentary about the follies of the sacredness surrounding the military. Thus, anti-establishment elements are part of the tradition of the monkey performance, and the acts at Yoyogi Park follow this tradition.

On a higher level of abstraction, the performance does not simply present the inversion of the social structure or existing hierarchy. Instead, it portrays both the essential ambiguity and the ephemeral nature of hierarchy—a state in which trainer and monkey constantly exchange relative positions so that neither holds permanent hegemony over the other. Note that the hierarchies of both trainer over monkey and monkey over trainer are simultaneously present. This is accomplished by the skillful improvisation by Murasaki Tarō, whose repertoire includes the "order of disobedience."

The "order to disobey" given by the human trainer to the monkey may be translated at yet a higher level of abstraction into a question of human identity. By ordering the monkey to be disobedient, the trainer Tarō in fact offers himself as a sacrificial victim at the altar where Jirō the monkey openly takes hegemony over Tarō the human, forcing

Photo 11. Jirō, the monkey, with Tarō, the trainer, in Jirō's house, especially built for him to provide him with enough space and a "relaxing atmosphere." (From *Shūkan Asahi* 1986:5–9. Photograph by Masahiko Takai. Reproduced by permission of Asahi Shimbun)

spectators to question human uniqueness and superiority. In this process, then, Tarō is no longer a traditional trainer whose role is to have a monkey take center stage. Tarō takes on new roles—that of clown and trickster. He offers himself as the target of Jirō's disobedience, and consequently as the

203

target of laughter from the spectators. He is a clown. But he is also a metaphysical trickster, who fools unsuspecting spectators into laughing at themselves by making them believe that they are laughing only at Jirō and Tarō. He is therefore strikingly similar to the monkey in the Medieval play *Utsubozaru*.

The hierarchy that exists between humans and monkeys is a permutation of the nature/culture transformation that takes place during the performance. The hierarchy of humans over monkeys correlates with the transformation of culture, or the human way of life, into nature, that is, clumsy imitations of humans by monkeys. Conversely, the hierarchy of monkeys over humans correlates with the transformation of nature (monkeys) into culture (performing monkeys).

Discussion

While in the Medieval play the monkey is more of a trickster, we see full-blown clowning in the contemporary monkey performance. It is a performance during which the monkey becomes a scapegoat, the target of laughter both from the trainer and the spectators, while it, on the other hand, mocks the spectators as humans and as Japanese and urges them to contemplate their self. Furthermore, through his repertoire that includes "ordering disobedience," the trainer too offers himself as a scapegoat, mocked by the monkey and the target of laughter from the spectators who, while laughing at the monkey's defiance of the trainer, realize, albeit vaguely, that it is they, as humans, who are being challenged by the monkey.[5]

---

[5] When I spent a day with Murasaki Tarō and his group at his house in Tachikawa, a suburb of Tokyo, I offered my interpretation of "Murasaki Tarō, the trickster-clown." I explained that clowning presupposed a distance from oneself in order to offer the self as a target of laughter. We discussed how self-confidence and self-respect are necessary for a special status person to identify himself in public and, even more, to be able to let

The multiple structures of meaning, consisting of structure and its inversion, characterize both the processual and contextual structures of meaning of the monkey performance in the play *Utsubozaru*, written in the late Medieval period. The same holds for the monkey performance I observed at the rural festival in 1980. The contextual structure of meaning of the monkey performance at Yoyogi Park, however, was markedly different from these two. A repeated succession of structure and its inversion orchestrated by the trainer engendered many readings by the spectators. Among the contemporary urban Japanese, who constituted the majority of spectators, the structure and its inversion that were present throughout the performance did not correspond to a simple division between the dominant Japanese and the special status people; rather, both groups seemed to maintain the structure and its inversion simultaneously.

---

others laugh at him by being a clown. Murasaki Tarō told me that he was not aware of this dimension of his acts, although he had been strongly influenced by the idea of manzai, the genre of door-to-door comic performance that has a close historical connection to the monkey performance, as noted in Chapter 5.

The trainers of both the Tokyo and the Hokkaido group were quite open and stressed that they believed in understanding their past; only then could they deal squarely with the present state of oppression. As part of an effort to understand their collective self, they have engaged in extensive research into the history of the monkey performance. As they pointed out, however, their attitude is different from many of the members of the special status group who would rather eradicate their special identity, and who therefore do not wish anyone to probe into their past.

PART FOUR

FROM THE MEDIATING MONKEY

TO THE REFLEXIVE MONKEY:

HISTORICAL TRANSFORMATIONS

AND RITUAL STRUCTURE

9

Structures of Meaning in History, Myth, and Ritual

IN MY ATTEMPT to understand culture over a long span of time, I have chosen to examine monkey symbolism, the cultural meanings of the special status people, and the meanings assigned to the monkey performance in Japanese culture since the beginning of the eighth century. This chapter summarizes the major findings of the preceding chapters and explores their implications for anthropological theories about ritual, history, symbolic forms and meanings, and the interrelationships among them.

MONKEY PERFORMANCE: TEXT, CONTEXT, AND PERFORMANCE

The monkey performance at horse stables and as a street entertainment in Medieval Japan and in contemporary Japan presents a challenging task for the anthropological understanding of ritual. Unlike the Balinese cockfight (Geertz 1973), which does not involve heterogeneous people, the monkey performance cannot be summarized as a story the special status people tell by themselves about themselves. If a story is told, it is not always heard by the spectators the way it is told. Nor does it lend itself to the phenomenological possibility of the same cultural text having as many

209

readings as there are observers. Most of all, it defies most anthropological readings of ritual that assume the presence of only one meaning or structure of meaning.

Contextual Construction of Text

The processual-contextual structure of the monkey performance is not an automatic function of individual differences, or of intra-cultural differences, or even of the differences between the indigenous text and that of the anthropologist. It is determined by the complex interplay between the structure of meaning of the polysemes involved and the particular context of performance that is uniquely characterized by the simultaneous presence of two groups of Japanese.

In the case of the monkey performance at stables, framing is the only factor. Or, more specifically, the belief in the power of the monkey to cure the illnesses of horses, which underlies the framing of the performance as a stable ritual, determines the structure of meaning of the performance. This meaning is shared by trainers and spectators. By contrast, the context of the monkey performance as street entertainment involves the hierarchical relationship between two groups in Japanese society: the trainers and the spectators. The Medieval street performance is exceptionally complex in that there is more than one structure of meaning simultaneously present throughout the performance, with each structure being transformed during the course of the performance. The two structures of meaning are not haphazard, however; they constitute a structure, underlying the views of the dominant Japanese who make up the spectators, and its inversion, underlying the views of the trainers who belong to the special status group. During the performance, each of the structures is transformed: the structure becomes inverted and the inversion becomes the structure. The structure and its inversion are transformed in like manner but in opposite directions, thereby metaphorically exchanging places in the reflexive mirror. A similar but not identical picture holds true for the 1980 festival performance, during which the structure and its inversion are present, characterizing the views of the trainers from the special status group and those of the spectators from the dominant group, respectively. They talk, as it were, right past each other. In the case of the contemporary monkey performance in a park, both the structure and its inversion are simultaneously present, but in a wholly different configuration. Here, the structure and its inversion underlying the participants—trainers and spectators.

The monkey performance of various times and places in Japanese culture, then, defies several basic assumptions of anthropological theories, with far-reaching implications for our understanding of performance. It defies the concept of "multiple exegesis" of the same text. The text is not "objectively there" to be read. The text of the monkey performance that served as a Medieval street entertainment not only depends on a variety of binary opposition of polysemic symbols, but exists as it does precisely because it is read differently by two groups of Japanese. An important implication for semiotic analysis, then, is that a text exists as it does because it is read differently; that is, *a text is predicated upon a diametrically opposed interpretation of what it may signify.*[1] The same holds true with the 1980 performance, despite the fact that it occurs in a different historical period.

The multiple structures of meaning of the monkey performance, therefore, is a notion different from the multiple structures of thought present in a culture at large. My work

---

[1] After reading the first draft of this manuscript, Professor Donald Handelman of Hebrew University advised me that I did not capitalize enough on this point. His suggestion helped me further articulate the problem involved.

on the Ainu (Ohnuki-Tierney 1976, 1981a:100–103) reveals that in their shamanistic ritual, the women and their cooking activities are given high cultural valuation and are assigned the power of transforming nature into culture. In contrast, both in their sociopolitical structure and in group rituals, such as the bear ceremony, it is the men who convert nature into culture and who hold high cultural valuation. The phenomenon of the inverted structure of meaning symbolically expressed in minor rituals is widespread throughout the world.[2] However, these findings point only to the presence of more than one structure in a culture at large, not to their simultaneous presence during a collective activity. In the case of the monkey performance, *the structure and the inverted structure are not only simultaneously present, but their predication depends upon the presence of two groups of Japanese in a hierarchical relationship.*

Yet the presence of the two groups of Japanese does not in itself engender multiple structures of meaning. Note that the two groups of Japanese are always present at a monkey performance. When a monkey performance is held as a ritual at horse stables, the dominant Japanese, who always constitute the spectators, share the same structures of meaning, both processual and contextual, with the trainers, who are from the special status group; both observe the transformation of nature into culture facilitated jointly by sacred and human mediators. As for contemporary performances, the historical context—in which many of the young, urban spectators in changing Japan are unaware of the social identity of the trainers as burakumin—produces multiple structures of meaning underlying the views of both trainers and spectators.

This finding has important implications for the question of what is "public," "shared," or "collective." The structure

---

[2] E. Ardener (1975) and S. Ardener (1975) refer to the inarticulated structure of meaning as the "muted" structure.

of meaning at the processual and contextual level is not always shared. It is the polysemes of each symbolic object and action—in other words, the reservoir of meaning—that is public in the sense that they have been shared by both groups of Japanese throughout history. Both groups are, in theory, capable of drawing on any of the several meanings of a symbolic object or action. But the processual and contextual structure of meaning, which lies closer to observable behavior, is not always shared.

Consequently, the story told by the trainer during the performance is not always heard or understood by the spectators. Indeed, in the case of the Medieval street performance and the 1980 festival performance, the story is heard upside down, as it were. These findings force us to qualify the basic semiotic definition of *ritual* as a communicative event, since the two groups of Japanese who read the ritual in inversion do not engage in direct communication, either during the ritual or afterward. Instead they engage in a complex mode of communication during which the hierarchy of and differences in their respective thought structures are broached, but only vaguely. Importantly, therefore, the fact that the trainer and the spectators "communicate" past one another is not clearly recognized either by the trainer or by the spectators. This situation is made possible because communication is effected through the ambiguous language of ritual (Leach 1965), in which the meanings of symbolic objects and actions retreat further away from an intentional theory of communication (Tambiah 1981). This is an important point with profound implications for culture change or its lack, as will be further discussed later in this chapter.

Moreover, the story told by trainers via their monkeys is less about themselves as special status people than about the culture and society of the dominant Japanese. The story is ultimately about the centrality of ambiguity and the ephemeral nature of cultural and social categories.

213

Contextual Denial of Indexicality

The performative approach to ritual in anthropology looks at ritual performance with an emphasis on the actor who is a nonidentical individual doing more than expressing collective representations. In this line of argument, the actor is seen to state his or her own case or tell his or her own story while following "conventionalized" forms, just as an English speaker using the personal pronoun "I" proclaims his or her own, unique individuality—referred to as "indexicality" in linguistics[3]—while using the linguistic code "I." In his application of indexicality to the performative dimension of ritual, Tambiah emphasizes the actors/participants as social personae or individuals in a social setting who are "creating, affirming, or legitimating their social positions and powers" (Tambiah 1981:154).[4]

While this is often the case with performances involving a homogeneous group of people, the involvement of the two groups of Japanese makes it nearly impossible for the trainer to use either his personal identity or his social per-

---

[3] Within the framework of the well-known trichotomy of the symbol, icon, and index proposed by Charles Peirce, index differs from both symbol and icon in that it is a sign that signifies its object through an existential connection to that object or to a sign of that object (Burks 1948–1949; the original definition of index by Peirce includes an existential connection only to the object itself, not to its sign. See also Barthes 1979:22–23; Jakobson 1971:esp. 132–33; Silverstein 1976). Unlike a symbol and an icon, an index relies upon the act of pointing, thereby involving message and process, rather than exclusively referring to codes and structures, as do symbols and icons. Shifters, such as personal pronouns, are simultaneously a symbol and an index and therefore have a duplex structure. The personal pronoun "I" is a symbol in that it represents the speaker by a conventional linguistic rule, and yet it is simultaneously an index since it must be in existential relation to its object (the speaker) in order to represent it. In other words, the personal pronoun "I" refers to a code—the abstract meaning of "I"—and at the same time it points to the nonidentical individual, "Mary."

[4] It should be added that Tambiah extends the difference between symbol/icon and index and equates the former with cosmology, culture, and structure, and the latter with hierarchy, society, process, and the individual.

sona to assert, negotiate, or legitimate his individual identity or his social position. This is because the spectators always are primarily the dominant Japanese. In their eyes, the fact that a person is a monkey trainer puts him in the straitjacket of the special status group, allowing no room for a particular trainer to be an individual. This is the case with both the stable and street performances. As for the social persona or the social position of the trainer, the monkey performance, as noted earlier, does not constitute an arena of direct communication. The story told by the trainer either falls on deaf ears, is heard in its inversion, or is only vaguely communicated.

Worse yet, the monkey performance may even increase the social distance between trainers and spectators, rather than narrowing it. Toward the end of the Medieval period and during the Early Modern period, the leaders of the special status people who performed the ritual at the Imperial Court and the Shogunal Palace were clearly distinguished from other members of the special status group in their having considerable wealth and political power over their fellow members. Their proximity to the symbolic and political authorities in Japanese society, facilitated through the performance of monkey dancing, likely served to enhance their special position within their own community.

Yet, no matter how much the trainers were distinguished as individuals among the special status group, their performance identified them as members of that group in the eyes of the spectators. It placed and (as in the case of the 1980 performance) continues to place them in the straitjacket of a stereotype, denying them any assertion as unique individuals. Since there is no physical characteristic that identifies the members of the special status group, they can go unnoticed. Yet, by the very act of the monkey performance, they are suddenly labeled as such by the dominant Japanese. In other words, the monkey performance may serve to highlight the social distance that otherwise

215

might not be recognized. In the eyes of the spectators, be they an emperor or a shogun of an earlier period or the contemporary Japanese who know the art as a marker of the special status group, the trainer's "I" represents at all times the collective self of the special status people. The indexical "I," in the sense of either a unique individual or a social persona, may, therefore, be achieved only in the trainer's mind or in the eyes of fellow members of the group.

It follows, then, that, contrary to the ideology which sees the individualism of a unique person as the logical opposite or contradiction of a group and its collective sentiment, indexicality within the performative dimension presupposes the sharing of group identity and culture; only then do differences among members emerge as unique individuality.

Metaphysical Imagination without Power

Some anthropologists, such as V. Turner (e.g., 1969:42–43), who stress the "evocative" power of symbols, consider rituals and symbols to have the power to evoke participants to take action. Others see limited power in symbolic communication. For example, Langer (1980:153) emphasizes the logical nature of the feelings expressed in ritual—feelings that usually do not have "cathartic" value. Tambiah elaborates upon the "distancing" nature of ritual performance, which "separates the private emotions of the actors from their commitment to a public morality" (Tambiah 1981:124).

In addition to the contextual denial of indexicality, the monkey performance shares other constraints that are common in ritual performance in particular and symbolic communication in general, and that reduce its evocative power. In the case of the monkey performance, the ambiguity of ritual/symbolic communication is even more pronounced because communication between trainers and spectators is carried out indirectly through the monkey. In short, the monkey performance embodies a powerful moral message and sophisticated metaphysical contemplation, but it is unlikely that it prods people into social mobilization—a point I will return to in a later section.

STRUCTURAL REGULARITIES IN TRANSFORMATION

Polysemes of Anomalous Symbols

The material presented in this book reveals that identical meanings have been assigned to the monkey and the special status people, both occupying a structurally peripheral position in the respective categories of deities and humans. Thus, two "marginals," one among the sacred (nature deities) and the other in human society, have been assigned the meaning and power of a mediator, trickster-scapegoat, and clown.

In ethnographic literature, these meanings are assigned to so-called marginal or anomalous/ambiguous symbols and have received much attention in anthropology. However, these studies have usually located a mediator here, a trickster there, and so on, either in separate contexts within a culture or even from different cultures. In short, ethnographic treatment of these symbols has provided us only with a synchronic series of still photos, as it were, without systematically examining either ethnographic or theoretical relationships among them.

The data from Japanese culture testify that all of these meanings are assigned to two polysemic symbols with structurally marginal status—the monkey and the special status people—as a historical-ethnographic fact, rather than as logical possibilities proposed in the abstract by anthropologists. The historical-ethnographic evidence found in Japanese culture tells us that all of these meanings are indeed closely related, and that particular symbolic figures— the monkey and the special status people—are assigned

217

structurally related roles and meanings in contexts that differ in time and space.

As noted in Chapter 6, all the meanings assigned to the monkey and the special status people are structurally or logically related to each other. To recapitulate, the structural marginality provides these figures with the basis for becoming mediators when cross-categorical traffic is in need, and for becoming scapegoats when the structure calls for the reinforcement of boundary markers. This does not necessarily halt traffic between categories. Taboos and scapegoats may be necessary precisely because there is cross-categorical traffic; taboos and scapegoats help retain useful interaction between categories without eradicating the boundaries by permitting taboos to be broken as long as purification restores the original state. I coined the term "breakable taboos" to refer to these taboos and scapegoats. If scapegoats can create a distance from themselves, then they can laugh at themselves while laughing at the system itself; this is when scapegoats become clowns. All these roles derive from the structural marginality assigned to these objects and beings.

Importantly, it is the fundamental character of the dualistic universe that gives rise to "breakable taboos," since the most basic principles of the dualistic universe are flexible boundary lines and the accommodation of opposite principles.

Metonym and Metaphor: Transformation and Counter-Transformation

An intriguing characteristic of the symbolism of the monkey and of the special status people is that both involve the two basic modes of human symbolization—metonym and metaphor. Although metonym and metaphor represent complex concepts variously defined by scholars, I use the term *metonym* to refer to a symbol whose relationship to its referent is characterized by contiguity, and I use *metaphor* to mean a symbol that represents its referent through a similarity or analogy between the two. An important requirement for a metaphor is that at the denotative level, an object, a being, or a phenomenon chosen as a metaphor must be in a separate category in the classificatory system from that which it represents (Basso 1981). In the case of the monkey as a metaphor for humans, for example, the monkey belongs to the category of animals (deities), while humans occupy a separate category of beings.

The monkey as mediator between deities and humans in early history reveals the Japanese perception of contiguity between humans and monkeys; the monkey was chosen as mediator precisely because of the proximity which the early Japanese saw between it and humans. But it is the similarities perceived by the Japanese between themselves and monkeys that is the basis for the proximity between the two. Unlike other animals, monkeys were seen to be similar to humans and, therefore, contiguous with them; that is, the metaphoric relationship between monkeys and humans underlies the metonymic relationship between the two. The monkey as scapegoat involves a mechanism whereby the Japanese establish an analogy between the monkey and the negative side of the humans: the monkey represents a part—that is, the negative side—of the whole—that is, the Japanese. Again, this metaphoric relationship places the Japanese and the monkey in a contiguous relationship.

Being Japanese, the special status people have always been contiguous with the dominant Japanese. But their peripheral position rendered them mediators in early history. Like the monkey, they too became scapegoats. As scapegoats, they have stood in a metaphoric relationship with the dominant Japanese, since the negative meaning assigned to special status people is the projection of the negative side of the dominant Japanese. While the monkey can be an explicit metaphor projecting the negative side of humans, the special status people as scapegoats carrying and reflecting the negative side of the Japanese is only an implicit metaphor. Nevertheless, both metaphoric and metonymic modes of symbolization are involved here, as in the case of the monkey.

Because of the simultaneous presence of distance and proximity between the Japanese, on the one hand, and the monkey and the special status people, on the other, the latter two stand *simultaneously* in a metaphoric and metonymic relationship to the Japanese. The monkey, which is "naturally" discontinuous from humans, has been a metaphor for culturally perceived contiguity between humans and monkeys. The special status people, on the other hand, who are "naturally" contiguous or identical with the dominant Japanese, are a metaphor for the negative side of the Japanese—the association indicating that a distance and a distinct categorical identity between the two groups are presupposed. These meanings, then, represent more than transformations between the syntagmatic (metonymic) chains and the paradigmatic (metaphoric) relations.[5] They are simultaneously in a metonymic and metaphoric relationship to their referent, that is, the Japanese.

From the point of view of historical changes, the structural relationship between the metonymic and metaphoric meanings of these symbols indicates that the transformations of their meanings through history have been structurally patterned.

The Japanese material offers a broader implication for our understanding of mediator and scapegoat. In short, the relationship between mediator and scapegoat in general is

---

[5] For discussions of transformations between metaphor and metonym, see Fernandez (1974:125–26, 1982:558–62) and Lévi-Strauss (1966:150).

characterized by transformation and counter-transformation between metonym and metaphor. That is, mediator and scapegoat are transformations of the same structural meaning.

HISTORICAL REGULARITIES

Leaving the synchronic analysis, I now turn to the historical dimensions of this study. From a historical perspective, a major finding pertaining to the meaning of these symbols is that, while these meanings have persisted from the earliest times to the present, the dominant meaning has shifted from mediator to scapegoat and finally to clown in different historical periods. These historical regularities constitute another finding: the transformations of these meanings took place about the same time for the monkey as they did for the special status people, and, in addition, the transformations in the meanings of these symbols coincided with two periods of major transformations in Japanese society and culture in general.

After a brief discussion of historical actors, the rest of this section will be devoted to the issue of change over time versus structural stability.

Historical Actors

Historical transformations do not take place in a vacuum. They are always mediated by the perceptions and actions of historical actors who experience with feelings and thoughts various cultural and social representations and transformations. The importance of historical actors as forces for change in meaning of the special status people is clearly evident in the role played by Hideyoshi, "the monkey regent." It was he who created the legally defined caste of kawata to which the special status people were assigned. Up to that time, the special status people had been only loosely grouped together and had enjoyed considerable freedom. And although the tendency toward increased rigidity in the social structure and the value system had been underway, it took Hideyoshi, a particular historical actor, to institutionalize the tendency. Institutionalization of rigidity in turn accelerated the process by which the special status people not only were legally placed outside society but also were assigned the negative moral value of impurity.

Another example of the importance of historical actors is found in contemporary monkey trainers. It is they who revived the then-extinct art of the monkey performance and developed it into a clowning act. There is a long tradition of clowning in Japanese culture, and the contemporary monkey performance is a development related to, if not born of, this tradition. Yet, the particular form and content of the clowning act staged by Murasaki Tarō are of his own creation. His clowning focuses on juggling the social hierarchy and the hierarchy of humans and animals—and, by implication, on his own identity as a member of the special status group—rather than on sex, for example, which is the focus of clowning in many societies.

However, Murasaki Tarō as historical actor is not the same as Toyotomi Hideyoshi as historical actor. Murasaki Tarō does not directly or immediately affect the course of history. He neither negotiates his social position nor provokes spectators into action. His power as historical actor remains primarily metaphysical: in the atmosphere of play, he gently prods spectators to contemplate their society.

In this way, a subtle but potentially powerful historical event is produced at the seat of action—a creation by a genius in a performing art who acts upon the structure of thought and the structure of society in the process of creating a metaphysical masterpiece.

Polysemes and Their Transformations

The essentially Saussurian model of structure and process—analytically separate concepts that fuse in reality—is one powerful model used to explain the mechanism of change. The lack of fit and arbitrariness between language and the world, or between signs and actual objects, phenomena, and so forth, provide room for change. The contradiction between homonymy and synonymy produces a situation whereby "the signifier tries to have functions other than its own," while "the signified tries to be expressed by means other than its sign" (Karcevskij 1982:54).

While the Saussurian model is basically capable of explaining changes, it makes the implicit assumption that a symbol is univocal, that is, a signifier has one signified. The assumption derives from the fact that the Saussurian model is a linguistic model and is concerned only with the denotative meaning of a signifier. Symbols, including linguistic ones, however, are rarely univocal (cf. Ohnuki-Tierney 1981b).

As a signifier, a polysemic symbol can take on additional meanings; in fact, it always has more than one meaning. Polysemic symbols therefore embody an inherent mechanism to overcome the basic contradiction between the signifier (form) and the signified (meaning). Put another way, a polysemic symbol often prevents a situation in which the meaning of a symbol "outruns" the symbol (cf. Barthes 1979:38).

Since polysemes always have several meanings to which individuals can relate, multivocality may facilitate changes whereby polysemes take turns being the dominant meaning. On the other hand, the same mechanism, coupled with the ambiguity of ritual communication which does not immediately reveal non-sharing of meaning among participants, may inadvertently retard culture change by disguis-

223

ing fundamental contradictions. At the very best, we can predict that the cumulative effect of shrouded messages in a ritual such as the monkey performance will take a subtle form and a long time to make known their impact on the course of history.

Transformations as Structural Continuity

The decisive advantage of a study that takes in a long period of time is that it enables us to compare a series of transformations, whether they are changes in the meaning of a symbol or changes in a culture and society at large. Instead of looking at a stage of development, we can examine the entire cycle of transformation, thereby moving beyond the simple conclusion that a particular change represents transformation; that is, we can identify the nature of that particular transformation.

This study points to two findings: the persistence of the internal logic of the order of meaning and historical regularities in the timing of changes. These two findings are closely related, and together they raise two interrelated questions. First, what changes in the form or meaning of a symbol constitute true transformation? Put the other way, how do we assess different types of change—reproduction, random change, and transformation? Second, what is the meaning of historical regularities in regard to the dynamics of change? Let me address these questions in turn.

Broadly speaking, there are three types of change: reproduction, random change, and transformation. Reproduction signifies no change in structure, and random change refers to changes that are haphazard, showing little regularity or no pattern in the way they occur. Both types of change seldom take place in reality. Although the term "transformation" has been abused too often to be meaningful, I continue to use it to refer to one type of change that opposes both reproduction and random change. While there are several types of transformation (cf. Needham 1979:38–47; Yalman 1967:77), they are all permutations of the same structure.

The structural regularities between the meanings assigned to the monkey and those assigned to the special status people suggest that the changes may be seen as transformations within the structure, since they are neither simple reproductions nor random changes. This means, then, that the symbolic structure of the Japanese has undergone little basic change since the first recorded documents were published in the eighth century. This is a somewhat astounding finding, given that the more than one thousand years of recorded history encompassed by this study have included wars, famines, earthquakes, replacement of emperors by military governments during both the Early Modern period and World War II, and even conquests of other peoples as well as the conquest of the Japanese by the Allied forces. These major historical changes have rocked the very foundations of Japanese culture and society.

There are other studies that support the finding of long-term stability in regard to certain features and principles of Japanese culture and society. R. Smith (1962) has meticulously demonstrated the stability of kinship terms over the last twelve thousand years, while Najita (1974) sees what he calls "bureaucratism (bureaucratic pragmatism)" and "intuitive idealism" as the two dominant principles that have governed the behavior of the Japanese ever since the Early Modern period.[6]

[6] My argument here on the continuation of the basic structure should be clearly separated from an a priori assumption that the stability of Japanese culture demonstrates its superior nature; this assumption is held by some scholars of *nihonjinron* (theories about the Japanese), a genre of Japanese scholarship whose focus is on the identity of the Japanese and their culture. The publications of these scholars in turn have received the attention of Western scholars of Japan, who view them as a part of the "ethnography" of Japan.

In using the terms "stability," "continuity," "distinct," and "unique," I

Studies of other cultures also point to the stability of the basic sociocultural structure. A collaborative work by De Craemer, Vansina, and Fox (1976) indicates that Central African cultural patterns have been flexible but stable, and that the common religion has been remarkably stable, probably for millennia. In a general statement about history, Braudel comments that "the social content can renew itself almost completely without ever reaching certain deep-seated structural characteristics," and that "structure" becomes "stable elements for an infinite number of generations" (Braudel 1980:12, 31).

On the other hand, to dismiss these changes in the meaning system of Japanese culture simply as transformations of the unchanging basic structure gives us merely an illusion of an understanding, preventing further scrutiny about the nature of change.

To this end, I will engage in two tasks. First, I will reexamine the polysemes assigned to the monkey and the special status people and identify differences between the various meanings. Second, I will compare and contrast the historical contexts in which each of these meanings occupied a dominant position.

Transformations as Historical Changes

From Mediator to Scapegoat   Of all the meanings assigned to the monkey and the special status people, the mediator alone presupposes a belief in their supernatural power. Thus, the transformation in meaning from mediator to scapegoat reveals that some type of "secularization" has taken place. But we must be careful about using the term

---

do not imply any value judgment. I do think, however, that every culture is unique, and I concur with Vansina (1970:177), who argues that the uniqueness of a culture emerges with "a unique combination of factors which are not unique in themselves." Again, a systematic examination of historical regularities often can powerfully demonstrate the distinctiveness of a particular culture.

"secularization" when we are dealing with religions such as those of the Japanese, because the distinction between the sacred and the secular is quite different from that in the Judeo-Christian tradition. The Japanese, or at least the folk Japanese, have always behaved like magicians, manipulating supernatural beings who are assigned various roles having to do with the well-being of humans. Furthermore, "religion" has never been a separate category of activity for the Japanese. In Japanese culture, entertainment, art, and performing art were all inseparable in early history, and all were endowed with religious meaning. This is reflected in the early history of the special status people. As we saw in Chapter 4, some of the special status people at the time who were funeral attendants were called *asobi-be* (people who "play"), and their "religious" performance was accompanied by the "play" of dancing, music, and merrymaking. Even in later history and, in fact, today, some of the entertainments are believed to have "magial power," if not "religious" power.

While the "magical" attitude toward supernaturals continues to exist in contemporary Japan (cf. Ohnuki-Tierney 1984a:123–66), both the monkey in the monkey performance and the special status people have gradually lost their supernatural power to mediate. There is a radical difference between the monkey that is assigned supernatural power, in which people individually or collectively believed, and the monkey that is laughed at as simply "a human minus three pieces of hair."

A profound implication of the "secularization" process has been the loss of the non-formalized power that once accrued to the special status people. Without such power, the special status people have been left only with the negative value of impurity and with a fate as scapegoats.

There is another important point about the difference between mediator and scapegoat. The transformation of meaning from mediator to scapegoat indicates profound shifts in the rigidity or flexibility of the structure of culture. A structure of thought that encourages mediation as a way of facilitating inter-categorical traffic is far more flexible than a structure that facilitates the traffic through breakable taboos. We might think of a culture as an entity that tightens or relaxes its grids, or categorical principles. Changes in the degree of flexibility of the system, even in the absence of changes in the basic structure, are profound qualitative changes.

From Scapegoat to Clown   The shift of meaning to clown also represents a radical change. A clown is radically different from both mediator and scapegoat. While the meanings of mediator and scapegoat are on the same level of abstraction, as noted in Chapter 2, the meaning of a clown is at a higher level of abstraction. Thus, while both mediator and scapegoat are intimately involved in the reflexive structure of the Japanese, they themselves are not reflexive; that is, these figures do not represent the capacity to distance oneself from oneself, or to render oneself a sign. A clown alone is capable of being outside of its own structure, that is, outside its culture and society. Only the clown is truly reflexive, in that he represents a figure whose distance from himself enables him to mock himself as a representation of the structure or order of meaning. This capacity enables him to offer metasocial commentaries about the structure.

In short, the two types of transformation of meaning represent changes, and these changes took place historically, as I summarize in the next section.

Historical Contexts   While the above examination of the differences in meaning is illuminating, it does not tell us why a particular transformation took place; that is, the structural relationships, or the internal logic of the system of meaning, provide only possible directions for change. Why one among several possible meanings is selected must be explained in terms of historical contexts.

I do not subscribe here either to assigning primacy to "external" factors or to giving autonomy to the internal logic of the symbolic structure. Rather, I am interested in examining historical contexts in order to understand their relationships to the transformations in the meaning of the monkey and the special status people.

I contend not only that there is no simple "historical causality" for symbolic transformations, but also that no single dimension of a culture holds primacy over other dimensions of that culture, although any one subsystem may be "a dominant site of symbolic production" in a given culture (Sahlins 1976:211). Thus, I do not take a Durkheimian position, as does Douglas who argues that social systems "generate" conceptual categories (Douglas 1975:e.g., 296).[7]

[7] Neither do I side with the practice argument (well delineated but argued against by Sahlins 1976). I must admit, however, that in order to engage in sophisticated argument about the "political economy of meaning," to borrow Eickelman's (1979) phrase, I would need to engage in an intensive "serial history" (Braudel 1980); that is, I would have to qualitatively assess quantitative data on, for example, the income of various occupations held by the special status people, and I would have to examine Japan's political economy in general. But even in the absence of such evidence, reasons for refuting a simple "practical reason" explanation abound. During the late Medieval period, when Japan was involved in cyclical conquests by warlords, those who engaged in manufacturing leather goods were economically quite successful, since their skill was needed to armor warriors and their horses. However, their economic success did not lead them to upward social mobility. In fact, those whose achievements were in religion and the arts, rather than in manufacturing goods, fared better in their upward mobility during the late Medieval period, which saw an efflorescence of the arts. Thus individual members of the special status group who excelled in their achievements were able to denounce their ascribed status until the Early Modern period, when legal sanctions and cultural rigidity terminated such freedoms. To take one more example, leaders of the group during the Early Modern period were as wealthy as some feudal lords, and they were politically in command of a large number of special status people. Yet, it was during the Early Modern period that their "outcaste" status was legally codified for the first time in history. In his analysis of the Indian caste system, Dumont (1970) argues to restrict

The social structure of the Early Modern period, then, was *not*, in my view, the determinant of the rigidified conceptual structure; both social structure and conceptual structure became rigidified roughly at the same time through a process in which each influenced the other. The emergence of scapegoats was its expression.

The findings presented in this book reveal that the two major transformations in the meaning of the monkey and the special status people coincided with two periods in which major transitions in Japanese history took place—the latter half of the Medieval period to the Early Modern period and the present.

Importantly, the contrast between mediator and scapegoat that is based on structural principles is paralleled by the contrast between the periods in which the two meanings occur. Culture and society were relatively flexible during the earlier part of Japan's history. Although the society was stratified, there was considerable mobility, and the cosmology was pervasively dualistic, admitting no absolute hegemony by a single set of values or sector of society. But around the late Medieval period, increasing rigidity became apparent in all spheres of Japanese culture, a tendency that reached its height during the Early Modern period. We saw that the latter half of the Medieval period was pregnant with opposing forces in culture and society, but that it eventually developed into the society of the Early Modern

---

economic-political criteria to the power accessible to the four castes in the middle in Indian society, but not to the Brahmans and Untouchables whose positions are based upon religious values of purity and impurity. Dumont's argument artificially separates the economic-political and the religious-symbolic. I would argue that the meaning assigned to the economic-political activities is crucial in determining the allocation of power/authority in the economic and political arenas. Geertz's (1980:13) insight that in Bali "[p]ower served pomp, not pomp power," and Evans-Prichard's (1940:215) observation that "the *diel* [aristocrats] have prestige rather than rank and influence rather than power," are cross-cultural findings that challenge economic determinism.

period. Within, the society became further stratified along the lines of occupational specialization and sex, a shift that had dire consequences for the special status people and for women in general. Without, trade and other forms of contact with foreigners were virtually forbidden.

This historical transition in Japanese society coincided with the transformation of the monkey and the special status people from mediator to scapegoat. The parallel transformations offer a good fit. The stratified society with highly developed occupational specialization must rely on the interdependence of people, and the monkey trainers were vital to the welfare of the horses of farmers and warriors. Yet maintenance of the "caste system" also depended on sharp boundary lines between the two groups.

A parallel phenomenon was present in the symbolic structure at the time. As noted earlier, taboos and scapegoats function both to facilitate cross-categorical traffic and to mark boundaries. Embodying the impurity caused by boundary transgressions and requiring purification by ritual, breakable taboos and scapegoats highlight boundaries while accommodating inter-categorical traffic. In short, scapegoats in society and symbolic scapegoats both were manifestations of the rigidified system of the Early Modern period.

There is another dimension to the parallel between society and symbolic structure. We noted that the Early Modern period began with the closure of the society to foreigners, who in the symbolic structure represented stranger-deities and the source of the vital energy of purity needed to rejuvenate the self of humans. In their absence, another means of rejuvenation had to be utilized—hence, the emphasis on scapegoats. In contrast to rejuvenation by bringing in the positive element from outside—the role assigned to mediators—scapegoats provided a means whereby people rejuvenated themselves by getting rid of their negative side, dumping it, as it were, onto scapegoats.[8] Scapegoats became "naturally" impure, providing justification for the prejudice harbored by the dominant Japanese toward them. Thus, we see again interrelated expressions of the rigidity of the system both in the social structure and in the symbolic structure.

The two structures—one with mediators and one with scapegoats—may share the same classificatory principles, yet they operate in a radically different manner. Thus, we can argue that increasing systemic rigidity was responsible for transforming structural marginals, that is, the monkey and the special status people, from mediators to scapegoats. We cannot afford to dismiss a change in the degree of flexibility/rigidity of a structure by calling it "essential stability," since this type of change constitutes a basic qualitative change in the structure. The structural principles may remain the same, and in that sense the structure does not change through time. But the degree to which the structural principles operate may loosen or tighten, and these changes are fundamental.

To reiterate, neither the social structure nor the conceptual structure of the Early Modern period served as the causal agent of the other, although both structures mutually influenced the other, and this in turn affected the direction toward increased rigidity of Japanese culture. Put another way, the arrows of causation must be seen as two-directional: the social structure and the symbolic structure mutually influenced each other in their process of change, and they also had an impact on the system at large, which in turn influenced the subsequent course of change in both the social structure and the symbolic structure. A concrete example of this process is the codification of the "caste system" by Hideyoshi at the very end of the Medieval period. What he did was to codify the "naturalization" of impurity

---

[8] Cf. Burke's (1955:407) analysis of the Jews in Nazi Germany.

232

that had been developing. But his codification in turn reinforced the degree to which the impurity of the special status people was seen as "natural." In short, the structure of thought, the structure of values, and the social structure were mutually acting upon each other in a process whereby the caste system and the naturalization of impurity of the special status people became historical facts.

The second period in which the meaning of the monkey and the special status people was transformed is contemporary Japan. Any assessment of contemporary Japan must be tentative. The myriad waves and ripples of history have not settled enough yet for us to evaluate the degree of lasting impact they will have upon the basic structure of culture. However, there is no doubt that it is a period of exhilarating transition.

This period is similar to the latter half of the Medieval period, on the one hand, and is the inversion of the trends during the Early Modern period, on the other. Fluidity of the social structure in contemporary Japan is manifested both internally and externally. Internally, various opposing forces are at work, just as they were in the late Medieval period. Externally—again similar to the latter half of the Medieval period—the Japanese people are exploring the outside, as manifested in the millions of Japanese tourists in countries all over the world, including the People's Republic of China, which once provided Japan with a writing system, technology, a political structure, and a host of other vital cultural apparatus.

A fundamental change unique to contemporary Japan, however, concerns the changing perception of the Japanese self associated with the country's recent technological development. It is technology that once defined the superiority of Western civilization in the eyes of the Japanese near the end of the nineteenth century, when the country was reopened. Symbolically, foreigners represent the transcendental self to be emulated by the Japanese. The Japanese effort to excel in technology is motivated by the symbolic position that technology occupies. By superseding the technology of the West, the Japanese no longer feel inferior to the other. Their "conquest," as many Japanese see it, of the world market in "high tech," the automobile industry, and other economic-technological spheres therefore should not be seen as economic success as such. As a representation of the transcendental self, the symbolic value of technology and industry has motivated the Japanese to excel in this area, and the Japanese achievement in technology in turn has had a profound impact on their concept of the collective self. We see a complex picture in which the internal logic of the symbolic structure provides symbolic meaning to "external" phenomena, such as foreigners. It is the symbolic meaning of technology that has been at least partially responsible for the Japanese effort in technological advancement, which in turn has affected the structure of reflexivity. Causal arrows are again operating in two directions.

From the perspective of the structure of reflexivity, therefore, the present is a new era for the Japanese, who feel for the first time in their history that they have "mastered" the outside, the other, whose negative power devastated the country in 1945. Therefore, while contemporary Japan is similar to the late Medieval period, from the perspective of the Japanese relationship to the other, it constitutes an inversion of the traditional hierarchy between the self and the other. This inversion is a drastic change and is happening for the first time to the Japanese, over whom the Chinese and Westerners had always claimed superiority.

It is a period of intense reflexivity. It is not a simple coincidence, then, that we see the emergence of a reflexive monkey. However, the monkey is not just passively reflecting the reflexivity of the contemporary Japanese. It is definitely urging the Japanese to examine critically the basic as-

234

sumptions of Japanese culture and society, thereby contributing to ever-moving historical forces.

In assessing the changes in contemporary Japan, we must refrain from making premature judgments about the long-term impact of these changes upon the structure of meaning. Eventually, our reflexive monkey will tell us again about the changes we observe in contemporary Japan by donning yet another meaning—if not clown, something else.

For our perennial problem of *plus ça change*, the study of a culture over a long period enables us to see the complex picture of the system of meaning, both its stability and its changes. Like polysemes, Japanese culture has multiple structures, consisting of flexible and "egalitarian" tendencies on the one hand and rigid and "hierarchical" tendencies on the other.[9] Historical events and historical actors interact with these principles, creating the dynamic processes of history. At some times, as during the late Medieval period, both tendencies become conspicuous because they are in competition with each other. At other times, as during the Early Modern period, one claims hegemony over the other. Had we looked at one particular period of history, we would have had a snapshot of one phase of the total structure and process. The significance of the monkey as a reflexive metaphor cannot be understood without examining the changing phases of its complex structure of meaning, as each phase is historically actualized.

HISTORY, MYTH, AND RITUAL

A long-term study of a culture has another advantage. It enables us to examine the relationship between history on the one hand and a specific body of myth and a particular ritual

[9] It should be clearly noted here that the "egalitarian" and the "hierarchical" in the context of Japan are quite different from egalitarian and hierarchical principles as conceived or practiced in some Western societies.

on the other. We can also avoid an a priori equation of myth and ritual with history, and of historicity, or the way people conceive of history, with history itself. For example, we can attempt to determine whether the myth of the stranger-deity has served as a model for interpreting events—such as the Japanese interaction with Mongols, Chinese, and Westerners—during different historical periods. If we discover that the stranger-deity has not served as a model for interpreting forces outside Japan in different historical periods, the myth remains a myth, rather than a part of history. If it did, however, as I argued in Chapter 6, the myth becomes a part of the historical process.

A long-term historical study also enables us to compare the structure of consciousness and its transformations as expressed in *historical processes* with the structure of consciousness as expressed in a specific myth and ritual. Both myth and ritual have a tendency to retain a structure of meaning independent of historical changes and the intentionality of the actors involved. In the case of the monkey and the special status people, their meanings as mediator, scapegoat, and clown are found in data dated to different historical periods. They therefore constitute historical transformations. The same set of meanings is found in both ritual and myth. We saw the monkey as mediator in stable ritual, and as scapegoat and clown in different types of street entertainment. In the myth-history of the *Kojiki* and the *Nihongi*, we saw that the Monkey Deity (Saruta Biko) was a mediator, scapegoat, and clown all at once.

Despite close correlations, there are some differences between the structure of meaning as expressed in the performance and the one expressed in history. In the case of the monkey performance during the Medieval period and contemporary monkey performances in the parks, we see all the meanings: the monkey is a mediator, a scapegoat, and a trickster turning into a clown. In other words, in both cases the monkey embodies all the meanings and their

236

transformations as unfolded in Japanese history. Here, the symbolic structure during a ritual is an exact replica of the historical transformation of these meanings. However, in the other types of monkey performances, only one meaning is expressed. In short, there seems to be at times a complete fit and at other times a partial fit between the structure of meaning expressed in a given ritual and the one expressed in the course of history.

Likewise, a close but not isomorphic correspondence is found between the structure of meaning of myth and that of history. However, the Monkey Deity as a clown-scapegoat who offers himself as a target of the spectators' laughter is radically different from the monkey as a scapegoat in history, which received a value of radical negativity.

Nevertheless, one may argue that the myth of the eighth century was indeed a charter for both ritual and history, and that the latter two are simply permutations of the basic structure already embedded in the myth. I must reiterate, however, that the sequence of the changes in the meaning of the monkey and the special status people—from mediator to scapegoat to clown—was ordered by historical processes; the particular sequence of transformation was not a given of the structural constraints.

Similarly, the stranger-deity with dual power who resides outside has served as a model for interpreting outsiders as well as marginals throughout history. The dialectic definition of the self in relation to the other as embedded in the monkey metaphor has served as a model that extends interdependence only to insiders and marginates outsiders who become insiders. Although these models are tools that the Japanese have used to interpret Chinese and Westerners, as well as such outsiders as enemies in wars, their role as models for interpretation is most vividly illustrated in the changing meaning of the special status people. As migrant religious/artistic specialists, they were endowed with positive power and welcomed by the members of a settlement when they visited. However, once they became residents, as they were forced to, they became scapegoats. As outsiders, then, they could enter the settlement only temporarily and under prescribed circumstances, but they were punished with negative marking when they stayed permanently. Therefore, the stranger-deity and the monkey metaphor as conceptual models dialectically interacted with historical events. They powerfully chartered the way people conceived of historical events, thereby constructing historical processes.

Time is continuous, while history is discontinuous, punctuated by the people who interpret temporal flow and historical events. History is not repeatable. Myths and ritual, on the other hand, are repeatable, or, more accurately, time is arrested in myths and ritual, in which we find dynamic synchronicity. All three provide sources for historicity, which exercises its own selection in people's construction of history. The findings presented in this book suggest a good although not isomorphic fit between history on the one hand and myth and ritual on the other. I must emphasize here that my method is inductive. I did not directly extract history from the myths, nor did I extract historical transformations of the meaning of these symbols from ritual. Despite their interrelatedness, history, myth, and ritual are treated as analytically separate.

Musings on the Reflexive Monkey

The monkey, like clowns and tricksters in many other societies, transcends its contradictions and challenges many cherished assumptions of the Japanese. But if we confine our observation to a short period and only to the most empirical level, there are limitations to the symbolic power of the monkey and the monkey performance. As metaphors, their revelations are indirect, and they conceal the meanings of their referents, the Japanese. Moreover, the monkey performance suffers from the ambiguity of symbolic communication.

Scholars have stressed the impotence of clowns and tricksters in facilitating social mobility. Beidelman (1980) argues that the intellectual/symbolic centrality of the trickster seldom translates into social centrality. Socially, Pierrot or Tonio Kröger muses at the periphery, or outside the trees in order to see the forest, as Peacock (1971) would put it. Commenting on symbolic productions in general, Fernandez (1980:22) argues that they "act more to excite the moral imagination than to alert it to its duty."

In most societies, clowns have neither led a revolution nor mobilized a crowd to mass demonstration. Yet I think we risk being short-sighted if we completely write off the practical power of clowns. We must be patient and look for the long-term effect of that power, not anticipate an immediate or direct effect upon Japanese culture and society. In the absence of concrete evidence of that effect I must simply speculate that these metaphysical voices are not simply on the fringe like pale shadows, but somehow nibble away at the core of the structure, albeit gradually and quietly. Their cumulative effect may be more powerful than a revolution, like raindrops imperceptibly transforming the shape of a rock. Had we not had during the Medieval period the monkey charming the lord into a compassionate human with a love of dancing, or had we not had during the 1930s the monkey dropping a torpedo while making a dash into enemy territory, the course of Japanese history might have been different. These monkeys have represented the forces that oppose the rigid hierarchical tendency in Japanese culture and society, always calling the structure into question and reminding people that there are alternatives. They have kept the moment of opposition going. Who knows how many contemporary spectators, young and old, think about the centrality of ambiguity and the darker side of their society, which has made a scapegoat out of the monkey and the special status people? If they do not reflect upon it now, they may do so years later. Such subtle changes are nearly invisible and are slow to show their effect on the reordering of society. Only history will tell, perhaps only several hundred years from now. But observing Tarō and Jirō performing in an open area under a blue sky and amidst the laughter of spectators, I became much more optimistic about the effect on society that these trainers and special status people have had and will have than when I first observed the performance during its frail revival in 1980.

Watching the monkey performance at the park, I suddenly realized that the monkey was the embodiment of the transformational process itself—both historical and cultural. Historically, it is transforming the past through the present into the future; it is the seat of historical transformation. Culturally, the monkey is transforming nature into culture, illness into health, the savage lord into a dancing human, and thereby transforming Japanese culture and history. Above all, the monkey represents the generative power of the Japanese who are engaged in the never-ending quest for the transcendental self—the force that drives the Japanese to reach for the moon—economic, technological, and, above all, reflexive. The quest, then, is not a matter of pragmatic achievements, as it appears on the surface. Rather, it is a quest with an aesthetic nature: the effort for and the process of transcendence provide the Japanese with an aesthetic experience; the practical achievements are but by-products.

References

Akima, Toshio. 1972. Shisha no uta: Saimei Tennō no Kayō to Aso-bibe (The songs of the dead: Songs of Emperor Saimei and Asobibe). *Bungaku* 40(3):97–112.

———. 1982. The songs of the dead: Poetry, drama, and ancient rituals of Japan. *Journal of Asian Studies* 41(3):485–509.

Akisada, Yoshikazu. 1978. Suiheisha Undō to Yūwa Seisaku (The Suiheisha Movement and the Yūwa Policy). In *Buraku Mondai Gaisetsu* (Introduction to Buraku Problems). Buraku Kaihō Kenkyūsho, ed. Osaka: Kaihō Shuppansha. Pp. 161–88.

Amino, Yoshihiko. 1980. *Nihon Chūsei no Minshūzō—Heimin to Shokunin* (Portrait of the Folk in Medieval Japan—The Common People and the "Professionals"). Tokyo: Iwanami Sho-ten.

———. 1983. *Muen Kugai Raku—Nihon Chūsei no Jiyū to Heiwa (Muen, Kugai, and Raku*—Freedom and Peace in Medieval Japan). [1978] Tokyo: Heibonsha.

———. 1984. Chūsei no tabibitotachi (Travelers during the Medieval period). In *Hyōhaku to Teijū* (Wandering and Settlement). Y. Amino et al., eds. Tokyo: Shōgakukan. Pp. 153–266.

Appadurai, Arjun. 1986. Theory in anthropology: Center and periphery. *Comparative Studies in Society and History* 28(2):356–61.

Ardener, Edwin. 1975. The "problem" revisited. In *Perceiving Women*. S. Ardener, ed. London: J. M. Dent & Sons/New York: John Wiley & Sons. Pp. 19–27.

Ardener, Shirley. 1975. Introduction. In *Perceiving Women*. S. Ardener, ed. London: J. M. Dent & Sons/New York: John Wiley & Sons. Pp. vii–xxiii.

Asakura, Haruhiko, Shōji Inokuchi, Hirohiko Okano, and Takeshi Matsumae, eds. 1969. *Shinwa Densetsu Jiten* (Dictionary of Myths and Folktales). [1963] Tokyo: Tōkyōdō.

Asquith, Pamela. 1984. Reichōruigaku no hōkō (Trends in the study of primates). *Shisō* 3:36–51.

Aston, W. G., trans. 1956. *Nihongi: Chronicles of Japan from the Earliest Times to A.D. 697*. [1896] London: George Allen & Unwin.

Babcock, Barbara. 1980. Reflexivity: Definitions and discriminations. *Semiotica* 30(1/2):1–14.

———. 1984. Arrange me into disorder: Fragments and reflections on ritual clowning. In *Rite, Drama, Festival Spectacle*. J. J. MacAloon, ed. Philadelphia: Institute for the Study of Human Issues. Pp. 102–28.

Babcock, Barbara, ed. 1978. *The Reversible World*. Ithaca: Cornell University Press.

Bakhtin, Mikhail. 1984. *Rabelais and His World*. [Original publication in Russian in 1965.] Bloomington: Indiana University Press.

Barnes, Barry. 1973. The comparison of belief-systems: Anomaly versus falsehood. In *Modes of Thought*. R. Horton and R. Finnegan, eds. London: Faber and Faber. Pp. 182–98.

Barthes, Roland. 1979. *Elements of Semiology*. [Original publication in French in 1964.] New York: Hill and Wang.

Basso, Keith. 1981. "Wise Words" of the Western Apache: Metaphor and semantic theory. In *Language, Culture and Cognition–Anthropological Perspectives*. R. W. Casson, ed. New York: Macmillan Publishing Co. Pp. 244–67.

Bateson, Gregory. 1974. *Steps to an Ecology of Mind*. [1972] San Francisco: Chandler.

Beidelman, T. O. 1980. The moral imagination of the Kaguru: Some thoughts on tricksters, translation and comparative analysis. *American Ethnologist* 7(1):27–42.

Bellah, Robert. 1970. *Tokugawa Religion: The Values of Pre-Industrial Japan*. [1957] Boston: Beacon Press.

Benedict, Ruth. 1967. *Chrysanthemum and the Sword: Patterns of Japanese Culture*. New York: New American Library.

Berger, Peter L., and Thomas Luckmann. 1967. *The Social Construction of Reality*. New York: Doubleday.

Blacker, Carmen. 1975. *The Catalpa Bow: A Study of Shamanistic Practices in Japan*. London: George Allen & Unwin.

Bloch, Marc. 1961. *Feudal Society*. L. A. Manyon, trans. [Original publication in French in 1949.] Chicago: University of Chicago Press.

Boon, James A. 1984. Folly, Bali, and anthropology, or satire across cultures. In *Text, Play, and Story: The Construction and Reconstruction of Self and Society*. E. Bruner, ed. *1983 Proceed-*

ings of the American Ethnological Society. Washington, D.C.: American Ethnological Society. Pp. 156–77.

Bouissac, Paul. 1976. *Circus and Culture: A Semiotic Approach.* Bloomington: Indiana University Press.

Braudel, Fernand. 1980. *On History.* Chicago: University of Chicago Press.

Bulmer, Ralph. 1967. Why is the Cassowary not a bird?—A problem of zoological taxonomy among the Karam of the New Guinea Highlands. *Man* 2:5–25.

Buraku Kaihō Kenkyūsho, ed. 1978a. *Buraku Mondai Gaisetsu* (Introduction to *Buraku* Problems). Osaka: Kaihō Shuppansha.

———. 1978b. *Buraku Mondai Yōsetsu* (Outline of *Buraku* Problems). Osaka: Kaihō Shuppansha.

Burke, Kenneth. 1955. *A Grammar of Motives.* New York: George Braziller, Inc.

———. 1966. *Language as Symbolic Action.* Berkeley: University of California Press.

Burks, Arthur W. 1948–1949. Icon, index and symbol. *Philosophy and Phenomenological Research* 9:673–89.

Cazja, Michael. 1974. *Gods of Myth and Stone.* New York: Weatherhill.

Chiba, Tokuji. 1975. *Shuryō Denshō Kenkyū* (Research on Hunting Lore). Tokyo: Kazama Shobō.

———. 1977. *Shuryō Denshō Kenkyū Kōhen* (Research on Hunting Lore, Cont.). Tokyo: Kazama Shobō.

Clifford, James. 1983. Ethnographic authority. *Representations* 1(2):118–46.

De Craemer, Willy, Jan Vansina, and Renée C. Fox. 1976. Religious movements in Central Africa: A theoretical study. *Comparative Studies in Society and History* 18(4):458–75.

DeVos, George, and H. Wagatsuma, eds. 1966. *Japan's Invisible Race: Caste in Culture and Personality.* Berkeley: University of California Press.

Doi, Tsugiyoshi. 1973. *Hasegawa Tōhaku* (Hasegawa Tōhaku). *Nihon no Bijutsu* (Fine Arts of Japan). Vol. 8, no. 87. Tokyo: Shibundō.

Donoghue, John. 1966. The social persistence of outcaste groups. In *Japan's Invisible Race: Caste in Culture and Personality.* G. DeVos and H. Wagatsuma, eds. Berkeley: University of California Press, Pp. 138–52.

Dorson, Richard M. 1962. *Folk Legends of Japan.* Tokyo and Rutland, Vermont: Charles E. Tuttle Co.

Douglas, Mary. 1966. *Purity and Danger*. London: Routledge & Kegan Paul.

1975. *Implicit Meanings*. London: Routledge & Kegan Paul.

Dumont, Louis. 1970. *Homo Hierarchicus*. M. Sainsbury, trans. [Original publication in French in 1966.] Chicago: University of Chicago Press.

Eickelman, Dale. 1979. The political economy of meaning. *American Ethnologist* 6(2):386–93.

Eliade, Mircea. 1971. *Patterns in Comparative Religion*. New York: World Publishing Co. Meridian Book.

Elison, George. 1981. Hideyoshi, the bountiful minister. In *Warlords, Artists and Commoners: Japan in the Sixteenth Century*. G. Elison and B. L. Smith, eds. Honolulu: University Press of Hawaii. Pp. 222–44.

Ema, Tsutomu. 1932. Saruhiki monogatari (A story of monkey trainers). *Fūzoku Kenkyū* (no. 140):14–18.

Ema, Tsutomu, Nishioka Toranosuke, and Hamada Giichirō, eds. 1967. *Kinsei Fūzoku Jiten* (A Dictionary of Customs During the Early Modern period). Tokyo: Jinbutsu Ōraisha.

Evans-Prichard, E. E. 1940. *The Nuer*. Oxford: Clarendon Press.

Fernandez, James. 1974. The mission of metaphor in expressive culture. *Current Anthropology* 15(2):119–45.

1980. Reflections on looking into mirrors. *Semiotica* 30(1/2):27–39.

1982. *Bwiti: An Ethnography of the Religious Imagination in Africa*. Princeton: Princeton University Press.

Frankenberg, Ronald. 1957. *Village on the Border: A Social Study of Religion, Politics and Football in a North Wales Community*. London: Cohen & West.

Freedman, Maurice. 1969. Geomancy. In *Proceedings of the Royal Anthropological Institute of Great Britain and Ireland for 1968*. London: Royal Anthropological Institute of Great Britain and Ireland. Pp. 5–15.

Fujiwara, Akihira. 1979. Shin-Sarugakuki. In *Kodai Seiji Shakai Shisō* (Polity, Society and Thought Structure in Ancient Japan). Tokuhei Yamagishi et al., ed. Tokyo: Iwanami Shoten. Pp. 133–52.

Fukuyama, Toshio. 1968. Nenjū gyōji emaki ni tsuite (Notes on the picture scrolls of annual events). In *Nihon Emakimono Zenshū* (A Collection of Japanese Picture Scrolls). Kadokawa Shoten Henshūbu, ed. Vol. 24. Tokyo: Kadokawa Shoten. Pp. 3–23.

Geertz, Clifford. 1973. *The Interpretation of Cultures*. New York: Basic Books.

——— 1980. *Negara: The Theatre State in Nineteenth-Century Bali*. Princeton: Princeton University Press.

Goffman, Erving. 1974. *Frame Analysis: An Essay on the Organization of Experience*. Cambridge, Mass.: Harvard University Press.

Gonda, Yasunosuke. 1971. Sarumawashi (Monkey Performance). In *Ryūmin* (The Non-Settlers). H. Hayashi, ed. Tokyo: Shinjinbutsu Ōraisha. Pp. 317–18.

Graburn, Nelson H. H. 1977. Tourism: The sacred journey. In *Hosts and Guests: The Anthropology of Tourism*. V. L. Smith, ed. Philadelphia: University of Pennsylvania Press. Pp. 17–31.

Granet, Marcel. 1977. *The Religion of the Chinese People*. Maurice Freedman, trans. [Original publication in French in 1922.] New York: Harper and Row.

Hamaguchi, Esyun. 1982. *Kanjinshugi no Shakai: Nihon* (A Society of Contextualism: Japan). Tokyo: Keizai Shimposha.

——— 1985. A contextual model of the Japanese: Toward a methodological innovation in Japanese studies. *Journal of Japanese Studies* 11(2):289–321.

Hanawa, Hokiichi, ed. 1940. *Shinkō Gunsho Ruijū*. [1932] H. Matsumoto, ed. Vol. 22. [Original publication in 1819.] Tokyo: Naigaishoseki Kabushikigaisha.

Handelman, Don. 1981. The ritual-clown: Attributes and affinities. *Anthropos* 76:321–70.

Handelman, Don, and Bruce Kapferer. 1980. Symbolic types, mediation and the transformation of ritual context: Sinhalese demons and Tewa clowns. *Semiotica* 30(1/2):41–71.

Hannerz, Ulf. 1986. Theory in anthropology: Small is beautiful? The problem of complex cultures. *Comparative Studies in Society and History* 28(2):362–67.

Harada, Tomohiko. 1971. Danzaemon Yuishogaki kaidai (Introduction to "The Report by Danzaemon"). In *Nihon Shomin Seikatsushiryō Shūsei* (History of the Lives of the Common People in Japan). T. Harada, K. Nakazawa, and H. Kobayashi, eds. Vol. 14 (*Buraku*). Tokyo: Sanichi Shobō. Pp. 427–28.

——— 1978a. Buraku no zenshi (An early history of *buraku*). In *Buraku Mondai Yōsetsu* (Outline of *Buraku* Problems). Buraku Kaihō Kenkyūsho, ed. Osaka: Kaihō Shuppansha. Pp. 16–23.

——— 1978b. Kinsei hōken shakai to buraku keisei (The feudal society of the Early Modern period and the formation of *buraku*). In

Buraku Mondai Yōsetsu (Outline of *Buraku* Problems). Buraku Kaihō Kenkyūsho, ed. Osaka: Kaihō Shuppansha. Pp. 24–33.

Hastrup, Kirsten, and Jan Ovesen. 1976. The joker's cycle. *Journal of the Anthropological Society of Oxford* 7(1):11–26.

Hayashiya, Tatsusaburō. 1978. *Machishū* ("Town Folk"). [1964] Tokyo: Chūōkōronsha.

——— 1979. *Kabuki Izen* (Before Kabuki). Tokyo: Iwanami Shoten.

——— 1980. *Nihon Geinō no Sekai* (The World of Performing Arts in Japan). [1973] Tokyo: Nihon Hōsō Shuppan Kyōkai.

——— 1981. Chūsei geinō no shakaiteki kiban (The social foundation of arts during the Medieval period). In *Yōkyoku Kyōgen (Yōkyoku and Kyōgen)*. Nihon Bungaku Kenkyū Shiryō Kankōkai, ed. [1981] Tokyo: Yūseidō Shuppan Kabushiki Gaisha. Pp. 201–9.

Hearn, Lafcadio. 1904. *Japan: An Attempt at Interpretation*. New York: Macmillan.

Higo, Kazuo. 1942. *Nihon Shinwa Kenkyū* (Research on Japanese Myths). [1938] Tokyo: Kawade Shobō.

Hirono, Saburō. 1968. Shōrui awaremi no rei (The law requiring mercy towards all living things). In *Nihon Rekishi Dai-Jiten* (Encyclopedia of Japanese History). Vol. 5. Tokyo: Kawade Shobō. Pp. 606–7.

Hirose, Shizumu. 1978. Nihonzaru o meguru animaru roa no kenkyū (Research on animal lore of Japanese macaques). In *Shakai Bunka Jinruigaku* (Socio-Cultural Anthropology). T. Katō, S. Nakao, and T. Umesao, eds. Tokyo: Chūōkōronsha. Pp. 287–334.

——— 1979. *Saru* (Monkeys). Tokyo: Hōsei Daigaku Shuppankyoku.

Huizinga, Johan. 1970. *Homo Ludens: A Study of the Play Element in Culture*. [1944] New York and Evanston: Harper & Row.

Hyers, Conrad. 1973. *Zen and the Comic Spirit*. Philadelphia: Westminster Press.

Ichiko, Teiji. 1958a. Kaisetsu (Introduction). In *Otogizōshi* (Fairy Tales). T. Ichiko, ed. Tokyo: Iwanami Shoten. Pp. 5–21.

Ichiko, Teiji, ed. 1958b. *Otogizōshi* (Fairy Tales). *Nihon Koten Bungaku Taikei* (Anthology of Classical Literature in Japan). Vol. 38. Tokyo: Iwanami Shoten.

Iida, Michio. 1973. *Saru Yomoyama Banashi—Saru to Nihon no Minzoku* (Tales About Monkeys—The Monkey and Japanese Folk Ways). Tokyo: Hyōgensha.

——— 1983. *Mizaru Kikazaru Iwazaru—Sekai Sanzaru Genryūkō* (No See, No Hear, No Say—The Source(s) of the Three Monkeys in Various Cultures of the World). Tokyo: Sanseidō.

Ikeda, Yasaburō. 1974. Kami to geinō (Deity and performing arts). In *Nihon no Minzoku*, by M. Ueda et al. Tokyo: Asahi Shinbunsha. Pp. 281–321.

Inada, Kōji, and Tatehiko Ōshima. 1977. *Nihon Mukashibanashi Jiten* (Dictionary of Japanese Folktales). Tokyo: Kōbundō.

Inoue, Hisashi, et al. 1978. *Shinpojūmu Sabetsu no Seishinshi Josetsu* (Introduction to a Conceptual History of Discrimination—A Symposium). [1977] Tokyo: Sanseidō.

Inoue, Kiyoshi. 1967. *Tennō-sei* (Emperor System). [1963] Tokyo: Tōkyō Daigaku Shuppankai.

Irokawa, Daikichi. 1981. Kindai Nihon no kyōdōtai (Corporate groups in modern Japan). In *Shisō no Bōken* (Explorations into Thought Structure). K. Tsurumi and S. Ichii, eds. Tokyo: Chikuma Shobō. Pp. 235–76.

——— 1983. Yatsushirokai minshūshi—Minamatabyō jikenshi josetsu (A history of the people at Yatsushiro Sea—Introduction to the history of the Minamata disease incident). In *Minamata no Keiji—Yatsushirokai Sōgō Chōsa Hōkoku* (Teachings of Minamata—Report of the Investigation at Yatsushiro Sea). D. Irokawa, ed. Vol. 2. Tokyo: Tsukuma Shobō. Pp. 5–164.

Ishibashi, Fushiha. 1914. Minzokugaku no hōmen yori mitaru kagami (Anthropological interpretations of mirrors). *Jinruigaku Zasshi* 29(6):223–27.

Ishida, Eiichirō. 1966. *Kappa Komahikikō* (The *Kappa* Legend [*sic*]). Tokyo: University of Tōkyō Press.

Ishii, Ryōsuke. 1963. *Zoku Edo Jidai Manpitsu* (Essays on the Edo Period, Vol. 2). [1961] Tokyo: Inoue Shoten.

Itoh, Mikiharu. 1973. Nihon bunka no kōzōteki rikai o mezashite (Toward a structural analysis of Japanese culture). *Kikan Jinruigaku* 4(2):3–30.

Iwabashi, Koyata. 1920. Senshū manzai to Daikokumai, tsuketari sarumawashi (*Senshū manzai* and *Daikokumai*, and also monkey performance). *Minzoku to Rekishi* 3(2):321–30.

Jakobson, Roman. 1971. Shifters, verbal categories, and the Russian verb. In *Selected Writings* by Roman Jakobson. Vol. 2. The Hague: Mouton. Pp. 130–47.

Japan Monkey Center. 1967. *Nihonjin no Seikatsu no naka no Nihonzaru* (Japanese Macaques in the Lives of the Japanese). *Monkī* 11(2) (special issue).

Kadokawa Shoten Henshūbu, ed. 1961. *Nihon Emakimono Zenshū (13-kan)—Hōnen Shōnin Eden* (Collection of Japanese Scroll

Paintings, Vol. 13, Illustrated Deeds of St. Hōnen). Tokyo: Kadokawa Shoten.

1968. *Nihon Emakimono Zenshū (24-kan)—Nenjū gyōji Emaki* (Collection of Japanese Scroll Paintings, Vol. 24, Scroll Paintings of Annual Events). Tokyo: Kadokawa Shoten.

1969. *Nihon Emakimono Zenshū (28-kan)* (Collection of Japanese Scroll Paintings, Vol. 28). Tokyo: Kadokawa Shoten.

Kailasapathy, K. 1968. *Tamil Heroic Poetry.* Oxford: Clarendon Press.

Kaneko, Shigetaka, ed. 1969. *Chōjū Giga* (Scrolls of Animal Caricatures). Adapted by Shigetaka Kaneko from the Japanese text by Hideo Okudaira. Honolulu: East-West Center Press.

Kapferer, Bruce. 1977. First class to Maradana: Secular drama in Sinhalese healing rites. In *Secular Ritual.* S. F. Moore and B. G. Myerhoff, eds. The Netherlands: van Gorcum. Pp. 91–123.

1979. Introduction: Ritual process and the transformation of context. *Social Analysis* 1:3–19.

1983. *A Celebration of Demons.* Bloomington: Indiana University Press.

Karcevskij, Sergej. 1982. The asymmetric dualism of the linguistic sign. [1929] In *The Prague School: Selected Writings, 1929–1946.* P. Steiner, ed. Austin: University of Texas Press. Pp. 47–54.

Kita, Sandy. n.d. *Matabei as Machishū—Two Worlds of Ukiyo.* In progress.

Kitagawa, Morisada. 1981. *Morisada Mankō* (Essays by Morisada). [1853] Published in 1908 as *Kinsei Fūzokushi* (History of Customs During the Early Modern Period), by Bunchōsha Shoin. Tokyo: Tōkyōdō Shuppan.

Kitagawa, Tadahiko. 1972. *Zeami* (Zeami). Tokyo: Chūōkōronsha.

Kitahara, Taisaku. 1975. *Senmin no Kōei—Waga Kutsujoku to Hankō no Hansei* (The Descendants of the "Base People"—The First Half of My Life of Humiliation and Rebellion). [1974] Tokyo: Chikuma Shobō.

Kitamura, Nobuyo. 1970. *Kiyū Shōran* (Playful Essays). Vol. 2. Tokyo: Meicho Kankōkai.

Komatsu, Shigemi. 1983. *Yūzū Nenbutsu Engi* (The Origin of *Yūzū Nenbutsu Engi*). *Zoku Nihon Emaki Taisei* (Anthology of Japanese Picture Scrolls, Cont.). Vol. 11. Tokyo: Chūōkōronsha.

Koyama, Hiroshi. 1960. *Kyōgenshū (Jō)* (Collection of Kyōgen). Vol. 1. Tokyo: Iwanami Shoten.

Kubo, Noritada. 1961. *Kōshin Shinkō no Kenkyū: Nicchū Shūkyō Bunka Kōshōshi* (Research on Belief in *Kōshin*: A History of Cultural and Religious Exchange between Japan and China). To-kyo: Maruzen Kabushiki Gaisha.

Kuhn, Thomas S. 1962. *The Structure of Scientific Revolutions*. Chi-cago: University of Chicago Press.

Kurano, Kenji, and Yūkichi Takeda, eds. 1958. *Kojiki Norito (Kojiki and Norito)*. Tokyo: Iwanami Shoten.

Kuroda, Toshio. 1972. Chūsei no mibunsei to hisen kannen (The social stratification during the Early Medieval period and the concept of baseness). *Buraku Mondai Kenkyū* 33:23–57.

Kuroita, Katsumi, ed. 1966. *Ryō no Shūge* (A Collection of Classical Notes on Ancient Legal Codes). *Kokushi Taikei*, Vol. 24. Tokyo: Yoshikawa Kōbunkan.

LaFleur, William R. 1983. *The Karma of Words: Buddhism and the Lit-erary Arts in Medieval Japan*. Berkeley: University of California Press.

Langer, Susanne K. 1980. *Philosophy in a New Key: A Study in the Symbolism of Reason, Rite and Art*. [1942] Cambridge, Mass.: Harvard University Press.

Leach, Sir Edmund R. 1963. Two essays concerning the symbolic representation of time. In *Rethinking Anthropology*. [1961] Lon-don: The Athlone Press. Pp. 124–36.

———. 1965. *Political Systems of Highland Burma*. [1954] Boston: Beacon Press.

———. 1967. Magical hair. In *Myth and Cosmos*. J. Middleton, ed. New York: Natural History Press. Pp. 77–108.

———. 1968. Anthropological aspects of language: Animal categories and verbal abuse. In *New Directions in the Study of Language*. [1964] E. Lenneberg, ed. Cambridge, Mass.: Massachusetts Institute of Technology Press. Pp. 23–63.

———. 1971. *Kimil*: A category of Andamanese thought. In *Structural Analysis of Oral Tradition*. P. Maranda and E. K. Maranda, eds. Philadelphia: University of Pennsylvania Press. Pp. 22–48.

———. 1976. *Culture and Communication*. Cambridge, England: Cam-bridge University Press.

———. n.d. Aryan invasions over four millennia. In *History and Symbol-ism* (tentative title). E. Ohnuki-Tierney, ed. In progress.

Lebra, Takie Sugiyama. 1976. *Japanese Patterns of Behavior*. Hono-lulu: University Press of Hawaii.

Leutner, Robert W. n.d. *Crescent Moon: A Romance (1806–1810)*, by Takizawa Kyokutei Bakin. R. W. Leutner, trans. Unpublished manuscript.

Lévi-Strauss, Claude. 1966. *The Savage Mind*. [Original publication in French in 1962.] George Weidenfeld and Nicolson Ltd., trans. Chicago: University of Chicago Press.

1967. *Structural Anthropology*. [1963. Original publication in French in 1958.] New York: Doubleday.

1969. *The Raw and the Cooked: Introduction to a Science of Mythology*. Vol. 1. [Original publication in French in 1964.] John and Doreen Weightman, trans. New York: Harper Torchbooks.

Maruoka, Tadao. 1975a, 1975b, 1975c, 1976a, 1976b, 1976c, 1976d, 1977a, 1977b. Suō jōgeyuki kō—Daidōgei "sarumawashi" o shudaini (Thoughts on *Suō jōge yuki*—Primarily on monkey performances as street entertainment). *Geinō Tōzai* No. 1 (1975a): 123–28; No. 2 (1975b): 132–37; No. 3 (1975c): 139–45; No. 4 (1976a): 124–29; No. 5 (1976b): 59–64; No. 6 (1976c): 139–44; No. 7 (1976d): 162–67; No. 9 (1977a): 122–27; No. 10 (1977b): 148–53.

Maruoka, Tadao, Shūji Murasaki, and Ei Kataoka, eds. 1982. *Sarumaiza* (Monkey dance company). Yamaguchi Prefecture: Sarumaiza.

Matsudaira, Narimitsu. 1977. *Matsuri—Honshitsu to Shosō: Kodaijin no Uchū* (Festivals—Their Essence and Multiple Dimensions: The Universe of Ancient Japanese). Tokyo: Asahi Shimbusha.

Matsumae, Takeshi. 1960. *Nihon Shinwa no Shin-Kenkyū* (New Research on Japanese Mythology). Tokyo: Ōhūsha.

Matsumoto, Shinpachirō. 1981. Kyōgen no Omokage (Images in *Kyōgen*). In *Yōkyoku Kyōgen* (*Yōkyoku* and *Kyōgen*). Nihon Bungaku Kenkyū Shiryō Kankōkai, ed. Tokyo: Yūseidō Shuppan Kabushiki Gaisha. Pp. 190–200.

Matsumura, Takeo. 1948. *Girei Oyobi Shinwa no Kenkyū* (Research on Ritual and Myth). Tokyo: Baihūkan.

1954. *Nihon Shinwa no Kenkyū* (Research on Japanese Myths). Vol. 1. Tokyo: Baihūkan.

Matsuyama, Yoshio. 1941. Nanshin dōbutsushi—Uma, saru, kaiko (Notes on animals in southern Shinshū—Horses, monkeys, and silk worms). *Dōbutsu Bungaku* 81:23–29.

McNeill, William H. 1986. *Mythistory and Other Essays*. Chicago: University of Chicago Press.

Miller, Roy A. 1967. *The Japanese Language*. Chicago: University of Chicago Press.

Minakata, Kumakusu. 1972. *Minakata Kumakusu Zenshū* (Collected Essays by Minakata Kumakusu). Vol. 1. [1971] Tokyo: Heibonsha.

Miyaji, Denzaburō. 1973. Shōwa sanzaru (Three monkeys of the Shōwa period). *Monkī* 17(2):12.

———. 1981. Sarumawashi engi (The origin of monkey performances). *Monkī* 25(4):28–30; 25(5):22–24; 25(6):21–23.

Miyamoto, Tsuneichi. 1981. *Emakimono ni Miru Nihon Shomin Seikatsushi* (Life of the Common People in Japan as Depicted in Picture Scrolls). Tokyo: Chūōkōronsha.

Miyata, Noboru. 1975. *Kinsei no Hayarigami* (Popular Deities during the Early Modern Period). Tokyo: Hyōronsha.

Mizuo, Hiroshi. 1965. *Nihon no Bijutsu, 25-kan—Sōtatsu to Kōrin* (Fine Arts of Japan, Vol. 25—*Sōtatsu* and *Kōrin*). Tokyo: Heibonsha.

Moore, Sally Folk, and Barbara G. Myerhoff, eds. 1977. *Secular Ritual*. Amsterdam: van Gorcum.

Morinaga, Taneo. 1967. *Runin to Hinin—Zoku Nagasaki Bugyō no Kiroku* (The Exiled and the *Hinin* Outcastes—The Records of the Commissioner of Nagasaki *Bugyō*, Cont.). [1963] Tokyo: Iwanami Shoten.

Morita, Yoshinori. 1978. *Kawara Makimono* (The Scrolls of the "River Banks"). Tokyo: Hōsei Daigaku Shuppankyoku.

Motoori, Norinaga. 1971. *Motoori Norinaga Zenshū* (A Collection of Essays by Motoori Norinaga). Ōno Susumu, ed. Vol. 7. Tokyo: Chikuma Shobō.

Motoyama, Keisen. 1942. *Nihon Minzoku Zushi* (Illustrated Chronicle of Folk Customs in Japan). Vol. 2. Tokyo: Tōkyōdō.

Murasaki, Yoshimasa. 1980. *Sarumawashi Fukkatsu* (The Revival of Monkey Performances). Kyoto: Buraku Mondai Kenkyūsho Shuppanbu.

———. 1983. *Sarumawashi Jōgeyuki* (The Upward and Downward Travels of Monkey Trainers). Tokyo: Chikuma Shobō.

Myerhoff, Barbara. 1980. *Number Our Days*. [1978] New York: Simon & Schuster.

Myerhoff, Barbara, and Jay Ruby. 1982. Introduction. In *A Crack in the Mirror—Reflexive Perspectives in Anthropology*. J. Ruby, ed. Philadelphia: University of Pennsylvania Press. Pp. 1–35.

Nagahara, Keiji. 1979. The Medieval origins of the *eta-hinin*. *Journal of Japanese Studies* 5(2):385–403.

Najita, Tetsuo. 1974. *Japan*. New Jersey: Prentice-Hall.

Nakada, Sadanosuke. 1970. *Meiji Shōbai Ōrai* (Business During the Meiji Period). Tokyo: Seiabō.

Nakajima, Junji. 1979. *Hasegawa Tōhaku* (Hasegawa Tōhaku). *Ni-*

hon Bijutsu Kaiga Zenshū (Collection of Japanese Paintings).
Vol. 10. Tokyo: Shūeisha.

Nakamura, Hajime. 1978. *Ways of Thinking of Eastern Peoples: India-China-Tibet-Japan.* Honolulu: University Press of Hawaii.

Nakamura, Teiri. 1984. *Nihonjin no Dōbutsukan—Henshintan no Rekishi* (Japanese Views of Animals—History of Tales about Metamorphoses). Tokyo: Kaimeisha.

Nakayama, Tarō. 1976. Mizukagami Tenjin (Mizukagami Tenjin). *Nihon Minzokugaku* 1:181–88. Tokyo: Yamato Shobō.

Namihira, Emiko. 1979. Hare to ke to kegare (Sacred, profane, and pollution). In *Kōza Nihon no Minzoku Shūkyō 1: Shintō Minzokugaku* (Folk Religions of Japan 1: Ethnography of *Shintō*). S. Gorai, T. Sakurai, and N. Miyata, eds. Tokyo: Kōbundō. Pp. 78–93.

Needham, Rodney. 1963. Introduction. In *Primitive Classification*, by E. Durkheim and M. Mauss. [1901–1902] Chicago: University of Chicago Press. Pp. vii–xlviii.

——— 1972. *Belief, Language, and Experience.* Chicago: University of Chicago Press.

——— 1979. *Symbolic Classification.* Santa Monica, Calif.: Goodyear Publishing Co.

——— 1980. *Reconnaissances.* Toronto: University of Toronto Press.

Nihon Meicho Zenshū Kankōkai, ed. 1929. *Nihon Meicho Zenshū* (Anthology of Masterpieces in Japanese Literature). Vol. 7 (*Edo Bungeinobu*—Literary Arts of Edo). Tokyo: Nihon Meicho Zenshū Kankōkai.

Nihon Rekishi Daijiten Henshū Iinkai (Editorial Board of the Encyclopedia of Japanese History), ed. 1968. *Nihon Rekishi Daijiten* (Encyclopedia of Japanese History). Vols. 1 and 4. Tokyo: Kawade Shobō.

Ninomiya, Shigeaki. 1933. An inquiry concerning the origin, development, and present situation of the *eta* in relation to the history of social classes in Japan. *Transactions of the Asiatic Society of Japan* 10:47–154.

Noguchi, Michihiko. 1978. Chūsei no shomin seikatsu to hisabetsumin no dōkō (The life of the common people and movements of the discriminated people during the Medieval period). In *Buraku Mondai Gaisetsu* (Introduction to *Buraku* Problems). Buraku Kaihō Kenkyūsho, ed. Osaka: Kaihō Shuppansha. Pp. 86–99.

Nonomura, Kaizō, ed. 1968. *Kyōgenshū (Jō)* (Collection of *Kyōgen*). Vol. 1. [1953] Tokyo: Asahi Shinbunsha.

Nonomura, Kaizō, and Tsunejirō Andō, eds. 1974. *Kyōgen Shūsei* (Collection of *Kyōgen*). Tokyo: Nōrin Shoin.

Norbeck, Edward. 1952. Pollution and taboo in contemporary Japan. *Southwestern Journal of Anthropology* 8(3):269–85.

Ochiai, Shigenobu. 1972. *Mikaihō Buraku no Kigen* (Origin of *Buraku*). Kobe: Kōbe Gakujutsu Shuppan.

Oda, Kōji. 1967a, 1967b, 1967c, 1968a, 1968b, 1968c, 1968d, 1968e, 1968f, 1968g. Kinsei daidō geinin shiryō—Sarumawashi no fukei (Data on roadside performing artists during the Early Modern period—The history of monkey trainers). *Geinō* 9(8) (1967a): 48–52; 9(9) (1967b): 48–53; 9(10) (1967c): 41–46; 10(1) (1968a): 33–36; 10(3) (1968b): 40–43; 10(4) (1968c): 31–35; 10(5) (1968d): 34–37; 10(6) (1968e): 34–42; 10(7) (1968f): 38–42; 10(9) (1968g): 37–40.

——— 1978. Nihon geinōshi eno atarashii hikari (New light toward the history of Japanese performing arts). In *Suō no Sarumawashi* (Monkey Performances at Suō). Suō Sarumawashinokai Jimukyoku, ed. Hikari City, Yamaguchi Prefecture: Suō Sarumawashinokai Jimukyoku. P. 15.

——— 1980. Suō ni okeru sarumawashi (Monkey performances at Suō). In *Suō Sarumawashi Kinkyū Chōsa Hōkokusho* (Report on urgent investigation of monkey performances at Suo). Yamaguchiken Kyōiku Iinkai Bunkaka, ed. Yamaguchi Prefecture: Yamaguchiken Kyōiku Iinkai. Pp. 3–29.

Ohnuki-Tierney, Emiko. 1976. Shamanism and world view: The case of the Ainu of the northwest coast of southern Sakhalin. In *The Realm of the Extra-Human: Ideas and Actions*. A. Bharati, ed. The Hague: Mouton. Pp. 175–200.

——— 1981a. *Illness and Healing among the Sakhalin Ainu—A Symbolic Interpretation*. Cambridge, England: Cambridge University Press.

——— 1981b. Phases in human perception/cognition/symbolization processes: Cognitive anthropology and symbolic classification. *American Ethnologist* 8(3):451–67.

——— 1984a. *Illness and Culture in Contemporary Japan: An Anthropological View*. Cambridge, England: Cambridge University Press.

——— 1984b. Monkey performances—A multiple structure of meaning and reflexivity in Japanese culture. In *Text, Play and Story: The Construction and Reconstruction of Self and Society*. E. Bruner, ed. *1983 Proceedings of the American Ethnological Society*. Washington, D.C.: American Ethnological Society. Pp. 278–314.

Okawa, Naomi. 1975. *Edo Architecture: Katsura and Nikkō*.

A. Woodhull and A. Miyamoto, trans. New York: Weather-hill/Tokyo: Heibonsha.

Ono, Hideo. 1968. *Meiji Wadai Jiten* (Dictionary of Conversation Topics of the Meiji Period). Tokyo: Tōkyōdō Shuppan.

Ooms, Herman. 1985. *Tokugawa Ideology: Early Constructs, 1570–1680*. Princeton: *Princeton University Press*.

Origuchi, Shinobu. *1965a, 1965b, 1976a, 1976b, 1976c. Origuchi Shinobu Zenshū* (Collected Papers of Shinobu Origuchi). Vol. 1 (1965a); Vol. 2 (1965b); Vol. 7 (1976a); Vol. 9 (1976b); Vol. 10 (1976c). Tokyo: Chūōkōronsha.

Ortiz, Alfonso. 1969. *The Tewa World: Space, Time, Being and Becoming in a Pueblo Society*. Chicago: University of Chicago Press.

Ouwehand, Cornelius. 1958–1959. Some notes on the god Susano-o. *Monumenta Nipponica* 14(3–4):138–61.

———. 1964. *Namazu-e and Their Themes: An Interpretative Approach to Some Aspects of Japanese Folk Religion*. Leiden: Brill.

———. 1979. *Namzue—Minzokuteki Sōzōryoku no Sekai* (Catfish Pictures—The World of Folk Imagination). Tokyo: Serika Shobō.

Ozawa, Shōichi. 1978. Sarumawashi Fukkatsu (The revival of the monkey performances). In *Suō no Sarumawashi*. Suō Sarumawashinokai Jimukyoku, ed. Hikari City, Yamaguchi Prefecture: Suō Sarumawashinokai Jimukyoku.

Peacock, James L. 1968. *Rites of Modernization*. Chicago: University of Chicago Press.

———. 1971. Class, clown, and cosmology in Javanese drama: An analysis of symbolic and social action. In *Structural Analysis of Oral Tradition*. P. Maranda and E. K. Maranda, eds. Philadelphia: University of Pennsylvania Press. Pp. 139–68.

Philippi, Donald L., trans. 1959. *Norito: A Translation of the Ancient Japanese Ritual Prayers*. Tokyo: The Institute for Japanese Culture and Classics, Kokugakuin University.

———. 1969. *Kojiki*. Princeton: Princeton University Press/Tokyo: University of Tōkyō Press.

Plath, David W. 1982. Resistance at forty-eight: Old-age brinksmanship and Japanese life course pathways. In *Aging and Life Course Transitions*. T. K. Hareven and K. Adams, eds. New York: Guilford Press. Pp. 109–25.

Pollack, David. 1983. The informing image: "China" in *Genji Monogatari*. *Monumenta Nipponica* 38(4):359–75.

Porkert, Manfred. 1974. *The Theoretical Foundations of Chinese Medicine: Systems of Correspondence*. Cambridge, Mass.: Massachusetts Institute of Technology Press.

Price, John. 1966. A history of the outcaste: Untouchability in Japan. In *Japan's Invisible Race: Caste in Culture and Personality*. G. DeVos and H. Wagatsuma, eds. Berkeley: University of California Press. Pp. 6–30.

Putzar, Edward D. 1963. The tale of Monkey Genji, *Sarugenjizōshi. Monumenta Nipponica* (nos. 1–4):286–312.

Rohlen, Thomas. 1974. *For Harmony and Strength: Japanese White-Color Organization in Anthropological Perspective*. Berkeley: University of California Press.

Sahlins, Marshall. 1976. *Culture and Practical Reason*. Chicago: University of Chicago Press.

———. 1981. *Historical Metaphors and Mythical Realities: Structure in the Early History of the Sandwich Islands Kingdom*. Ann Arbor, Mich.: University of Michigan Press.

———. 1982. The apotheosis of Captain Cook. In *Between Belief and Transgression: Structuralist Essays in Religion, History and Myth*. M. Isard and P. Smith, eds. Chicago: University of Chicago Press. Pp. 73–102.

———. 1985. *Islands of History*. Chicago: University of Chicago Press.

Saigō, Nobutsuna. 1967. *Kojiki no Sekai* (The World of the *Kojiki*). Tokyo: Iwanami Shoten.

Sakamoto, Tarō, Saburō Ienaga, Mitsusada Inoue, and Susumu Ōno, eds. 1967. *Nihon Shoki*. Vol. 1. Tokyo: Iwanami Shoten.

Sakurai, Tokutarō. 1981. Kesshū no genten—Minzokugaku kara tsuikyū shita shōchiiki kyōdōtai kōsei no paradaimu (The source of solidarity—Folklorists' search for a paradigm for the structure of corporate groups). In *Shisō no Bōken* (Explorations into Thought Structure). K. Tsurumi and S. Ichii, eds. Tokyo: Chikuma Shobō. Pp. 187–234.

Sakurai, Tokutarō, Kenichi Tanikawa, Hirofumi Tsuboi, Noboru Miyata, and Emiko Namihira. 1984. *Hare, Ke, Kegare* ("Sacred," "Profane," and "Pollution"). Tokyo: Seidosha.

Samson, George B. 1943. *Japan: A Short Cultural History*. New York: Appleton-Century-Crofts.

Satake, Akihiro. 1970. *Gekokujō no Bungaku* (Literature of the *Gekokujō* [the below conquering the above]). [1967] Tokyo: Chikuma Shobō.

Schutz, Alfred. 1971. *Collected Papers. Vol. II: Studies in Social Theory*. The Hague: Martinus Nijhoff.

Schwartz, Benjamin I. 1975. Transcendence in ancient China. *Daedalus* (Spring 1975): 57–68.

Seki, Keigo. 1979. *Nihon Mukashibanashi Taisei* (Collection of Japanese Folktales). Vol. 1, Dōbutsu Mukashibanashi (Animal Folktales). Tokyo: Kadokawa Shoten.

Shack, William A., and E. P. Skinner, eds. 1979. *Strangers in African Societies*. Berkeley: University of California Press.

Shibuzawa, Keizō, ed. 1965, 1966a, 1966b, 1968. *Emakimono ni Miru Nihon Jōmin Seikatsu Ebiki* (The Lives of the Folk as Illustrated in Picture Scrolls). Vol. 2 (1965); Vol. 3 (1966a); Vol. 4 (1966b); Vol. 5 (1968). Tokyo: Kadokawa Shoten.

Shimazu, Hisamoto. 1933. *Kokumin Densetsu Ruijū* (Collection of Legends). Vol. 1. Tokyo: Ōokayama Shoten.

Shimonaka, Yasaburō, ed. 1941. *Shintō Daijiten* (Encyclopedia of Shintō). Vol. 2. Tokyo: Heibonsha.

Silverstein, Michael. 1976. Shifters, linguistic categories, and cultural description. In *Meaning in Anthropology*. K. Basso and H. A. Selby, eds. Albuquerque: University of New Mexico Press. Pp. 11–55.

Simmel, Georg. 1950. *The Sociology of Georg Simmel*. Glencoe, Ill.: The Free Press.

Smith, Robert J. 1962. Stability in Japanese kinship terminology: The historical evidence. In *Japanese Culture: Its Development and Characteristics*. R. J. Smith and R. K. Beardsley, eds. Chicago: Aldine. Pp. 25–33.

——— 1974. Town and city in pre-modern Japan: Small families, small households, and residential instability. In *Urban Anthropology*. A. Southall, ed. Oxford, England: Oxford University Press. Pp. 163–210.

——— 1983. *Japanese Society*. Cambridge, England: Cambridge University Press.

Smith, Robert J., and Ella L. Wiswell. 1982. *The Women of Suye Mura*. Chicago: University of Chicago Press.

Smith, W. Robertson. 1972. *The Religion of the Semites*. [1889] New York: Schocken Books.

Steiner, Franz. 1967. *Taboo*. [1956] Middlesex, England: Penguin Books.

Sugiura, Minpei. 1965. *Sengoku Ransei no Bungaku* (Literature of the Turbulent World during the Cyclical Conquest). Tokyo: Iwanami Shoten.

Suō Sarumawashinokai Jimukyoku, ed. 1978. *Suō no Sarumawashi* (Monkey Performances at Suō). Hikari City, Yamaguchi Prefecture: Suō Sarumawashinokai Jimukyoku.

Suzuki, Mitsuo. 1974. *Marebito no Kōzō* (The Structure of Marebito [Stranger]). Tokyo: Sanichi Shobō.

1979. Marebito (Visitors). In *Kōza Nihon no Minzoku* (Folk Cultures of Japan). Vol. 7, *Shinkō* (Belief Systems). T. Sakurai, ed. Tokyo: Yūseidō Shuppan. Pp. 211–39.

Tachibana, Narisue. 1966. *Kokon Chomonshū* (Stories Heard from Writers Old and New). Y. Nagazumi and I. Shimada, eds. [1254] Tokyo: Iwanami Shoten.

Takasaki, Masahide. 1956. "Hina" no kuni (The country of "Hina"). *Kokugakuin Zasshi* 56(5):4–26.

Takayanagi, Kinpō. 1981. *Edo Jidai Hinin no Seikatsu* (The Life of the *Hinin* during the Edo Period). Tokyo: Yūzankaku Shuppan.

1982. *Edo no Daidōgei* (Street Entertainment in Edo). Tokyo: Kashiwa Shobō.

Takenaka, Shinjō. 1977. *Tabū no Kenkyū* (Research on Taboo). Tokyo: Sankibō Busshorin.

Takizawa, Bakin. 1958. *Chinsetsu Yumiharizuki*. Vol. 2. Edited by T. Gotō. [1807] Tokyo: Iwanami Shoten. For the English translation, see Leutner (n.d.).

Tambiah, S. J. 1969. Animals are good to think and good to prohibit. *Ethnology* 8(4):423–59.

1981. A performance approach to ritual. (Radcliffe-Brown Lecture, 1979). *Proceedings of the British Academy* 65:113–69.

Toda, Teiyū. 1978. *Bokkei, Gyokan* (Bokkei and Gyokan). Tokyo: Kōdansha.

Toda, Teiyū, Hiroshi Kanazawa, Susumu Hayashi, and Suzuki Hiroshi. 1982. *Kangakei Jinbutsu* (Portraits in the Chinese Tradition). *Nihon Byōbue Shūsei* (Collection of Japanese Paintings on Screens). [1980] Tokyo: Kōdansha.

Tsuji, Nobuo. 1981. *Iwasa Matabei* (Iwasa Matabei). *Nihon Bijutsuega Zenshū* (Japanese Fine Arts Series). Vol. 13. Tokyo: Shūeisha.

Tsurumi, Kazuko. 1974. *Kōkishin to Nihonjin* (Curiosity and the Japanese). [1972] Tokyo: Kōdansha.

Turner, Terence S. 1977. Transformation, hierarchy and transcendence: A reformation of van Gennep's model of the structure of rites de passage. In *Secular Ritual*. S. F. Moore and B. G. Myerhoff, eds. The Netherlands: van Gorcum. Pp. 53–70.

Turner, Victor. 1967. *The Forest of Symbols*. Ithaca: Cornell University Press.

1969. *The Ritual Process*. Chicago: Aldine.

1975. *Dramas, Fields, and Metaphors: Symbolic Action in Human Society*. Ithaca: Cornell University Press.

Ueda, Kazuo. 1978a. Buraku no bunpu to jinkō (Distribution of *buraku* settlements and population). In *Buraku Mondai Gaisetsu* (Introduction to *Buraku* Problems). Buraku Kaihō Kenkyūsho, ed. Osaka: Kaihō Shuppansha. Pp. 3–10.

——— 1978b. Kodai senminsei to buraku kigensetsu (The "base people" in ancient Japan and the origin of the *buraku*). In *Buraku Mondai Gaisetsu* (Introduction to *Buraku* Problems). Buraku Kaihō Kenkyūsho, ed. Osaka: Kaihō Shuppansha. Pp. 73–85.

——— 1978c. Kinsei hōken shakai to mibunsei (The feudal society of the Early Modern period and the hierarchical system). In *Buraku Mondai Gaisetsu* (Introduction to *Buraku* Problems). Buraku Kaihō Kenkyūsho, ed. Osaka: Kaihō Shuppansha. Pp. 100–118.

Umehara, Takeshi. 1967. Jō to yū kachi (Purity as a value). In *Bungaku Riron no Kenkyū* (Research on Literary Criticisms). T. Kuwahara, ed. Tokyo: Iwanami Shoten. Pp. 78–97.

Umezu, Jirō. 1972. *Emakimono Sōshi* (A Collection of Picture Scrolls). Kyoto: Hōzōkan.

Ushioda, Tetsuo. 1973. *Hakimono* (The Footgear). Tokyo: Hōsei Daigaku Shuppankyoku.

van Gennep, Arnold. 1961. *The Rites of Passage.* [1909] Chicago: University of Chicago Press.

Vansina, Jan. 1970. Cultures through time. In *A Handbook of Method in Cultural Anthropology*. R. Naroll and R. Cohen, eds. Garden City, N.Y.: Natural History Press. Pp. 165–79.

Watsuji, Tetsurō. 1959. *Rinrigaku* (Ethics). Vol. 1. Tokyo: Iwanami Shoten.

White, Hayden, 1983. *Metahistory: The Historical Imagination in Nineteenth-Century Europe.* [1973] Baltimore: Johns Hopkins University Press.

Willis, Roy. 1974. *Man and Beast.* London: Hart-Davis, Mac-Gibbon.

Wittgenstein, Ludwig. 1968. *Philosophical Investigations.* Third edition. New York: Macmillan.

Yalman, Nur. 1967. "The raw:the cooked :: nature:culture"—Observation on *Le Cru et le Cuit.* In *The Structural Study of Myth and Totemism*. E. Leach, ed. London: Tavistock. Pp. 71–89.

Yamaguchi, Masao. 1977. Kinship, theatricality, and marginal reality in Japan. In *Text and Context: The Social Anthropology of*

Tradition. R. K. Jain, ed. Philadelphia: Institute for the Study of Human Issues. Pp. 151–79.

1978. *Bunka to Ryōgisei* (Culture and Ambiguity). [1975] Tokyo: Iwanami Shoten.

Yamaguchiken Kyōiku Iinkai Bunkaka (Cultural Section, Kyōiku Iinkai, Yamaguchi Prefecture), ed. 1980. *Suō Sarumawashi Kinkyū Chosa Hōkokusho*. Yamaguchi Prefecture: Board of Education, Yamaguchi Prefecture.

Yanagita, Kunio. 1979, 1981, 1982a, 1982b, 1982c, 1982d, 1982e, 1982f. *Teihon Yanagita Kunioshū* (Collected Writings of Kunio Yanagita). Vol. 4 (1981 [1968]); Vol. 6 (1982a [1968]); Vol. 8 (1982b [1969]); Vol. 9 (1982c [1969]); Vol. 11 (1982d [1969]); Vol. 12 (1979 [1969]); Vol. 27 (1982e [1970]); Vol. 30 (1982f [1970]). Tokyo: Chikuma Shobō.

Yanagita, Kunio, ed. 1951. *Minzokugaku Jiten* (Ethnographic Dictionary). Tokyo: Tōkyōdō.

Yokoi, Kiyoshi. 1980. *Gekokujō no Bunka* (Literature of the *Gekokujō* [the below conquering the above]). Tokyo: Tōkyō Daigaku Shuppankai.

1982. *Chusei Minshū no Seikatsu Bunka* (The Life of the Common People during the Medieval Age). [1975] Tokyo: Tōkyō Daigaku Shuppankai.

Yonemura, Ryūji. 1979. *Junkyō to Minshū—Kakure Nenbutsukō* (Martyr and People—A Study on Hidden Buddhism). Kyoto: Dōbōsha.

Yoshida, Teigo. 1981. The stranger as god: The place of the outsider in Japanese folk religion. *Ethnology* 20(2):87–99.

Yoshino, Hiroko. 1984. *Inyō Gogyō to Nihon no Minzoku* (Yin-Yang and the Five Elements—Their Presence in the Lives of the Japanese). [1983] Kyoto: Jinbun Shoin.

Yu, Anthony, trans. 1977–1983. *The Journey to the West*. Vols. 1, 2, 3, and 4. Chicago: University of Chicago Press.

Index

Authors referred to only in citation forms are not indexed. Similarly, such concepts as *mediator* and *scapegoat* are indexed only when they are discussed in theoretical terms. Following the Japanese convention, well-known Japanese historical figures are listed by last and first names, without a comma in between. No distinction between the text and footnotes is made, since the notes generally are as important as the text for the arguments in the book.

261

93, 94, 95, 96
eta, 91–92, 93, 94, 96
eta hinin, 83, 84, 85, 93
Evans-Prichard, E., 230

Fernandez, J., 129, 151, 220, 239
foreigners (Chinese, Westerners,
   outside forces), 26, 27, 28, 29,
   31, 144–47, 199, 230, 231, 233,
   234, 235, 237
Fox, R., 226
framing, 164, 179–82, 210
Frankenberg, R., 129
Freedman, M., 130
Fujiwara, A., 109
fujō (impurity). *See* impurity
Fukuyama, T., 104

game, as opposed to ritual, 181–82
Geertz, C., 3, 128, 209
gekokujō ("the below conquering
   the above"), 15, 73
gibbons, in Japanese paintings,
   26–31, 34, 63
Goffman, E., 179
gohei (ritual staff used in Shintoism), 44
Gonda, Y., 119
Graburn, N., 147
Granet, M., 132

Hamaguchi, E., 23
Handelman, D., 37, 155, 180
han-japa (Japanese children raised
   overseas), 148
Hannerz, U., 4
Harada, T., 76, 95, 117
hare (sacred). *See* sacred
Hastrup, K., and J. Ovesen, 37
Hayashiya, T., 30, 85, 88, 89, 109,
   169
healing, meaning of, 50, 167
healing power of monkey, 49, 50,
   168, 210
Hearn, L., 146
heimin, 84

Hieda-no-Are, 111
hierarchy: between humans and
   animals, 9, 176, 200, 201, 202,
   204, 222; in Japanese society, 9,
   93, 153, 174–75, 176, 182, 210,
   213, 222. *See also* stratification
hierarchy of meaning, 18, 28, 29,
   34–36, 154. *See also* levels of abstraction
Higo, K., 129
hijiri (saints), 86
hinin, 86, 93, 94, 96, 117
Hirose, S., 24, 31, 47, 48, 50, 56,
   57, 58, 64, 116
hisabetsu burakumin, 76. See also
   burakumin
historians. *See* history, as a discipline
historical actors, 221–22, 235, 236
historical causality, 229–30, 232,
   234
historical regularities, 220, 221, 224
historicity, 12, 236, 238
history: as a discipline, 3, 4, 5; in
   relation to myth and ritual, 235–
   38; long-recorded, 4, 5, 11 (*see
   also* long-term study of culture)
Huizinga, J., 180, 181
human-animal relationship, 20–21,
   32–34, 176. *See also* hierarchy: between humans and animals
humans, as defined in Japanese
   culture, 23, 24, 25. *See also* self
   and other, dialogic definition of
Hyers, C., 200

Iida, M., 27, 29, 44, 46, 53, 55, 58,
   68, 69, 70, 114, 116, 117
Ikeda, Y., 80
imi (avoidance), 141
impurity, 8, 35, 38, 81, 88, 89–93,
   98, 99, 100, 137–44, 231. *See also*
   defiled/defiling; dirt; polluted/
   polluting; purity
indexicality, 214, 216
Inoue, K., 79

Library of Congress Cataloging-in-Publication Data

Ohnuki-Tierney, Emiko.
The monkey as mirror.

Bibliography: p.
Includes index.
1. Japan—Civilization. 2. Monkeys—Japan—
Social aspects. 3. Animals and civilization—
Japan. 4. Buraku people. I. Title.
DS821.03627 1987   306'.0952   87-45530
ISBN 0-691-09434-9